ANTI-LANGUAGE
IN THE APOCALYPSE OF JOHN

ANTI-LANGUAGE
IN THE APOCALYPSE OF JOHN

John E. Hurtgen

MELLEN BIBLICAL PRESS

Lewiston/Queenston/Lampeter

Library of Congress Cataloging-in-Publication Data

Hurtgen, John E.
    Anti-language in the Apocalypse of John / by John E. Hurtgen.
       p.   cm.
    Revision of the author's thesis (Ph.D.)--Southern Baptist
Theological Seminary, Louisville, Ky., 1990.
    Includes bibliographical references.
    ISBN 0-7734-9839-7
    1. Bible. N.T. Revelation--Language, Style. 2. Sociology,
Biblical. I. Title.
BS2825.2.H86 1993
228'.066--dc20   93-5985
                                            CIP

A CIP catalog record for this book
is available from the British Library.

The Edwin Mellen Press   The Edwin Mellen Press
Box 450   Box 67
Lewiston, New York   Queenston, Ontario
USA 14092   CANADA L0S 1L0

The Edwin Mellen Press, Ltd.
Lampeter, Dyfed, Wales
UNITED KINGDOM SA48 7DY

Printed in the United States of America

For John's and Pam's parents:
Thomas Henry and Evelyn Ann Hurtgen
Charles Wayne and Doris Jean Arnold

CONTENTS

TABLE OF ABBREVIATIONS

AA	*American Anthropologist*
AB	Anchor Bible
ANRW	*Aufstieg und Niedergang der römischen Welt*
AUSS	*Andrew's University Seminary Studies*
BAGD	W. Bauer, W. F. Arndt, F. W. Gingrich, and F. W. Danker, *Greek-English Lexicon of the New Testament*
BDF	F. Blass, A. Debrunner, and R. W. Funk, *A Greek Grammar of the New Testament*
BETL	Bibliotheca Ephemeridum Theologicarum Lovaniensium
CBQ	*Catholic Biblical Quarterly*
CNT	Commentaire du Nouveau Testament
CI	*Critical Inquiry*
ETL	*Ephemerides theologicae lovanienses*
EWNT	Exegetisches Wörterbuch des Neuen Testaments
FV	*Foi et Vie*
GNTLHR	A. T. Robertson, *A Greek Grammar of the New Testament in the Light of Historical Research*
HDR	Harvard Dissertations in Religion
HNT	Handbuch zum Neuen Testament
HTR	*Harvard Theological Review*
ICC	International Critical Commentary
JEvTh	*Journal of Evangelical Theology*
JR	*Journal of Religion*

JSNT	*Journal for the Study of the New Testament*
KPG	Knox Preaching Guides
LS	*Language in Society*
NA	New Accents
NCB	New Century Bible
NICNT	New International Commentary on the New Testament
NovT	*Novum Testamentum*
NovTSup	Novum Testamentum, Supplements
NTC	New Testament Commentaries
NTM	New Testament Message
NTS	*New Testament Studies*
PTL	*P[oetry and] T[heory of] Literature: A Journal for Descriptive Poetics and Theory*
RE	*Review and Expositor*
RSR	*Religious Studies Review*
SBLDS	Society of Biblical Literature Dissertation Series
SBLSP	Society of Biblical Literature Seminar Papers
SBT	Studies in Biblical Theology
ST	*Studia Theologica*
TDNT	G. Kittel and G. Friedrich (eds.), *Theological Dictionary of the New Testament*
UBS	United Bible Societies
WUNT	Wissenschaftliche Untersuchungen zum Neuen Testament
ZNW	*Zeitschrift für die neutestamentliche Wissenschaft*

FOREWORD

Hurtgen's dissertation on anti–language in the Apocalypse of John is a welcomed addition to the growing body of social scientific interpretation of New Testament documents. And it is welcomed on several accounts. First of all, it is a model of clarity in procedure. The models the author utilizes are clearly set forth on their own terms. And secondly, it is a study in sociolinguistics, an area not sufficiently probed by biblical scholars. A reading of his chapters dealing with this subject allows for a ready introduction to sociolinguistics and anti–language as applicable in textual interpretation. Finally, the author duly applies his chosen models to the sample central passage in John's revelation selected as a sort of sounding area: the seven tableaux of Revelation 11:19–15:4.

Like social scientific criticism in general, sociolinguistics demonstrates that biblical interpretation intent upon discovering original meanings requires the interpreter to seek out those meanings from the social system shared by an author and his initial audience. If one does not take the pain to reconstruct that social system, one will simply have to make do with the social system in which one has been enculturated. Meanings in language derive from social systems.

Sociolinguistics deals with the interpersonal and/or collective dimensions of language. Its opposite is psycholinguistics, that is, language as it is performed by an individual person. Psycholinguistics is psychological, focused on the individual, concerned with the individual speaker or writer. Most literary criticism is psycholinguistically oriented, often concerned with the impact a given writing has on an individual, usually contemporary, reader. This impact is most often assessed aesthetically, in terms of the emotions and/or feelings elicited by a reading. Such impact is ascribed to the linguistic ability of the document in question rather than to the personality, mood and social situation of the contemporary reader.

Sociolinguistics is concerned with groups and their social interactions. The purpose of this dissertation is to gather up the disparate but relevant elements of various studies on Revelation into one sociolinguistic framework. Within such a framework, Hurtgen assesses the language of Revelation as an instance of anti–

language, the creative critique of one group, endowed with the spirit of prophecy, addressing another group dialectically. Such anti–language is rooted in social opposition, opposition rooted in social structures. The linguistic features typical of such anti–language include concealment, word play, and creation of alternate social and conceptual realities. The language of one world is set up over against the language of another in conscious opposition. Anti–language is a language which is determinedly relexicalized and often overlexicalized to focus on the interpretation of existence offered by some person or community.

Some would consider the procedure followed by Hurtgen as a "cookie cutter approach" (Howard C. Kee) since it processes data through models. The fact is that any adult interpretation of any complex phase of life takes place on an abstract level and requires using models (Kee's cookie cutter). Only some interpreters are more honest than others since they inform their readership about the types of models they utilize in their investigation. Such scholarly honesty can only be applauded. The attention of critics would then focus on where it belongs, on the models and the question of fit between data set (here Revelation) and the models. Such an approach allows for growth in knowledge. Surely that is a step beyond the prevailing hand count of those who (will) agree or disagree with the author. It further allows others to build on the work by either consciously fine tuning the models or reapplying other text–segments to the model to further demonstrate its validity or non validity.

Others consider such a procedure "hypothetics–deductive" (Susan R. Garrett). They prefer some presumably "objective," model–less, inductive procedure that sounds more like mystical magic than critical assessment. For induction and its selection of data are surely rooted in some deductive hypothesis, even if only in faith in "immaculate perception." Obviously, some biblical interpreters are willing to examine everything but their own thinking.

Be that as it may, it would seem that all scientific approaches are rooted in hypothesis. However the approach followed in this dissertation is not hypothetics–deductive, but hypothetics–abductive or hypothetico–retroductive. The process is as follows:

> "In the process of abductive discovery, two separate pieces of data, d1 and d2 could both be explained by a hypothesis H1; if this hypothesis were true, further data should exist which would corroborate the existence of H1; this corroborative data is cd3. Similarly d4 and d5 could be explained by H2 and its existence could be corroborated by the finding of cd6. Supposing the corroborative

data to have been found, Hl and H2 both suggest a common explanation E. If E were true, then it would suggest another hypothesis H3, which could be corroborated by cd7" (Linda Woodson, *A Handbook of Modern Rhetorical Terms.* Urbana: National Council of Teachers of English, 1979, p. 1).

Hurtgen's dissertation is a fine example of the application of appropriate models to a selected text–segment for the purpose of verifying or disproving an insight – the insight that John's Apocalypse is an instance of anti–language, hence should be assessed accordingly. Whether Hurtgen is successful or not is, of course, left to the judgment of the reader, who is here invited to enter that interesting world of social–scientific criticism of the Bible.

Bruce J. Malina
Creighton University

PREFACE

The present work, which is a revision of my doctoral dissertation (The Southern Baptist Theological Seminary, Louisville, Kentucky, 1990), is a study that finds its place among a growing number of studies which analyze Biblical texts following methods of research employed in the social sciences. Social science paradigms--from cultural anthropology and sociology of knowledge to sociolinguistics--are applied to the Apocalypse of John in order better to understand the social and cultural environment of the Biblical world and to illumine the time/space differences that separate the twentieth–century reader or hearer from the first–century reader or hearer. The title alone may imply a negative rather than a positive usage of language; the opposite, however, is the case with the prophet John. He employs a mode of dialectical address, quite literally, "back talk," to assert creatively the overarching reality of the power and presence of a God of both grace and vengeance.

I am grateful for the release of "Anti–language in the Apocalypse of John" by the Mellen Biblical Press. I hope that the publication of the work may enable Bible students to hear "the voice like a trumpet" in new ways and that it also may stimulate further research in the Book of Revelation and in the application of social science models for Biblical interpretation.

I am ever cognizant that the accomplishment of a project represents the help of many persons. I must again express appreciation to my doctoral committee of instruction, The Southern Baptist Theological Seminary: James Blevins, R. Alan Culpepper, and Wayne Ward, who gave initial guidance and support. Mike Harris, colleague at Southern Seminary, offered directions for research and engaged in many informal, informative chats. Bruce Malina of Creighton University provided insight at the doctoral stage of study and has continued to give helpful direction and encouragement. Watson Mills, Editor at the Mellen Biblical Press, has carefully arranged the publication of the work. John Mason, pastor of Trinity Baptist Church, Norfolk, Virginia, ably supplied technical support services. Jerry Kibbons and Robert Street of the Christian Studies Division at Campbellsville

College, Campbellsville, Kentucky, supported their new colleague by providing a generous divisional grant for the completion of the project.

I must express my gratitude to a gracious and supportive family: my wife Pam and three sons, Eric, Joseph, and Peter, were patient and understanding as husband and father spent a few hours away to pursue the interest embodied in this text.

Chapter 1

THE VOICE LIKE A TRUMPET

So off we went our several ways, me belching arrgh on the cold coke I'd peeted. I had my cut-throat britva handy in case any of Billyboy's droogs should be around near the flat-block waiting, or for that matter any of the other bandas or gruppas or shaikas that from time to time were at war with one.

A Clockwork Orange,
Anthony Burgess

And another, third, angel, followed them, saying with a loud voice: "If anyone worships the beast and his image and receives a mark upon his forehead or upon his hand, he also will drink of the wine of the wrath of God that he has been mixed purely in the cup of his wrath; and he will be tormented with fire and sulphur before his holy angels and before the Lamb. And the smoke of their torment will ascend for ever and ever, and those who worship the beast and his image and if anyone receives the mark of his name--they have no rest day and night. Here is the patience of the saints, those who keep the commandments of God and the faith of Jesus."

Revelation 14:9-12
The prophet John

The antilanguage is a language of social conflict--of passive resistance or active opposition; but at the same time, like any other language, it is a means of expressing and maintaining the social structure--in this case, the structure of antisociety.

Language as Social Semiotic,
Michael Halliday

The literary and aesthetic power of the Apocalypse of John has in it the "voice like a trumpet," compelling its listeners to "come up here!" and be instructed by it (Rev. 4:1). The "voice" has both frightened and confused, encouraged and instructed the saints for nearly two millennia. Interpreters and interpretations continue to multiply, yet the attraction of this prophetic, apocalyptic book multiplies as well. The power of the language of the Apocalypse derives not merely from the vivid color and description of its visions but from an incessant verbal contest against ungodly forces. It is a language of believers who oppose the devil and the Roman Empire and who are called to be faithful witnesses of Jesus in the end time.

One notes irony, however, in the fact that the "voice like a trumpet" has for centuries been criticized as full of grammatical irregularities and mistakes, dissonant notes in its music. Henry Swete noted how Dionysius of Alexandria (ca. A.D. 190–265) "was struck by the many departures from the rules of syntax which mark the Apocalypse, and charges its author with writing incorrect Greek and even occasional solecisms."[1] Apparently no systematic effort was made in the early centuries to correct its "poor" Greek.[2] Recently much scholarly effort has issued in order to understand better John's simple though often lexicogrammatically irregular Greek.

G. Mussies sought to describe the morphology of John's *Koine* Greek to discern the influence of Aramaic and Hebrew in the formation of the lexical inventory of the language.[3] Several scholars, Klaus Beyer, Max Wilcox, Steven Thompson, and Stanley Porter among them, have investigated the nature of the syntax, with a similar concern to distinguish the extent of semitic influence on word order.[4] The attempt to see the language of the book of Revelation as either hebraicized Greek or as fairly unsemiticized *Koine* has a long history. Steven Thompson gave an excellent overview of the history of the struggle from the beginning of this century to the present and concluded from his study that the Greek of the Apocalypse "was little more than a membrane, stretched tightly over a Semitic framework, showing many essential contours from beneath."[5] However

---

[1]Henry Swete, *Commentary on Revelation* (1911; rpt. Grand Rapids, Michigan: Kregel, 1977), p. cxxiii.

[2]Ibid.

[3]G. Mussies, *The Morphology of Koine Greek as used in the Apocalypse of Saint John*, NovTSup 27 (Leiden: E. J. Brill, 1971).

[4]Klaus Beyer, *Semitische Syntax im Neuen Testament* (Göttingen: Vandenhoeck & Ruprecht, 1961); Max Wilcox, "Semiticisms in the New Testament," *ANRW*, vol. 2, 25.2, ed. Wolfgang Haase (Berlin: Walter de Gruyter, 1974), pp. 978–1029; Steven Thompson, *The Apocalypse and Semitic Syntax* (Cambridge: Cambridge University Press, 1985); Stanley E. Porter, "The Language of Apocalypse in Recent Discussion," *NTS*, 35 (1989), 582–603.

[5]Thompson, *Apocalypse*, p. 108. Thompson went on to suggest a rationale for the Greek "membrane" and Hebrew "framework": "Perhaps the necessity of expressing sacred themes in a gentile tongue was rendered less distasteful so long as it preserved the tenses and other essential syntactical features of the sacred language?" (p. 108). A better solution may be to regard the language as anti–language, in which case, the speakers of the anti–language would evince verbal contest at the phonological, morphological,syntactical, as well as semantical levels of language.

one chooses to view the grammatical irregularities, either as mistakes or hebraicized Greek, the question remains of how the symbolic language of the Apocalypse of John—the "voice like a trumpet"—functions. The following study will attempt to describe its language as anti–language, that is, a language displaying all kinds of verbal play that a group employs to register its opposition to a dominant group in the culture.

The State of Research

To understand how a language functions one must understand the situation that gave rise to it. Recent sociological studies have had a generative impact on the interpretation of the New Testament, opening up new categories for ascertaining meaning from a text with reference to the socio–cultural matrix which is presupposed by it.[6] An excellent example is Bruce Malina's discussion of the first century values honor/shame, the dyadic personality, limited good, and purity rules, which has allowed others similarly to investigate the Biblical text.[7] Employing models from Malina's research, Leland White and David May have been successful

---

[6]The major works are: John H. Elliott, *A Home for the Homeless, A Sociological Exegesis of 1 Peter, its Situation and Strategy* (Philadelphia: Fortress Press, 1981); John G. Gager, *Kingdom and Community: The Social World of Early Christianity* (Englewood Cliffs: Prentice–Hall, 1975); Ronald F. Hock, *The Social Context of Paul's Ministry, Tent–Making and Apostleship* (Philadelphia: Fortress Press, 1980); Bengt Holmberg, *Paul and Power: The Structure of Authority in the Primitive Church as Reflected in the Pauline Epistles* (Philadelphia: Fortress Press, 1980); Edwin A. Judge, *Rank and Status in the World of the Caesars and St. Paul*, University of Canterbury Publication 29 (Canterbury: University of Canterbury, 1984); Howard Clark Kee, *Christian Origins in Sociological Perspective* (Philadelphia: The Westminster Press, 1980); Abraham J. Malherbe, *Social Aspects of Early Christianity*, 2nd rev. ed. (Philadelphia: Fortress Press, 1983); Bruce J. Malina, *The New Testament World: Insights from Cultural Anthropology* (Atlanta: John Knox, 1981), *Christian Origins and Cultural Anthropology: Practical Models for Biblical Interpretation* (Atlanta: John Knox, 1986); Wayne A. Meeks, *The First Urban Christians, The Social World of the Apostle Paul* (New Haven: Yale University Press, 1983); Carolyn Osiek, *What are They Saying About the Social Setting of the New Testament?* (New York: Paulist Press, 1984); Gerd Theissen, *Sociology of Early Palestinian Christianity*, trans. John Bowden (Philadelphia: Fortress Press, 1978), *The Social Setting of Pauline Christianity*, ed. and trans. John H. Schuetz (Philadelphia: Fortress Press, 1982), *Studien zur Soziologie des Urchristentums*, WUNT 19 (Philadelphia: Fortress Press 1983); David C. Verner, *The Household of God: The Social World of the Pastoral Epistles*, SBLDS 71 (Chico, California: Scholars Press, 1983).

[7]*The New Testament World: Cultural Insights from Cultural Anthropology* (Atlanta: John Knox, 1981), pp. 25–152.

4

in their attempts to open new perspectives on the gospels of Matthew and Mark respectively.[8]

While Malina has been sharply criticized for failure to document sources, shallowness in the use of primary sources and exegetical interpretation; he has consistently demonstrated, however, that profound work with primary sources and careful exegesis alone do not allow one to explain what is happening in a Biblical text.[9] He insists that interpreters, in dealing with any alien or foreign culture and language, must learn to become "eavesdroppers"; for we live in a socio–cultural matrix that is radically different from that of the seven churches of Asia Minor.[10] According to Malina, social scientific method in conjunction with historical–critical method provides the appropriate approach to get at the tacit meanings within the Biblical text.

Particularly helpful to this writer has been Malina's recent analysis of *The Gospel of John in Sociolinguistic Perspective* (1985). In it he combined a model of social location of thought with sociolinguistic perspective, namely, anti–language, in order to "look into the social system revealed in and presupposed by Jn [sic] to generate insight into the distinctive features of this text."[11] A similar study in the book of Revelation will help to achieve further insight into its dynamic language. This dissertation will analyze the language of the Apocalypse as an

---

[8]Leland J. White, "Grid and Group in Matthew's Community: The Righteousness/Honor Code in the Sermon on the Mount," *Semeia*, 35 (1986), 61–90; and David M. May, "The Role of House and Household in the Markan Social World," (Ph.D. dissertation, The Southern Baptist Theological Seminary, 1987).

[9]Malina was so criticized by John G. Gager in his review of Malina's *The New Testament World* in *Interpretation*, 37 (1982), 194–197. See Malina's critique of Gager in "Normative Dissonance and Christian Origins," in John Elliott (ed.) *Semeia*, 35 (1986), 35–59. Malina, most recently in Bruce Malina and Jerome Neyrey, *Calling Jesus Names: The Social Value of Labels in Matthew* (Sonoma: Polebridge Press, 1988), p. xvi, has argued that the exegete must emphasize the social dimension of meaning in one's method: "In this sense, all knowledge is social, totally within the shared paradigms and accumulated experiences of a group of knowers, a social group." Without making explicit the first century worldview, the interpreter will appear "ethnocentric," insensitive to non–Western values (p. xv).

[10]Bruce Malina, *Christian Origins and Cultural Anthropology: Practical Models for Biblical Interpretation* (Atlanta: John Knox Press, 1986), p. 12.

[11]Malina, *The Gospel of John in Sociolinguistic Perspective*, Center for Hermeneutical Studies in Hellenistic and Modern Culture Colloquy 48 (Berkley, California: Center for Hermeneutical Studies, 1985), p. 1.

"anti–language," that is, a language that is antithetical to the norm society.[12] The communities of Revelation are seen as anti–society on the outside of the dominant social structure. This social placement is indicated by the use of anti–language, which is characterized by "relexicalization" (new words for old words) and "overlexicalization" (multiple words for the same concept).[13] Four practical functions of anti–language are (1) secrecy, (2) verbal play, (3) solidarity, and (4) alternative social and conceptual reality.[14] Both secrecy and verbal context are valued in the anti–language, for they help to facilitate solidarity within the group as it seeks to maintain its alternative social and conceptual reality in the face of cultural opposition.

The method of research that I will follow is based in large part on Malina's *The Gospel of John in Sociolinguistic Perspective*. In this work Malina attempted to get at the reason why the Fourth Gospel is considered "'the Maverick gospel'"

---

[12]Ibid., p. 11.

[13]There are two brief examples of anti–language on page 1. The first is the voice of Alex, the leader of a teenage gang, from the novel by Anthony Burgess, *The Clockwork Orange*, which example was quoted by Roger Fowler, *Language as Social Discourse* (Bloomington, Indiana: Indiana University Press, 1981), p. 152. Alex's (anti–)language is characterized by relexicalization (*peet, britva,* and *droog* are simple arbitrary relexicalizations for 'drink,' 'razor,' and 'friend') and overlexicalization (*bandas or gruppas or shaikas* all refer to marauding teenage gangs). His language is also filled with all kinds of verbal play. "Presumably, these devices are meant to signify energy,confidence, creativity: to emphasize their freedom from the patterns of the language and so their freedom from the norms of the society" (p. 153).
The second voice is presumably that of the apocalyptic prophet John in Revelation 14:9–12. Note the relexicalization (Rome and Imperial Cult are designated as 'beast' and 'his image,' with participation in the cult as hideous 'mark' ($\chi\acute{\alpha}\rho\alpha\gamma\mu\alpha$) to be avoided at all costs) and the overlexicalization (note the number of images for God's judgment: 'he will drink of the wine,' 'he will be tormented with fire,' 'smoke of his torment ascends,' 'they have no rest day and night'). John's language is also filled with verbal play (there is, in the Greek, a concatenation of genitives (in the phrase 'of the wine of the anger of God which has been poured out unmixed'); also note several repetitions which are presumably meant to signify energy and creativity ('*upon* his forehead and *upon* his hand'; '*before* the holy angels and *before* the Lamb; solemn pronouncement twice on those who *worship* the beast and those who receive the *mark*).
The connection between Alex the gang leader and John the apocalyptic prophet is not to infer that they are identical (Alex had problems that, one hopes, John never even dreamed of). Yet they are alike in that they both stand on the outside of the norm society and "language" in much the same way. This is anti–language, then and now. What will help the present writer to understand John's voice more clearly is to attempt to make my own voice and socio–cultural matrix explicit, as well as John's. This will be undertaken by means of social location of thought.

[14]Ibid., p. 147.

6

(Kysar's term).[15] Creating and applying models is Malina's specialty, and in order to understand the nature of the language of the Gospel he 'kitbashe[d]' Mary Douglas's "group and grid" model from cultural anthropology, over which he superimposed Hayden White's "metahistorical" model, and then added the concept of anti–language from the sociolinguistics of Halliday.[16]

Malina brought together these individual elements to first place the writing within a particular social location of thought (Douglas's group and grid/White's metahistory) and second to describe the language—the anti–language—that emanates from this social location of thought. Thus he accounted for the differences between the Synoptics and John in reporting the story of Jesus. My reason for using Malina's model will not be to explain how the Apocalypse of John differs from other New Testament writings but to show how its language can be understood as anti–language, emanating from a particular social location of thought. One need not place anti–language solely in Douglas's weak group/low grid social location, for there is every indication of the presence of anti–language in the strong group/low grid communities of Revelation.

Apocalyptic and Apocalyptic Language. Since my work will focus on the Apocalypse of John, I cannot neglect an area that is somewhat lacking in the Gospel of John, namely, apocalyptic and apocalyptic language. Recent study of apocalyptic language tends to confirm the sociolinguistic notion of anti–language. Adela Yarbro Collins noted that apocalyptic literature was "often *literature evoked by a crisis*" (underscore mine).[17] One cannot, in a definition of apocalypticism,

---

[15]Malina, *Gospel of John*, p. 1.

[16]Malina referred to this process as "'kitbashing'" (from the term in model railroading that indicates the creation of one model train out of several individual parts), which he regarded as "selective model building" (*Christian Origins*, p. iii). Malina has been criticized by James V. Spickard, "A Guide to Mary Douglas's Three Versions of Grid/Group Theory," *SA*, 50 (1989), 151–170, for not getting Douglas's grid and group model neither conceptually nor ontologically correct.   Some alteration of Douglas's model was necessary to make it usable. Spickard, however, may be the one who has wrongly classified (ontologically) Douglas's social model; in this regard, see Richard Jung, "A Quaternion of Metaphors for the Hermeneutics of Life," in John A. Dillon Jr., (ed.), *GS*, 30 (1987), 25–31; and Frederick L. Bates and Walter Gillis Peacock, "Conceptualizing Social Structure: The Misuse of Classification in Structural Modeling," *AMS*, 54 (1989), 565–577.

[17]*Crisis and Catharsis: The Power of the Apocalypse* (Philadelphia: The Westminster Press, 1984), p. 84.

specify the particular conflict for every writing, but a survey of the history of apocalyptic, beginning in postexilic prophecy, only reinforces the above maxim by Collins.[18] Apocalyptic language, as one finds it in the last book of the New Testament, functions as 'resistance literature' in the midst of crisis within and without the churches.[19]

The renewed interest in the book of Revelation has been fueled by a renewed interest in apocalyptic in general. Apocalyptic, according to Klaus Koch, began to experience a renaissance with the appearance of Ernst Käsemann's 1960 essay "The Beginnings of Christian Theology," in which Käsemann boldly stated that "'Apocalyptic was the mother of all Christian theology—since we cannot really class the preaching of Jesus as theology.'"[20] Since that time we have witnessed a profusion of works on apocalypticism, its genre, setting, and function.

The Old Testament Pseudepigrapha, edited by James H. Charlesworth, appeared in 1983 (Vol. 1) and 1985 (Vol. 2), which consisted of new introductions, translations, and notes of Jewish apocalyptic literature and testaments (some of which contain apocalyptic sections). About the same time three statements were put forward to identify and define "apocalypse."[21] This dissertation will build

---

[18]John J. Collins pointed out this lack of specificity in apocalyptic definition in *The Apocalyptic Imagination* (New York: Crossroad, 1987), pp. 31–32. For a history of the development of apocalyptic see the following: John J. Collins, *The Apocalyptic Imagination* (New York: Crossroad, 1988); Paul D. Hanson, *The Dawn of Apocalyptic* (Philadelphia: Fortress Press, 1975; Klaus Koch, *The Rediscovery of Apocalyptic*, trans. Margaret Kohl, SBT, new series 22 (Naperville, Illinois: Allenson, 1972); Christopher Rowland, *The Open Heaven* (New York: Crossroad, 1982).

[19]Tina Pippin, "Political Reality and the Liberating Vision: The Context of the Book of Revelation" (Ph. D. dissertation, The Southern Baptist Theological Seminary), p. 4; Pippin applied a liberation theology and Marxist hermeneutic to the book of Revelation and interpreted its language as the language of politically oppressed persons.

[20]Koch, *Rediscovery*, p. 14.

[21]First, in 1979 the Society of Biblical Literature's Apocalypse Group published its results in *Semeia* 14 (*The Morphology of a Genre*), ed. John J. Collins. The following definition was proposed: "'Apocalypse' is a genre of revelatory literature with a narrative framework, in which a revelation is mediated by an otherworldly being to a human recipient, disclosing a transcendent reality which is both temporal, insofar as it envisages eschatological salvation, and spatial insofar as it involves another, supernatural world" (9). Second, in the same year the International Colloquium on Apocalypticism met at Uppsala, publishing its results in 1980 (David Hellholm, ed., *Apocalypticism in the Mediterranean World and the Near East* (Tübingen: Mohr–Siebeck, 1980), which, though it did look thoroughly at the shapes of various apocalypses, did not put forward a definition.

upon the fruits of these genre studies; my concern, however, will be to show how apocalyptic language has previously been understood in terms of function, as a prelude to analyzing the Apocalypse of John as anti–language.

Several brief and longer studies have appeared recently dealing with the function of the language as it relates to the social setting (sociological analysis in general has impacted all areas of New Testament research).[22] Placed alongside these works, my proposal will not introduce entirely new insights. Wayne Meeks, for example, in his functional analysis of Pauline apocalyptic language, spoke of the function of group solidarity, which one finds in the concept of anti–language as well.[23] The value of this study is that the language of Revelation will be considered from a unified, sociolinguistic perspective, employing a phenomenon—anti–language—that has been observed in diverse literary and social contexts.

Third, the problem of genre was again taken up in *Semeia* 36 (*Early Christian Apocalypticism: Genre and Social Setting*, ed. Adela Y. Collins (Decatur, Georgia: Scholars Press, 1986). David Hellholm,"The Problem of Apocalyptic Genre and the Apocalypse of John," argued that as well as discussing content, form, and function, one should look to syntagmatic aspects of apocalypses (that is, text–linguistic analysis (13–64). Hellholm would add to the *Semeia* 14 definition, "intended for a group in crisis with the purpose of exhortation and/or consolation by means of divine authority" (27). David Aune ("The Apocalypse of John and the Problem of Genre") suggested that more attention needs to be given to the differences between ancient and modern literature in attempting to solve the problem of genre. He looked at orality and textuality, the connection between literature and cult, and the relationship between apocalypses and ancient revelatory magic (65–96). John J. Collins (*The Apocalyptic Imagination* (New York: Crossroad, 1984), pp. 7–8) stayed fairly close to the definition in *Semeia* 14 (he was uneasy with Hellholm's proposed definition, for it covers some but not all apocalypses), and he admitted that there will be related literature (non–apocalyptic) that will be relevant to apocalypses. Yet there must be some attempt to outline the shape of a literary genre.

[22]See, for example, David Aune, "The Social Matrix of the Apocalypse of John," *BR*, 26 (1981), 16–32; David Barr, "The Apocalypse as a Symbolic Transformation of the World," *Interpretation*, 38 (1984), 39–50 and "The Apocalypse of John as Oral Enactment," *Interpretation*, 40 (1986), 243–256; Adela Y. Collins, *Crisis and Catharsis* (Philadelphia: The Westminster Press, 1984) and Adela Y. Collins, ed., *Early Christian Apocalypticism: Genre and Social Setting*, *Semeia*, 36 (1986); John Collins, *The Apocalyptic Imagination* (New York: Crossroad, 1984); Elizabeth S. Fiorenza, *The Book of Revelation: Justice and Judgment* (Philadelphia: Fortress Press, 1985; John Gager, *Kingdom and Community: The Social World of Early Christianity* (Englewood Cliffs, New Jersey: Prentice–Hall, 1975); Paul Hanson, *Visionaries and their Apocalypses* (Philadelphia: Fortress Press, 1983); Christopher Rowland, *The Open Heaven* (New York: Crossroad, 1982).

[23]Wayne Meeks, "Social Functions of Apocalyptic Language in Pauline Christianity," in *Apocalypticism in the Mediterranean World and in the Near East*, ed. David Hellholm (Tübingen: Mohr–Siebeck, 1983), pp. 687–706.

Social Location of Thought. Social location of thought is "designated by the
common structural position occupied by a number of individuals in relation to a
larger social whole".[24] In this dissertation I will adopt Malina's method of getting
at the social location of thought of a New Testament text. He adopted Mary
Douglas's cultural anthropological model of group and grid, over which he
superimposed Hayden White's metahistory model. An initial question one poses is
"Why social location of thought?"

Every social group follows what Malina called "cultural scripts," which he
likened to "team sport rules."[25] The twentieth–century reader of a first–century
Biblical text is all too likely to interpret a narrative according to his or her own
cultural script or rules. While humans are somewhat the same, they are also
somewhat different in terms of how they organize themselves around and express
themselves relative to their own cultural scripts:[26]

> If language basically realizes or makes present meanings and
> feelings from a given cultural system and if the texts of the Bible are
> pieces of language, then to understand the documents of the Bible is
> to understand the meanings and feelings of an alien culture. To
> perform this task in some fair and adequate way, what is needed is a
> cross–cultural approach to grasping the meanings imparted by a
> foreign language. . . . It should be clear at this point that any dealings
> with communications from alien cultures require the reader/hearer to
> play the role of eavesdropper. While this might sound rather tiresome,
> the point is that, until the human family invents and discovers a
> language that might be called "Human" (something like the
> emotionless univocal speech of mathematics), people will simply have
> to make the added effort to understand foreigners in an adequate
> cross–cultural way if they wish to interpret the meanings shared by
> alien groups.

This quotation makes clear the case for social location of thought: cultural barriers--
particularly as the space/time distance between groups widens—necessitate the need
for cross–cultural social identification. I am convinced, along with Malina, that
Mary Douglas's group and grid model is an appropriate first step in becoming an
adequate eavesdropper, for the model attempts to make explicit the "cultural scripts"
of the "alien," Johannine culture.

---

[24]Richard L. Rohrbaugh, "'Social Location of Thought' as a Heuristic
Construct in New Testament Study," *JSNT*, 30 (1987), 115.

[25]Malina, *Christian Origins*, pp. 28–29.

[26]Ibid., p. 12.

Malina placed the Gospel of John in the weak group/low grid quadrant of the model but the book of Revelation in the strong group/low grid quadrant (because that is the script of groups "pressed to their ultimate, such as apocalyptic, chiliastic, millenarian, end–of–the–world groups by whatever designation one wishes to label them."[27] See Appendix A for particular group and grid scripts for Revelation.

Hayden White's model of metahistory is superimposed on Douglas's group and grid model to provide a further set of social locations. White originally distinguished between mode of emplotment, mode of argument, and mode of ideological implication in order to analyze the "deep structure of the historical imagination of nineteenth–century Europe"[28] In combining Douglas's and White's models Malina has established a method for distancing the scholar and his or her social focus of investigation. See Appendix B for White's metahistory model as it applies to the Apocalypse of John. Malina is careful to admit, however, that there is no "immaculate perception."[29] At the least, this process allows for a greater degree of objectivity.

Social location of thought raises several problems for the sociologist of knowledge, as Rohrbaugh has clearly shown. Perhaps the chief of these, as Rohrbaugh indicated, is that we do not have John the apocalyptic prophet available for interview.[30] We would want to ask him to tell us how he experienced and

---

[27]Ibid., p. 64.

[28]Hayden White, *Metahistory: The Historical Imagination in Nineteenth–Century Europe* (Baltimore, Maryland: The Johns Hopkins University Press, 1973), pp. 2, 29–31.

[29]Malina, *Gospel of John*, p. 7.

[30]Rohrbaugh, "Social Location," pp. 108–113. He listed the following problems with the construction of a group: (1) a human situation is characterizable only when one has also taken into account those conceptions which the participants have of it, how they experience their tensions in this situation and how they react to the tensions so conceived; (2) it is perilously easy to construct social locations without taking into account the overlapping character of social groups; (3) when separating out a single group for observation, it is easy to forget that groups are not only internally defined, but also defined externally by their relation to other groups; (4) conventional sociology of knowledge has concentrated on theoretical thought or, what is worse, the written ideas of intellectuals, instead of the common–sense 'life-world' of everyday experience; (5) generalizations about groups come more easily when yet another type of complexity is not in view, namely, that *conflicting* social values are often integrated *within a single group* (pp. 108–109).
Not that I will not proceed without caution, but I believe that social location is a workable hypothesis for my proposal for the following reason: problem number 3

reacted to the tensions in his social situation.[31] Whatever the nature and degree of the conflict that is reflected in Revelation may be (and there seems to be no consensus at present as to the extent of the "persecution"[32]), one can safely infer that it was sufficient to trigger within John, and prophets like him, an attempt to "language" in such a way as to show heated opposition to the world about his community, which is where the sociolinguistic perspective—and anti–language— comes in.

Sociolinguistics and Anti–language. The final stage of Malina's "kitbashing" (selective model building) is the addition of the sociolinguistic perspective. Malina relied mainly on the theory of the eminent British linguist M. A. K. Halliday in his *Language as Social Semiotic* (1978), which consists of a series of essays written between 1972 and 1976. The chapter on "Anti–Languages" appeared earlier (in somewhat longer form) in *American Anthropologist,* 78 (1976), 570–584.

At the heart of Halliday's theory is the idea of language as a signaling system (semiotic), which is embedded within an encompassing cultural matrix. Language thus becomes "a resource, a meaning potential."[33] Language has a meaning generating potential and possesses the ability to encode information on at least three levels (content, form, and expression, that is in linguistic terms,

---

above is directly answered in terms of the sociolinguistic perspective of anti–language, that is, it is precisely the nature of anti–language to make clear *metaphorically* the relation between the communities of the Apocalypse of John and the dominant society to which it stands opposed. As Halliday indicated, in anti–languages the social values are foregrounded, so that it is intended to be clear which group stands over against the other (Halliday, *Language*, p. 172).

[31]Of course, even if John were available for interview, he would not respond in terms of his own individual experience or reaction. Modern interpreters must guard against looking at the Biblical characters with the "introspective conscious of the West." See the excellent treatment on the dyadic personality in Mediterranean culture in Malina *New Testament World*, pp. 51–70 and in his "Dealing with Biblical (Mediterranean) Characters: A Guide for U.S. Consumers," *BTB*, 19 (1989), 127–141.

[32]Leonard Thompson, "A Sociological Analysis of Tribulation in the Apocalypse of John," *Semeia*, 36 (1986), 147–174, attempted successfully to relate the literary theme of tribulation and the sociopolitical situation of Christians in the Roman province of Asia. In doing so he provided a good review of the several positions taken as to the extent of "real" persecution.

[33]Halliday, *Language*, p. 187.

semantics, lexicogrammar, and phonology).[34] The functional components of this meaning generating system are ideational (language as reflection), interpersonal (language as action), and textual (language as texture, in relation to the environment).[35]

Halliday coined the term "antilanguage." Studying anti–language is like studying not the ear but the earache, not the tympanum but otitis media. Yet knowledge of the inflammation of the middle ear (otitis media) can tell us much about the function of the ear itself (under certain conditions). Anti–language, in other words, is pathological language, language at the other end of the spectrum, or, as Halliday maintained, it is "*both* the limiting case of a social dialect . . . *and* a language."[36] It is the limiting case of a social dialect because it stands over against the language of the dominant society; it is a language because, like the language of the dominant society, it is a (counter) reality generating system.

According to Halliday, anti–language "arises when the alternative reality is a *counter*–reality, set up *in opposition to* some established norm. . . . It is thus not the *distance* between the two realities but the *tension* between them that is significant."[37] Malina correctly applied the concept of anti–language to the Gospel of John. I should like to do the same in the Apocalypse of John. There is not only distance but also tension in the language of Revelation, as it reflects group and anti–group, society (of the Beast) and anti–society (of the Lamb).

In his study of the Gospel of John, Malina regarded the presence of anti–language as indicative of weak group/low grid collectivities. The presence of anti–language in Revelation does not mean a drop in group quadrant (from strong to low), for Revelation is certainly strong group/low grid. Anti–language in strong group may mean, rather, that someone, perhaps the prophet John, has taken the normative way of speaking apocalyptically (anti–language) and has taught/

---

[34]Ibid., p. 21.

[35]Ibid., pp. 186–188. Halliday suggested that one can learn from pathologies: "It has commonly been found with other aspects of the human condition—the social structure, or the individual psyche—that there is much to be learnt from pathological manifestations. . . . In the same way a study of sociolinguistic pathology may lead to additional insight into the social semiotic" (p. 164).

[36]Ibid., p. 179.

[37]Ibid., p. 171.

prophesied in this manner to the churches in Asia Minor, which are, nevertheless, categorized as strong group.[38] One may also explain that the presence of anti–language in the Apocalypse of John, a strong group/low grid collective, may also indicate that the notion of anti–language is more fluid between groups having the same or differing group/grid configurations.[39] Roger Fowler noted that "anti–language can be a code of the over–privileged just as well as of the under–privileged."[40]

What does anti–language look like? Halliday's initial study included samples from the counterculture of vagabonds in Elizabethan England, anti–society in modern Calcutta, and the subculture of Polish prisons and reform schools. According to Halliday, anti–language is language *re*lexicalized and *over*lexicalized.[41] Relexicalization is the occurrence of new words for old, the principle being "same grammar, new vocabulary." In Revelation examples of relexicalization are (1) within the letters to the seven churches the opponents, or false teachers, are no longer Jews but "those who call themselves Jews" (2:9); they belong not to the synagogue but to "the synagogue of Satan" (2:9); those who live in and about Pergamum live "where the throne of Satan is" (2:13); and Antipas is no longer (from the view of those who killed him) a perpetrator but is "my faithful witness" (2:13); and (2) glorious Rome is now a "beast from the sea" (13:1–10), a "whore" (17:1–18); the imperial cult is similarly a "beast from the land" (13:10–17).

Overlexicalization employs several words for one basic concept. Overlexicalization is found in terms for God, Jesus, Satan, Imperial Rome, the followers of Jesus, the followers of the Dragon (Satan). In two examples one finds overlexicalization par excellence: (1) "and from Jesus Christ, the faithful witness, the firstborn from the dead and the ruler of the kings of the earth" (1:5); (2) "And the great dragon was thrown (down), the old snake, the one who is called the devil and satan, the one who deceives the whole earth, he was cast down to the earth"

---

[38]This position was suggested to me by Malina in telephone conversation, February 12, 1988.

[39]Stephen Reid raised this critique in response to Malina's use of Douglas and Halliday (see Malina, *Gospel of John*, p. 30).

[40]Fowler, *Language*, p. 149.

[41]Ibid., pp. 165–166.

14

(12:8). Anti–languages originate out of opposition to the dominant society. Fowler, who has applied Halliday's concept to the novel, made an important modification of Halliday's initial study:[42]

> It is not a static mirror–image, but a medium of negotiation between two communities, a transaction through which conflicts of ideology and identity are actively waged. Similarly, it is not satisfactory to regard anti–language as creating a completely autonomous alternative reality (which might be *any* ideology); the alternative is most fruitfully seen as provoked by, and a creative critique of, the norm. It is in this sense of dialogue between ideologies, reflected in linguistic transformations, that I am going to apply the concept of anti–language to literature.

Anti–language for Fowler was not so static a concept as (he thought) it was for Halliday; rather, anti–language is not only a variety but a process as well.

What function does the anti–language serve? The practical uses (which come from Halliday) to which Fowler puts this "creative critique" were four: (1) secrecy, (2) solidarity, (3) verbal play, and (4) facilitation of an alternative social and conceptual reality for their speakers.[43] As one surveys the recent social scientific literature on the Apocalypse of John, aspects of these four categories become familiar.[44] It is the purpose of this dissertation, however, to gather up the disparate elements of such studies into one unified sociolinguistic concept. What makes the study interesting for this writer is viewing the Apocalypse of John in terms of the verbal contest and verbal display (relexicalization and overlexicalization) that surfaces in the language of the oppressed Christians.[45]

Methodology and Organization

The basic methodology for this dissertation was "kitbashed" by Bruce Malina. Two areas of research, social location of thought and anti–language will combine to provide an adequate method for getting at the function of the language of the Apocalypse of John. The primary aim is to understand the language of

---

[42]Ibid., p. 150.

[43]Ibid., pp. 146–147.

[44]For the distinction between "sociological" and "social scientific" see John Elliott's "Social–scientific Criticism of the New Testament: More on Methods and Models," *Semeia*, 35 (1986), 1–33.

[45]Halliday says of oppressed groups: "Meaning is often the most effective form of social action that is available to them" (*Language*, p. 185).

Revelation as anti–language, the creative critique of one group, endowed by the Spirit of prophecy, addressing another group dialectically.

The third chapter will unfold the area of social location of thought. Given the kind of language one finds in the Apocalypse of John, from what social location would it have likely emerged? Before I discuss social location of thought, I will provide a sketch of the social *realia* of the text. Concerning the 'social facts' of the book, I will discuss author, location and destination of the writing (including the internal and external threats to the prophet John and his communities), and date. Building upon the latter historical exegesis, I will then discuss Malina's revision of Mary Douglas's group and grid model and superimposition of Hayden White's metahistory model, giving illustrations from the Apocalypse of John, which may be placed in the strong group/low grid quadrant (Douglas) and evinces a satiric–tragic mode of formal argument, emplotment, and ideological implication (White).

The fourth chapter will investigate the area of sociolinguistic perspective and anti–language. I will first provide a brief introduction to sociolinguistic theory, especially that of Halliday. The components of Halliday's sociosemiotic theory (language as a signalling system) are text, situation, register, code, the linguistic system, and the social structure. The major portion of the chapter will consist of an examination of four theorists of anti–language: Michael Halliday, Gunther Kress, Roger Fowler, and Bruce Malina. Anti–language is found to be the language of thieves and prisoners, poets, prose fiction characters, and the gospel writer John. The relexicalization, overlexicalization, and verbal play of the anti–language will then be compared to certain aspects of the speech of oral cultures, in which the "sounded word" is experienced "as power and action."[46]

The fifth chapter consists of an analysis of Revelation 11:19–15:4 as a test case for anti–language in the Apocalypse of John. I will employ Blevins's terminology for the above section, namely, "The Seven Tableaux," which are outlined as follows.

The First Tableau—Woman, Child, and Dragon (12:1–18)
The Second Tableau—The Beast from the Sea (13:1–10)
The Third Tableau—The Beast from the Land (13:11–18)
The Fourth Tableau—The Lamb with the 144,000 (14:1–5)
Interlude—Announcement of the Three Angels (14:6–13)
The Fifth Tableau—The Son of Man on a Cloud (14:14–16)
The Sixth Tableau—The Harvest of the Grapes (14:17–20)

---

[46]Walter J. Ong, *Orality and Literacy: The Technologizing of the Word*, NA, ed. Terence Hawkes (London: Methuen, 1982), pp. 31–33.

The Seventh Tableau—The Hymn of the Lamb (15:1–4)

I will begin with an examination of the overall structure of the book, defending the selection of 11:19–15:4, which I contend is a pivotal section of the Apocalypse.

Each of the seven tableaux will be analyzed not only in terms of anti-language but also in terms of indications of social location of thought that gave rise to the anti-language (Douglas and White). I will follow the categories below.

(1) Setting and Content of the Tableau
(2) Relexicalization in the Tableau
(3) Overlexicalization in the Tableau
(4) Verbal Play in the Tableau
(5) Anti-language and Strong Group/Low Grid

The first category, setting and content, will also look at a particular section from the perspective of White's metahistorical model; the perspective of Douglas's group and grid model is employed in the fifth category. Categories second through fourth are concerned with anti-language proper.

Chapter 2

SOCIAL LOCATION OF THOUGHT

Bruce Malina began his sociolinguistic analysis of the gospel of John by examining social location of thought. Social location of thought is a problem in the sociology of knowledge, which, stated simply, "relates ideas to their historical context."[1] He concluded that the Gospel's uniqueness, particularly its focus on the individual, is accounted for by reference to a cultural anthropological model. The latter model places the community that stands behind the Gospel in a particular locus in the social context, which further defines the kind of perceptions and language that the community will use.[2] Given the configuration of language and symbols in the Apocalypse of John, what can one say about the social placement of the communities to whom the Apocalypse of John is addressed? Social location of thought differs from an examination of the social, political, and economic *realia* of a text. Yet no interpretation should be considered complete without the employment of both.

Historical Exegesis and Social Location of Thought

William Ramsay and Colin Hemer in their works on the historical setting of the seven churches of Asia Minor in the Apocalypse of John attempted to explicate

---

[1]John Stanley, "The Use of the Symbol of Four World Empires to Inspire Resistance to or Acceptance of Hellenism in Daniel 2, Daniel 7, 4 Ezra 11–12, Revelation 13, and *Antiquities of the Jews*: Insights from the Sociology of Knowledge and Sect Analysis" (Ph.D. dissertation, Iliff School of Theology, 1986), p. 20.

[2]Thus Malina stated, "The model indicates that the reason the author of Jn tells the story in the way he does is not because he draws upon the 'objective' meaning of the events in the pre–existence—life—death—resurrection of Jesus, but because of constraints on perception deriving from his social location" (*The Gospel of John in Sociolinguistic Perspective*, Center for Hermeneutical Studies in Hellenistic and Modern Culture Colloquy 48 [Berkley, California: Center for Hermeneutical Studies, 1985], p. 11).

the social *realia* of each city in order to interpret the letters.[3] Hemer called his method "historical exegesis," which is concerned with ideological and cultural background and every reference or allusion to the contemporary scene, as reflected in a particular letter and other relevant sources.[4] Hemer's, as well as Ramsay's, "historical exegesis" is still a helpful resource of the historical social facts (*realia*) that aid one in interpreting the second and third chapters of the Apocalypse of John.

Historical exegesis is essential to the interpretation of the whole book. Yet inquiring after the social location thought of the Apocalypse of John is asking a different question.[5] Social location of thought is a matter of the application of sociological analysis to find the placement of a social group. One asks the question, as did Malina: "Given the information communicated in [a text], can one infer the type of situation in which that sort of information could have been imparted?"[6]

Richard Rohrbaugh has succinctly defined social location of thought as follows:

> In sum, then, a social location is to be designated by the common structural position occupied by a number of individuals in relation to a larger whole. Its specification would ideally designate the limited range of experience a position implies (showing how it is unique), together with the process by which that position comes to be occupied.[7]

Rohrbaugh's threefold definition of social location of thought entails the following. First, common structural position; second, limited range of experience the position

---

[3]William Ramsay, *The Letters to the Seven Churches* (1904; rpt. Grand Rapids, Michigan: Baker Book House, 1985); Colin Hemer, *The Letters to the Seven Churches of Asia in their Local Setting*, Journal for the Study of the New Testament Supplement Series 11 (Sheffield: JSOT Press, 1986). Hemer, who has the more recent work, consciously supplants Ramsay, particularly in the area of Old Testament background of the Apocalypse of John, which Hemer rightly understands as a serious lack in Ramsay.

[4]Hemer, *Letters*, p. 20.

[5]Carolyn Osiek, *What are They Saying about the Social Setting of the New Testament?* (New York: Paulist Press, 1984), pp. 4–6, distinguished between the need for social description and analysis, on the one hand, and for the application of social science theory, on the other.

[6]Malina, *Gospel of John*, p. 1; of course, Malina asked this question with special reference to the Gospel of John.

[7]Richard Rohrbaugh, "'Social Location of Thought' as a Heuristic Construct in New Testament Study," *JSNT*, 30 (1987), 115.

implies; and third, process by which that position comes to be occupied. The reasons for determining social location of thought are, according to Malina, (1) for the scholar to gain proper distancing, to become an adequate "eavesdropper"; and so (2) to provide a means for comparing one location over against another with questions that will be less ethnocentrically nuanced; and (3) for the scholar to determine his or her own social location and the implicit presuppositions that lie within it.[8]

Rohrbaugh has not only defined but also delimited social location of thought by his definition. Rohrbaugh's primary caution to those who attempt to draw lines between thought and social context in New Testament sociological exegesis is to beware of the incomplete nature of our data.[9] We do not have any of the actual participants of the prophet John's community available for examination. We cannot construct exactly all the overlapping relationships that obtained in any one given community nor the resulting significance that they would bear for interpretation. Bearing these restrictions in mind, one can cautiously proceed, even as Rohrbaugh encouraged, to investigate the social location of a given group or groups in order to determine (1) the position of a group in the social order, (2) something of the range of experience the location implies, and (3) how the position initially arose.[10] Even though we do not have all the data postulated by Rohrbaugh's ideal, yet with the help of his model one can advance an understanding of the book that sheds new light on its interpretation.

Historical Facts of the Apocalypse of John

Before examining the social location of thought of the Apocalypse of John, one should have a fairly clear understanding of one's view of the social *realia*, the historical facts of the case. Historical exegesis provides the basis for applying social scientific models to the text. The following social facts of the Apocalypse to be briefly sketched here are author, location and destination of the writing

---

[8]Malina, *Gospel of John*, p. 7.

[9]Rohrbaugh, "'Social Location,'" p. 103. According to Rohrbaugh, one is called upon to answer the following kinds of questions in determining social location of thought: "We would want to know if the relationship between belief and social structure is causative. Or dialectical? Or symmetrical? What is the relation between social structure and the distribution of belief?"

[10]Ibid., p. 115.

(including the contemporary internal and external threats to the prophet John and his communities), and date. These presuppositions will guide the present writer in his examination of social location of thought.

The Author of the Apocalypse of John. There can be no certainty in identifying the historical writer, as Adela Collins has ably shown.[11] While she could not find sufficient reason to associate John with a particular prophetic school, Collins, as well as David Aune, finds a satisfactory answer in asserting that John, whatever his exact identity, claimed to be a prophet to the churches of a certain geographical region of Asia Minor.[12] The Apocalypse departs from other apocalypses in the lack of a pseudonymous writer; John, though not giving a more complete identification, does not pretend to be a posthumous Moses, Adam, or Daniel. He sees himself as a living spokesperson to the early churches in Asia Minor.[13]

Location and Destination of the Apocalypse of John. Geographical locale is given by John. He writes from Patmos, which Hemer, favoring the probability, viewed as part of Asia Minor, and to the churches located at and about the representative seven churches of Ephesus, Smyrna, Pergamum, Thyatira,

---

[11]*Crisis & Catharsis: The Power of the Apocalypse* (Philadelphia: The Westminster Press, 1986), pp. 25–44. Collins reviewed the "historical quest" for, as well as the "social identity" of, the author of the Apocalypse and concluded that one cannot identify the historical person nor can one identify the author as part of a prophetic school (in the sense that Elisabeth Schüssler Fiorenza applied that term to John).

[12]Ibid., pp. 46–50; David Aune, "The Social Matrix of the Apocalypse of John," in *PCSBR*, vol. 26 (Chicago: Chicago Society of Biblical Research, 1981), pp. 17–22.

[13]John never directly calls himself a "prophet"; however, in the "apocalypse" that is given to him by Jesus he is equated with prophets (see, for example, the description of his eating of the "little scroll" at 10:8–11). In terms of Douglas's group and grid model, John may further be described as a "limit–breaking agent." Malina, *Christian Origins and Cultural Anthropology: Practical Models for Biblical Interpretation* (Atlanta: John Knox Press, 1986), p. 143: "People undergoing a ritual [status reversal, e.g.] do so because they find themselves in situations that they would like to leave, to get behind, and to get beyond or transcend. . . . In order to get beyond or transcend the socially imposed and culturally defined limits of the human condition, persons have recourse to limit–breaking agents who can take them over the limits in some socially accepted and satisfying way." See "strong group/low grid limit breakers" (pp. 145–146).

Sardis, Philadelphia, and Laodicea.[14] There were other cities to be sure that could have qualified to be on the "list" of representative churches. Size and power were apparently not the only criteria that John considered in the composition of his list. Hemer suggested Magnesia, Tralles, and Troas (as cities greater than, for example, Thyatira or Philadelphia), but he found the solution most satisfactory that the seven cities found in the Apocalypse of John were already a part of an established, circular route for itinerary prophets.[15]

The interpreter's interest in location and destination is focused on the internal and external threats to the churches that led to the vision in the first place. John leads one to this focus in the text from the beginning describing himself as "your brother and fellow partaker in the tribulation and kingdom and patient endurance in Jesus" (1:9). The notions of "tribulation" and "patient endurance" color the picture of "kingdom." Something is amiss. Scholars are divided as to the nature and extent of the threat to the churches. The notion of "tribulation" may be looked at from two sides. First, one may examine the nature of the communities John is addressing. Second, one may examine the nature of the enemies that stand opposed to the communities.

What kinds of groups were those churches of Asia Minor? John Stanley answered the question using the categories of contemporary sect analysis, particularly those of Bryan Wilson, and viewed the churches of the Apocalypse as "sectarian communities which resisted accommodation with Hellenism."[16] As

---

[14]Hemer, *Letters*, pp. 28–29.

[15]Ibid., pp. 14–15. Hemer made note of the proposal by John Bowman, followed by James Blevins, that the route topographically forms a menorah, geographically representing the seven lampstands (= the seven churches) of the vision. Doubts notwithstanding, the present writer does find Blevins's comment intriguing that "churches that are similar are paired with one another." See Hemer, *Letters*, p. 219; James Blevins, *Revelation*, KPG (Atlanta: John Knox Press, 1984), p. 10.

[16]John Stanley, "Use of Symbol," p. 1. Sect analysis, deriving from the sociology of religion, is not without its problems as an interpretive model for the New Testament, the chief of which is that, strictly speaking, there were no sects in the first–century Mediterranean world. See Bruce Malina's review of *Das Charisma des Gekreuzigten: Zur Soziologie der Jesusbewegung*, by Michael N. Ebertz (WUNT 45; Tübingen: Mohr [Siebeck], 1987) in *CBQ*, 51 (1989), 741–743. The main social forms available were the state, the household, and the unofficial association; see E. A. Judge, "The Social Identity of the First Christians: A Question of Method in Religious History," in *JRH*, 11 (1980), 201–217.
    Malina eschews the sociology of religion term ("sect") and points rather to the presence of "fictive kinship groups (such as the church) and factions. On these groups, see Malina's "Patron and Client: The Analogy Behind Synoptic

defined by Bryan Wilson, a sect is a "minority religion," which seems to be a fitting description of the churches one finds in the Apocalypse.[17]

Stanley used the term sect but was careful to define it as "a group so much in tension with its surrounding culture that it withdraws from the dominant culture usually under the influence of an authoritarian leader."[18] Wilson's "ideal sect" has the following five features: claim of a monopoly on religious truth, protest group, exclusivity, demand for complete allegiance, and made up of volunteers.[19] Further, Stanley, employing Wilson's categories, specifically classified the sects of the Apocalypse as both "millennial" (which projects "a vision of a different social order") and "adventist" (which is one type of millennial sect that emphasizes the Bible, expects an imminent judgment, views the world as opposed to God, and [as millennial] expects a new age and prepares for it).[20] Stanley then links sect analysis with models of sociology of knowledge, particularly of Karl Mannheim and the phenomenological cultural analysis of Peter Berger and Thomas Luckmann. A sect, in the view of sociology of knowledge, constructs a "symbolic universe" to deal with threats, real or imagined, that it confronts.[21]

Theology," *Forum*, 4 (1988), 1–32; and Torrey Seland, "Jesus as a Faction Leader: On the Exit of the Category Sect," in P. W. Bockman and R. E. Kristiansen, eds., *Context: festskrift til Peder Borgen* (Trondheim: Tapir, 1987), pp. 197–211. Religion was embedded in social institutions ("substantive religion") and was not "explicit" ("formal") religion: "First–century Mediterranean society did not have any organization whose *sole* and *only* tasks were those of what we call 'religion.' Just as there was no perceptible separation of politics and religion, or of kinship and religion, so there were no enduring social groups formed solely for and based solely on religious activities" (Malina, "Religion in the World of Paul: A Preliminary Sketch," *BTB*, 16 [1986], 97). Thus, in the first–century Mediterranean world there were no "sects," of Stanley's definition. Stanley's use of sect analysis, nevertheless, is helpful as corroborative evidence in determining the character of the "fictive kinship groups" that composed the seven churches of the Apocalypse. It is doubtless the case that these groups exhibit qualities that Stanley affirms indicate "sect."

[17]Bryan Wilson, *Religion in Sociological Perspective* (Oxford: Oxford University Press, 1982), p. 117.

[18]Stanley, "Use of Symbol," p. 2.

[19]Ibid., p. 182.

[20]Ibid., pp. 197–207.

[21]Ibid., pp. 236–237. Stanley, following Berger and Luckmann, listed the threats that faced the churches of the Revelation (which they shared with similar groups associated with Daniel and 4 Ezra) as follows: "These ordeals were (1) the awareness of a competing symbolic universe; (2) social displacement; (3) a significant upsetting of the status quo; (4) suffering; and (5) death.

There is no consensus as to who exactly the opponents to the churches of the Apocalypse of John were, and this is so because ultimately one cannot specify all the conflicts that obtained in the myriad of social relationships that made up the world of the narrative. By and large the majority of commentators have focused on the Roman Imperium, and often persecution under the emperor Domitian, as the chief source of persecution for the churches.[22] Roman oppression reaches its zenith, of course, in chapter 13, in which one finds the politico–economic measure of "no mark, no market" (13:16–17). Conflict had its source in other places as well, as one might expect from a millennial, adventist sect as described by Stanley above. Alan Beagley has recently attempted to prove that the 'Sitz im Leben' of the Apocalypse, while no doubt stemming from difficulties with Rome, should be focused more on the differences in response to Hellenism that obtained between the Church and Judaism.[23] Thus the chief opponent of the churches is "unbelieving and persecuting anti–Christian Judaism," which does not eliminate Rome's role in carrying out actual penalties against anti–Hellenists but shifts the focus away from Rome to Jerusalem.[24]

The list of opponents has been drawn most clearly by Adela Yarbro Collins. She viewed the "elements of crisis" in the historical situation as consisting of (1) conflict with Jews, (2) mutual antipathy toward neighboring gentiles, (3) conflict over wealth,[25] which took the form of resistance to Rome in the East, Jewish polemic against Rome, and social unrest in Asia Minor, (4) precarious relations

---

[22]See, for example, R. H. Charles, *A Critical and Exegetical Commentary on the Revelation of St. John*, vol. 1, ICC (Edinburgh: T. & T. Clark, 1920), pp. xci–xcvii; Henry Swete, *Revelation* (1911; rpt. Grand Rapids, Michigan: Kregel Publications, 1977), pp. lxxxiv–xciii, xcix–cvi; George Ladd, *A Commentary on the Revelation of John* (Grand Rapids, Michigan: Wm. B. Eerdmans, 1972), p. 8.

[23]Alan James Beagley, *The 'Sitz im Leben' of the Apocalypse with Particular Reference to the Role of the Church's Enemies* (New York: Walter de Gruyter, 1987), pp. 3, 24–25.

[24]Ibid., pp. 92–112.

[25]Malina expressed a preference for the word "greed," for in the world of the New Testament conflict centered on "social status" and not over wealth per se: "Thus significant social status did not derive from the accumulation of money, goods, or things but from birth into noble groups which commanded large resources of land and labor" (*Christian Origins*, p. 84); see also his "Dealing with Biblical (Mediterranean) Characters: A Guide for U.S. Consumers," *BTB*, 19 (1090), 127–141.

with Rome, and (5) experiences of trauma (particularly at the death of Antipas [2:13]).[26]

What makes Collins's list differ from that of Charles or Swete is that she qualifies the opponent or crisis with the notion of what John Gager has referred to as "*relative* deprivation."[27] What the interpreter finds of importance in the text is not so much the particular social troubles present but the response to persecution: "In other words, the crucial element is not so much whether one is actually oppressed as whether one *feels* oppressed."[28] One cannot determine the actual extent of persecution in the "real world" of the text; there is, nevertheless, struggle and death described in the Apocalypse. One should note further that relative deprivation is characteristic of a millennarian sect, which I posit the followers of John constitute.[29]

---

[26]Collins, *Crisis and Catharsis*, 1984), pp. 84–104.

[27]Ibid., pp. 84, 105–106. See also Leonard Thompson, "A Sociological Analysis of Tribulation in the Apocalypse of John," *Semeia*, 36 (1986), 163–170.

[28]Ibid., p. 84. Bryan R. Wilson, *Religion*, p. 116, explained that relative deprivation occurred ". . . either because they [persons experiencing deprivation] have done less well in life than they expected, or because they have not succeeded as well as those in the reference group against which they choose to compare themselves." Thus the above persons will turn to religion. Wilson, while admitting the plausibility of the thesis, offered his critique. He argued that the thesis tended to make religion a "dependent variable," that is, if the conditions are adverse enough there will be religion (pp. 116–117). Secondly, Wilson argued, relative deprivation can be detected "ex–post facto," and one cannot be sure just what the underlying causes were that produced the deprivation, how to measure subjective versus objective deprivation, nor how to predict what kind of circumstances lead one to a particular sect (pp. 117–118). The present writer suggests, as does Wilson, that the most the thesis of relative deprivation supplies is "plausible approximations" (p. 116). In this way Collins's interpretation of the social situation in the Apocalypse of John remains plausible as well.
Malina criticized the introduction of the notion of "relative deprivation" into the New Testament text because Gager has employed a social psychological category that obscures how life functioned in the first–century Mediterranean world. Relative deprivation (or "cognitive dissonance") was a part of this world; contemporary U.S. experience expects a match between values and experience: "Dissonance and inconsistency of norms are normal in a social situation in which traditional values are not realizable in daily living . . . . Moreover, given the anti–introspective, dyadic personality of the people involved . . . , normative dissonance would hardly prompt the modes of coping typical of U.S. individualists who might suffer cognitive dissonance ("Normative Dissonance and Christian Origins," *Semeia*, 35 [1986], 38). Malina preferred to use a model that stresses a relationship between "sociological ambivalence" and "legitimated inconsistency" ("Normative Dissonance," p. 49).

[29]Collins, *Crisis and Catharsis*, p. 84.

The thesis of relative deprivation moves from elements of tribulation to speak of "frustration":

> The response to elements of crisis and trauma reflects frustration. This frustration is not due to a recent encounter with a different culture perceived to be superior. Rather, it is due to the conflict between the Christian faith itself, as John understood it. A new set of expectations had arisen as a result of faith in Jesus as the Messiah and of belief that the kingdom of God and Christ had been established. It was the tension between John's vision of the kingdom of God and his environment that moved him to write his Apocalypse.[30]

For Collins the problem for the churches of the Apocalypse, which the prophet John addressed, was not only outer and inner tribulation but unfulfilled expectations about the near approach of the kingdom of God, which expectations provided the impetus for the visions. Leonard Thompson noted that Collins ran the risk of depriving the thesis of relative deprivation of explanatory power by forcing it to "characteriz[e] not only social relationships but also an individual or group's relations to aesthetic, religious, and ethical standards" (to explain the reason for a group's religious configuration).[31]

Date of the Apocalypse of John. The almost unanimous external testimony in early Christian tradition (Irenaeus, Clement of Alexandria, Origen, Victorinus, Eusebius, and Jerome) dates the Apocalypse of John to the last years of the reign of Domitian, who ruled A.D. 81–96.[32] Adela Yarbro Collins did not find sufficient evidence to contradict the early tradition.[33] She allowed that the composition of some sections of the Apocalypse was based on earlier sources, but she saw no reason to resort to theories of several editions (of the writing) as one finds in

---

[30]Ibid., p. 106.

[31]Thompson, "Sociological Analysis," p. 167. Thompson went on the support Collins's use of the theory because it suits the "so–called dualist structure" of the Apocalypse of John: "The so–called dualist structure of the Apocalypse of John can then be seen as the literary expression of, alternatively, the social experience of deprivation and the religious experience of compensation" (p. 167).

[32]Charles, *Revelation*, pp. xcii–xciii; see Swete, *Revelation*, p. c, for various date suggested in the early church.

[33]Collins, *Crisis and Catharsis*, pp. 54–83; and see Swete, *Revelation*, pp. c–cvi.

Charles and, more recently, Ford.[34] The Domitianic date also does not imply that one focus interpretation on widespread physical persecution alone. As shown above (pp. 35–39), tribulation in the Apocalypse of John came as a result of several social factors (political, economic, kinship, as well as religious). Collins dated the Apocalypse of John, in the form that we now possess it, at A.D. 95–96.

Bruce Malina and Social Location of Thought

The above sketch of the author, location and destination, and date of the Apocalypse serves as a foundation for the present task of viewing the Apocalypse in terms of social location of thought. Bruce Malina's kitbashed model consists of the group and grid model of Mary Douglas and the metahistory model of Hayden White. The purpose of this model, as indicated by Rohrbaugh above, is to designate (1) the common structural position of a social group, (2) the limited range of experience a position implies, (3) the process by which that position comes to be occupied. The latter, the process by which the position comes to occupied, may be partly answered by the social sketch above. According to Collins, the prophet John symbols the way he does because of outer and inner trauma and unfulfilled expectations of Christian belief. The visions are a response to this situation. For Collins the visions are intended to produce a cathartic effect in the hearer.[35] Gager, similarly, speaking of "the attainment of millennial bliss through myth," used a psychoanalytical model to describe the therapeutic effect of the text as overcoming time and bringing the millennium to the believer, if only for one fleeting moment.[36]

---

[34]Ibid., p. 54. Charles, *Revelation*, pp. xxix–lxi, spoke of the author John, then a first editor, later interpretations, lacunae, and dittographs; Ford, *Revelation*, AB, vol. 38 (Garden City, New York: Doubleday, 1975), pp. 50–56, spoke of John the Baptist's initial revelation, his disciples subsequent interpretation, and then Christian redaction.

[35]Collins, *Crisis and Catharsis*, pp. 152–154.

[36]John G. Gager, *Kingdom and Community: The Social World of Early Christianity* (Englewood Cliffs, New Jersey: Prentice–Hall, 1975), pp. 49–57. David Barr, "The Apocalypse as a Symbolic Transformation of the World: A Literary Analysis," *Interpretation*, 38 (1984), 49, was not content to speak of an emotional "ephemeral experience." The catharsis of the Apocalypse brings a more decisive change: "They [contemporary Asia Minor Christians] now live in another world. Persecution does not shock them back to reality. They live in a new reality in which lambs conquer and suffering rules. The victors have become victors" (p. 50). Despite Malina's objection that Collins and Gager get into a lot of introspective psychologizing at this point (see Malina's treatment of "the first–century personality" in *The New Testament World* [Atlanta: John Knox Press, 1981], pp. 51–70; and "Biblical Characters," pp. 128–131), Collins is correct in speaking of the "new reality" that Asia Minor Christians have revealed to them.

The above experiences, essentially, are what brought about the particular social location of the Apocalypse of John.

Mary Douglas and the Group and Grid Model of Cultural Analysis. Malina has been the chief spokesperson in New Testament research for the work of the British cultural anthropologist Mary Douglas. He has refined and applied in particular her primary contribution to the field of cultural anthropology, that is, her "group" and "grid" model of cultural analysis. He first made use of Douglas's model in his sociolinguistic analysis of the gospel of John, which later was applied more broadly to the New Testament and formed the basis for an investigation of the social value of titles for Jesus in the gospel of Matthew.[37]

Mary Douglas's early career as an anthropologist involved the description of African culture and ritual.[38] She later began to theorize as to the relationship between society and symbol, and, when she did, her "grid" and "group" model of cultural analysis attempted to be as earthy, everyday, as was her descriptive analysis of African peoples.[39] Mary Douglas, in her book *Natural Symbols*, sought to link social structures and symbolic structures, behavioral modes and symbol systems.[40] She accomplished this by devising two categories "grid," by which she meant "a system of shared classifications or symbols by which one brings order and intelligibility to one's experience," and "group," by which she designated "social pressure and is intended to indicate the extent to which an

---

[37]Malina employed Douglas's model in the following works: *Gospel of John*, p.2; *Christian Origins*, pp. 13–27, 28–44, 45–64; and, with Jerome H. Neyrey, *Calling Jesus Names: The Social Value of Labels in Matthew* (Sonoma, California: Polebridge Press, 1988), pp. 8–20. Malina's discussion of "rules of purity" in chapter six of *New Testament World* (Atlanta: John Knox, 1981), pp. 122–152, employed Douglas's discussion of purity in her *Purity and Danger: An Analysis of Concepts of Pollution and Taboo* (London: Routledge and Kegan Paul, 1966), but there he makes no explicit discussion of the grid and group model.

[38]Robert Wuthnow, James Davison Hujter, Albert Bergesen, Edith Kurzweil, eds., *Cultural Analysis: The Work of Peter L. Burger, Mary Douglas, Michel Foucault, and Jurgen Habermas* (Boston: Routledge & Kegan Paul, 1984), pp. 11–13, 77.

[39]Ibid., p. 77.

[40]Mary Douglas, *Natural Symbols: Explorations in Cosmology* (2nd ed. New York: Random House, 1973), pp. 94–95. See also Sheldon R. Isenberg and Dennis E. Owen, "Bodies, Natural and Contrived: The Work of Mary Douglas," *RSR*, 3 (1977), 5–6. One should note that Malina works from the grid/group model primarily as it is presented in the above article by Isenberg and Owen.

individual finds himself constrained and controlled by others."[41] Malina, an applier of Douglas's group and grid model, described "grid" as the "measurement of fit between socially shared conceptions and human experiences."[42] Thus high grid is the situation where human experiences match culturally shared assumptions, and low grid is the situation where the match between experience and culturally shared conceptions do not match. Malina described "group" as the "degree of social pressure exerted upon an individual or some subgroup to conform to the demands of the larger society, to stay within the 'we' lines marking off group boundaries."[43] Thus high group is the situation where individuals conform to the demands of the larger society, that is, a higher degree of embeddedness in the group, and low group is the situation where individuals do not conform to the demands of the larger society, that is, a lower degree of embeddedness in the group.

Placed on horizontal and vertical axes (see Appendix A), the grid and group model offers a method for analyzing, according to Mary Douglas, simple to complex societies. Each of the four quadrants (weak group/high grid; strong group/high grid; weak group/low grid; and strong group/low grid) is characterized by its own "cultural script" (Malina). Malina placed the gospel of John in the weak group/low grid quadrant to account for the particular features of that text. The Apocalypse of John fits the strong group/low grid quadrant.

Strong group/low grid for the Apocalypse of John means that the communities that adhere to John's message find that salvation is only to be found in company of the followers of the Lamb (high embeddedness, thus strong group) and that largely the experiences of these communities contradict the shared cultural assumptions of the larger society, both Jewish and Roman (high mismatch of experience versus perceptions, thus low grid). The "script features" (Malina) for all group and grid quadrants are as follows: purity, rite, personal identity, body, sin, cosmology, and suffering and misfortune.[44] Each quadrant will interpret the

---

[41]Isenberg and Owen, "Bodies," p. 6.

[42]Malina, *Christian Origins*, p. 13.

[43]Ibid.

[44]The "script features" and their definitions are taken from Malina, *Christian Origins*, pp. 14–15, 20–27. Malina delineated the weak group/low grid script for the gospel of John and, most recently, delineated the strong group/low grid script for the gospel of Matthew (see *Calling Jesus Names*, pp. 8–20). See also the definitions of Isenberg and Owen, "Bodies," pp. 7–8.

scripts vis a vis a particular group and grid. The "script features" for strong group/low grid (the Apocalypse of John) find the following explication.

Purity. Purity rules deal with the "us" versus "them" lines that are drawn by individuals and groups to mark off boundaries: "In sum, purity is about the socially contrived lines through time and space that human groups maintain in order to create and discover meaning."[45] Purity in strong group/low grid is characterized first "by a strong concern in respective groups to maintain social boundaries" (in others words, competing groups) and second by the "inside and outside of the social body under attack" (in other words, the "boundaries seem porous").[46]

The presence of competing groups in the Apocalypse of John is keenly felt. The visions are sent by one servant to other servants of God, who are further circumscribed as "a kingdom" and "priests to God" (1:1, 6). In the letters to the seven churches those who have ears to hear are warned against several competing groups: evil persons who falsely claim to be apostles (2:2); those who do what the Nicolatians do (2:6, 15); those who claim to be true Jews but actually comprise the synagogue of Satan (2:9); those who subscribe to the teaching of Balaam (2:14) and of Jezebel (2:20). In the visions proper the opposing groups are marked off with a heightened sense of concern for boundaries. The faithful are called to live consonant with the vision of God and the Lamb in chapters 4 and 5. Those who are evil, who do not follow the Lamb wherever it goes, belong necessarily in the group of those who worship the beast (14:9–12). The two opposed groups are instructed to remain as they are until judgment comes ("Let the unrighteous one be unrighteous still, and let the impure one be impure still, and let the upright one still do what is upright, and let the holy one be holy still" [22:11]).

---

[45]Malina, *Christian Origins*, p. 21.

[46]Ibid., p. 38.

[47]Douglas's basis for understanding primitive religions is the category of "hygiene": "As we know it, dirt is essentially disorder. There is no such thing as absolute dirt: it exists in the eye of the beholder. If we shun dirt, it is not because of craven fear, still less dread or holy terror. Nor do our ideas about disease account for the range of our behaviour in cleaning and avoiding dirt. Dirt offends against order. Eliminating it is not a negative movement, but a positive effort to organise the environment" (*Purity and Danger*, p. 2). Religions, primitive and modern, concern themselves with ordering the universe, putting matter in its place. Dirt, as Malina described it, is matter out of place (*Christian Origins*, p. 21). Purity is concerned with lines, boundaries, and cleanliness (and the opposite notion of pollution).

A primary, concrete phenomenon undergirds Douglas's abstract perception of purity rules, namely, dirt.[47] Malina described dirt as "matter out of place," that is, not dirty in itself (it has its place) but soil (ground, earth) where it should not be. One finds this notion of clean versus unclean in the Old Testament as well as in the New Testament, and in the Apocalypse of John in particular.[48] In the latter, for example, the notion of cleanness and whiteness of robes symbolizes the concern in strong group/low grid for maintaining strict social boundaries. Those who follow the Lamb will have white, clean garments; those who follow the beast are dirty (3:4; 6:11; 7:14; 19:8; 22:11).

For the strong group/low grid quadrant there is an intense concern for group identity. While boundaries are erected between respective groups (those of the Lamb versus those of Satan), the boundaries seem porous, that is, evil is able to lodge itself in the group and there is no effective means for expelling it.[49] The letters to the churches describe negative forces, as above, yet one must note that these forces are within the churches themselves. A Jezebel–like prophetess is able to infiltrate and "to lead [Jesus'] servants astray to fornicate and to eat food offered to idols" (2:20). Porousness of boundaries is also portrayed on a mythical, universal scale in chapter 12: the woman with child stands face to face with a dragon that is intent on killing her offspring. Those who consider themselves to be saints also may find that impurities have become lodged in them. The example of those at the Laodicean church who may have to be vomited out the mouth of Jesus (3:16) clearly illustrates the problem with purity (and pollution) in strong group/low grid.

---

[47]Douglas's basis for understanding primitive religions is the category of "hygiene": "As we know it, dirt is essentially disorder. There is no such thing as absolute dirt: it exists in the eye of the beholder. If we shun dirt, it is not because of craven fear, still less dread or holy terror. Nor do our ideas about disease account for the range of our behaviour in cleaning and avoiding dirt. Dirt offends against order. Eliminating it is not a negative movement, but a positive effort to organise the environment" (*Purity and Danger*, p. 2). Religions, primitive and modern, concern themselves with ordering the universe, putting matter in its place. Dirt, as Malina described it, is matter out of place (*Christian Origins*, p. 21). Purity is concerned with lines, boundaries, and cleanliness (and the opposite notion of pollution).

[48]See Mary Douglas's excellent study of the Levitical code in *Purity and Danger*, pp. 41-57; and Malina, *New Testament World*, pp. 122-152.

[49]Ibid., p. 39.

Rite. In the strong group/low grid quadrant rites focus on the boundary lines which an individual or group establishes. Rites can be either rituals, which concern crossing lines (for example, baptism), or ceremonies, which concern reinforcing lines (for example, Sunday worship): "Ceremonies, then, celebrate the status quo while rituals look to line crossings."[50] Because of the concern in strong group/low grid for boundaries (purity), one finds attention given to rituals, those rites which bring one into the group. Yet the Apocalypse of John is permeated as well with ceremony, in the form of worship, which serves, among other things, to reinforce the community's vision.[51]

In the Apocalypse of John the visionary speaks to his audience about the initiating ritual of Jesus that made them "a kingdom and priests to God and his Father" (1:5). The church in Sardis is called upon by Jesus to remember their ritual of entrance into the assembly: "Remember, therefore, how you received and heard and keep (it) and repent" (3:3). Within the vision itself there is the ritual of sealing, for the righteous (sealing of the 144,000 [7:1–8]) and the unrighteous (marked for the beast (13:16–17). Malina referred to rituals as "irregular time outs" (as in sports), "occur[ing] when situations or conditions that affect individuals or groups arise calling for a halt in the action."[52] The ritual of sealing allows for "status transformation," in which the person or, in the case of the Apocalypse, the group is allowed to take on a better (in the case of the 144,000 of chapter 7) or a worse (in the case of the beast's disciples of chapter 13) position.[53]

The invitation to ritual is offered throughout the text. The call to repentance—to ensure one's position within the boundary line of the church—is sounded five times in the letters to the churches (2:5, 16, 21–22; 3:3, 19). The note of repentance is heard in connection with those who do not worship God, but it is

---

[50]Ibid., p. 22.

[51]It is most likely that the hymns of the Apocalypse served as a basis for worship in the community. The hymns became the response of the church, that is, the church adopted the hymns in its own worship. Yet Leonard Thompson, "Cult and Eschatology in the Apocalypse of John," *JR*, 49 (1969), 348–349, has indicated that initially the impetus went the other way: "The writer of the Apocalypse used hymnic liturgical materials as they were used by prophets in the worship life of the Christian community: to realize in the present realities otherwise apprehended only as future eschatological events."

[52]Ibid., p. 140.

[53]Ibid.

usually appended to the description of (God's) severe physical judgment against them and consists in the statement that despite their torment they simply would not repent. The purity rules speak rather loudly about who is in and who is out, and one gets the impression that even though repentance is mentioned in connection with the unrighteous there is not the slightest hint that they would partake of the ritual. The Apocalypse sums up the situation by not calling for repentance but by urging the bad to remain bad and the good to remain good until the judgment (22:11; 13:10).

Ceremonies in the strong group/low grid quadrant focus on the boundary lines, not the crossing of them (as in rituals). As I have suggested above, ceremonies are indicated in the Apocalypse particularly in the hymnic sections of the text. They correspond to the choral odes of classic tragedies and act as commentary on the action. They can be viewed as ceremonies, for they function somewhat like what Malina terms "regular time outs" in a sporting event:

> Time–outs can be set up for the purpose of confirming the social institutions that structure the dimensions of communal living, in order to bolster the respective statuses of persons in those institutions and thereby effectively demonstrate the solidarity among all those persons who together realize and give concrete shape to the institution.[54]

As I mentioned above, the hymnic responses in the text function as ceremonies, for they serve to strengthen the faith of the community that God in fact holds the world's destiny in his hands and is to receive praise from his creation.[55] One is encouraged to think of the hymns as ceremonies particularly in view of the fact that

---

[54]Malina, *Christian Origins*, p. 140.

[55]James Blevins, *Revelation as Drama* (Nashville: Broadman, 1984), p.19, noted the function of the chorus in Greek tragedy and its counterpart in the book of Revelation with its some 30 hymns, which offer interpretation of the visionary action; Elisabeth Schüssler Fiorenza, *The Book of Revelation: Justice and Judgment* (Philadelphia: Fortress Press, 1985), pp. 166–167, also recognized the dramatic elements of the hymnic material but preferred to designate them as a "component–type" of the Apocalypse of John. See also Michael Harris, "The Literary Function of Hymns in the Apocalypse of John" (Ph.D. dissertation, The Southern Baptist Theological Seminary, 1988), who, while positing "little, if any, direct influence of the chorus upon the hymnic elements in the Apocalypse" (pp. 10–11), employed narrative critical perspectives in order to show how the hymnic material (which Harris restricted to eight units [p. 14]) related "the narratological code (plot development and narrative commentary), the ethnological code (shame/honor), and their function in relation to reader response" (p. 302).

33

the reading of the vision, and naturally its hymns, was to have a place in the worship of the community (1:3).

Personal Identity. Personal Identity in the strong group/low grid quadrant is characterized by a heightened concern for group identity, that is, a high degree of embeddedness in other persons. Malina described this phenomenon in the Mediterranean world of the New Testament as the "dyadic personality," which, differing greatly from the typical twentieth–century United States (low group) individuality, is characterized by an individual's need for another to understand his or her self.[56] Group membership is of prime importance; moreover, since religion was not an individual institution but was embedded in the family (as well as in polity), Christians belonged to the "fictive kin group" known as the church (ἐκκλησία).[57] In the Apocalypse of John, the Christian community is the group by which individuals will measure themselves and understand themselves. The text is addressed to the group: to the seven churches (1:4); to those who had been made into a kingdom and priests for God (1:5). In the seven letters to the churches both the second person plural and singular are used, but group identity is always in view. For example, in the letter to the angel of the church at Thyatira Jesus refers to the church using second person singular ("I know your [singular] work and love and faith and service and your [singular] patience, and your [singular] last works are greater than the first" [2:19]) in vv. 19–20. In 2:24–25 Jesus uses the second person plural to refer to the same group: "But I say to you [plural], to the rest in Thyatira, who [plural] have not this teaching, who [plural] have not known the depths of Satan, as they say; I am not laying upon you [plural] another burden, except hold on to what you [plural] have until I come." Finally, there is usage of the formulae in 26–28 and 29, both of which employ third person singular. In verses 26–28 the victor and the faithful [singular] are promised authority in the ages to come. In verse 29 the repetition of "Let the one [singular] who has ears hear what the Spirit is saying to the churches [plural]" begins with the singular; but this

---

[56]Malina, *New Testament World*, pp. 51–68; *Christian Origins*, pp. 19–20, 31, 39.

[57]Malina noted that in the first–century Mediterranean world "it seems that the kin group (family) is always primary with other groups replicating kinship values and structures" (*Christian Origins*, p. 39). Familial titles appear frequently in these groups (such as "brother," and "sister"). In the Apocalypse of John, the prophet addresses his hearers as "your brother" (1:9). See also his "Religion in the World of Paul," pp. 92–101.

is not to be taken in a highly individualistic sense, for the individual—as in the strong group mindset—will always have the group in view. Wherever one finds singular or plural number in the Apocalypse, one must always think in terms of the individual embedded in the group.

Body. In strong group/low grid body refers to how an individual in a group perceives his or her own physical body and, as a replication of which, the social body. Malina used the metaphor of the road map as he explained the notion of body:

> Human groups make and maintain lines through social time and space, thus mapping out the social territory of the group. If one were to look for a portable road map of that social territory, the place to find it is in the way people map out and regard their individual, physical selves. Anthropologists suggest that the way individuals map out the time and space dimensions of their physical persons offers a rather perfect scale model of the cultural group to which they belong.[58]

Malina referred to this physical–social roadmap as replication, that is, a metaphorical congruence.[59] An individual or group will perceive the social body in much the same way the physical body is perceived.

The key perception in the Apocalypse of John for the physical body is transformation. Though one does not find the Pauline terminology of perishable/imperishable, physical/spiritual body (1 Cor. 15:42–54), there is the underlying assumption that, as is typical of the strong group/low grid quadrant, the body is in need of transformation. Malina stated that in strong group/low grid the body is not a "symbol of life," in its present state.[60] Like the Son of Man, his followers need to be changed. Jesus was dead but is alive again, though having a different kind of existence (as John described in 1:12–16). The change that obtains for believers, particularly the martyrs, is indicated by the receiving of the white garments (3:4–5; 4:4; 6:11; 7:9, 13–14; 19:14), which is a symbol for, among other things, transformed, spiritual bodies.[61]

---

[58]Ibid., pp. 22–23.

[59]Ibid., p. 23.

[60]Ibid., p. 39.

[61]Charles, *Revelation*, pp. 82–83, viewed the white garments, in the above verses, primarily as spiritual bodies which the faithful receive "in the resurrection life." This meaning is allowed by Mitchell Reddish, who followed Swete in asserting that "white garments" is a rich symbol and indicates purity, victory, festivity, as well

White garments have an obviously ethical connotation for the present in 3:18. The Laodicean church is to possess white garments now, which is indicative of the strong concern for purity in strong group/low grid, as well as pointing to physical transformation. The physical body in the present state is, for the saints, subject to abuse and death at the hands of the wicked (6:9; 11:7–13; 17:6; 20:4) but, for those who do not repent, the physical body is subject to the terrible wrath of God (e.g., 16:2, 8–11, 21). Awaiting transformation, the physical body of the saints can only receive God's temporary seal (7:2–8; 9:4; 14:4); evil persons receive a mark (of the beast) that reserves a place for them in eternal fire (13:16; 14:9, 11; 16:2, 19, 20; 20:4).

As a roadmap the physical body informs one as to how the social body is to be read. Like the physical body, the social body is not a symbol of life and needs transformation. The social body is personified by a prostitute, whose name is "Babylon" (14:8; 16:19; 17:5; 18:2, 10, 21). "She," the present world order, is guilty, impure, and destined for desolation. The transformed order will be nothing less than "a new heaven and a new earth" (21:1). Only God can bring about the transformation of body and society.

Sin. Sin, in the strong group/low grid quadrant, is deviance, that is, disturbance in the social order: "In strong group/low grid scripts deviance is seen as penetrating and then lodging itself within persons and groups mainly because the boundaries are so porous."[62] The prophet John himself was considered a deviant "because of the Word of God and the witness of Jesus" (1:9).[63] In the Apocalypse

---

as the heavenly state and that all these ideas are likely present. See Mitchell Reddish, "The Theme of Martyrdom in the Book of Revelation" (Ph.D. dissertation, The Southern Baptist Theological Seminary, 1982), pp. 145–146; Swete, *Revelation*, pp. 51–52; Prigent, *L'Apocalypse de Saint Jean*, CNT, vol. 14 (Paris: Delachaux & Niestlé, 1981), pp. 65–66.

[62]Malina, *Christian Origins*, p. 40.

[63]Thompson, "Sociological Analysis," pp. 149–150, argued that the language of 1:9–10, John's self-description of his whereabouts, need not be interpreted that John was "banished, deported, relegated, or imprisoned" on the island of Patmos; Collins, *Crisis and Catharsis*, pp. 102–104, however, has a more persuasive argument for holding to the traditional notion that John was on Patmos because of some form of Roman banishment (whether deportation, relegation, or otherwise imprisoned): given the anti–Roman character of his apocalyptic visions one would not be surprised that he was viewed as a threat to the *pax romana*. John's descriptive phrase, "on account of the word of God and the witness of Jesus" (1:9), would then, contrary to Thompson, refer to the grounds for his banishment to Patmos, that is, preaching that particular message.

of John the emphasis on sin or deviance is on disturbance inside and outside the church.

Porous group boundaries allow sin to enter in the confines of the community. The letters to the seven churches amply testify to the deviance that is present within the teaching authorities in the churches. False teachers are viewed as deviants. The whole concern about sin is that everyone and everything has a place. The place for deviants is outside the community. Following the makarism of 22:14 ("Blessed are they who wash their garments") is the place–telling statement of 22:15: "The dogs and the magicians and the prostitutes and the murderers and the worshippers of idols and everyone who loves and does a lie are outside."[64] Deviance has its place, and that place is not in the church, ideally.

The deceptive and coercive regimes of the beast (chapter 13) and prostitute (chapters 17–18) are viewed as sin. The beast as deviant will cause the world to stand in amazement before himself (13:3–4, 8, 12); he will blaspheme the name of God (13:6); he will persecute the saints (13:7); he will deceive those who are amazed by him (13:14); he will extend his deviance economically as well (13:16). The prostitute's regime is described more in terms of a drunken profligacy: she enticed all persons to drunkenness and immorality (17:2); in her profligate state she brought harm to God's people (17:6); the world stands in amazement at her (17:8); her economic deviance consists in extravagance at the expense of people (17:4; 18:13).

God and Christ alone can put an end to sin, that is, can effectively remove the pollution in the world. Until the end of regimes of deviance, John exhorts the churches to remember who and what belongs "outside" as well as "inside." Again, the statement in 22:15 states clearly the place of sinners (deviants): "outside."[65]

---

[64]Mike Hatfield, "The Function of the Seven Beatitudes in Revelation" (Ph.D. dissertation, The Southern Baptist Theological Seminary, 1987), pp. 124, noted that this seventh beatitude, like the first two (Rev. 1:3; 14:13), "connects salvation with behavior; consistent with the third makarism [16:15], it mandates the maintenance of garments."

[65]Boundaries are porous in strong group/low grid scripts. One detects a state of porousness, interestingly, in events surrounding the final destruction of evil. When the thousand year period of confinement of Satan is expired, Satan once again roams the earth (20:7–10). The notion of porousness is lessened somewhat by the fact that Satan is unloosed and does not loose himself (20:7); however, it is once again increased with the appearance of Gog and Magog, who gather an innumerable army against the saints and the beloved city (20:8–9). Caird, *The Revelation of St. John the Divine*, NTC (New York: Harper and Row, 1966), p. 257, noted that "the myth of Gog enshrines a deep insight into the resilience of evil. The powers of evil have a defence in the depth, which enables them constantly to summon reinforcements from

Cosmology. Cosmology "refers to the way in which social groups perceive their universe or world to be outfitted and to function."[66] In the strong group/low grid quadrant events are explained anthropomorphically, that is, in terms of "who" is the causal factor behind them.[67] In the communities of the Apocalypse of John, one asked "who," not "what," brought about certain events. There were persons who brought about negative circumstances (for example, false teachers and those who misrepresent themselves [chapters 2 and 3]), and yet there were supernatural beings as well who were responsible for evil (Satan and his messengers, including beasts and a prostitute).

The notion of porous boundaries again colors the way the world is viewed. Because good is not inviolable and evil cannot be restrained, the universe is perceived as a dualistic struggle between good and evil, love and hate, God and Satan, saints and wicked.[68] Dualism is, of course, a primary characteristic of the apocalyptic genre.[69] The Apocalypse of John paints the dualistic struggle in bold strokes: God versus Satan, Jesus versus Beasts, Holy Angels versus Evil Angels, Holy Woman versus Prostitute, Jerusalem versus Babylon, Saints versus Idolaters. In the cosmology of the strong group/low grid perspective of the Apocalypse of John, the supernatural struggle in heaven both causes and affects the struggle in the natural world. One notes the movement in chapters 12:1–13:18 from supernatural (woman, child, dragon, angelic war) to earthly tribulation (beasts and their regime among humanity).

---

beyond the frontiers of men's knowledge and control." In light of Mary Douglas's group and grid model, one might add that evil has this "resilience" (Caird) due, in part, to the perception of the porousness of boundaries in strong group/low grid scripts. John's allowance of the return of Satan also may be a literary strategy to heighten his swift demise (20:10). See also Ford (*Revelation*, p. 357) and Swete (*Revelation*, p. 270), who both referred to Satan's triadic punishment.

[66]Malina, *Christian Origins*, p. 26.

[67]Ibid., p. 40.

[68]Ibid.

[69]See Philip Vielhauer's description of apocalyptic dualism in *New Testament Apocrypha*, vol. 2, ed. Wilhelm Schneemelcher, trans. R. Mcl. Wilson (Philadelphia: The Westminster Press, 1965), pp. 588–589.

Suffering and Misfortune. The final group and grid script is suffering and misfortune.[70] The strong group/low grid quadrant answers the question about suffering and misfortune with the perception that they are "unjust and unwarranted intrusions by some personal causes into the life of the individual or group."[71] The cosmology of the strong group/low grid quadrant perceives the world in terms of personal causality; malevolent forces in the world are to blame for suffering and misfortune. Satan can thus ultimately be charged for oppression against Christians. In fact, John visualized Satan driven to earth to personally handle the hunting down of the woman's offspring (12: 13, 16–17). Only the transformation of the whole universe can bring an end to suffering and misfortune, which, though now a distant *ultima Thule*, John prophesies that a deathless, sorrowless, weepingless, painless world is soon to come (21:4; 7:17).

Hayden White's Metahistory Model. In his sociolinguistic analysis of the gospel of John, Malina superimposed on the above group and grid model of Douglas another model with which to situate the Apocalypse of John in its particular social location.[72] The model is Hayden White's "metahistory" model. In a book by the same name White sought to explore what he interpreted as the "deep structural content" of nineteenth–century histories.[73] The "deep structural content," which is the metahistorical aspect of a narrative, consists of a group of three modes, or strategies, that guide the historian ("at a deep level of consciousness") in telling his or her story. The three modes are (1) formal argument, (2) emplotment, and (3)

---

[70]Malina noted that Douglas extended the scripts in her 1978 work, *Cultural Bias*, to treat nature, cultural process, time, human nature, and society. This dissertation will deal with the seven scripts outlined here (purity, rite, personal identity, body, sin, cosmology, suffering and misfortune). See Malina, *Christian Origins*, p. 27.

[71]Ibid., pp. 40–41.

[72]Malina, *Gospel of John*, pp. 1–2.

[73]*Metahistory: The Historical Imagination in Nineteenth–Century Europe* (Baltimore: The Johns Hopkins University Press, 1973), p. ix. Narrative of all kinds,"from the folktale to the novel, from the annals to the fully realized 'history,'" is a "metacode," according to White: "narrative is a metacode, a human universal on the basis of which transcultural messages about the nature of a shared reality can be transmitted" ("The Value of Narrativity in the Representation of Reality," *CI*, 7 [980] 6, 17). White's *Metahistory* focused on the historical narratives of Hegel, Michelet, Ranke, Tocqueville, Burckhardt, Marx, Nietzsche, and Croce.

ideological implication.[74] Malina discovered that one could plot out these strategies on a corresponding group and grid quadrant.

The strategies or modes of formal argument, emplotment, and ideological implication provide the basis for how and to what effect the historian composes a narrative. When Malina begins to speak of the New Testament narratives, he broadens the notion of "historian" to include all those who tell a story "for some social reason."[75] The following description of White's model is taken from Malina.[76] How does an historian, a storyteller, go about making a narrative?

Chronicle and Story. White refers to "chronicle" and "story."[77] The Chronicle is an arrangement of events considered important by the historian into a temporal order. The chronicling process necessarily is a critical one, deciding which events to include and which to exclude. The story is a second step in which the chronicle becomes "a meaningful flow of action."[78] The strategies (modes) that pre–form the narrative which have heretofore remained undefined, shape how the story is told (mode of emplotment), what the point of the story is (formal argument), and what action the story urges upon its hearers (ideological implication). The metahistory model of White, superimposed on Douglas's group and grid model, yields further insight into the social location of thought of the Apocalypse of John. I will make application to the biblical text as I describe the above strategies.

Mode of Emplotment. Once the historian selects from his or her available sources (events and their recounting), the next task is to form a meaningful story. The first strategy in the process is called by White the "mode of emplotment," which refers to the flow of events or plot.[79] Malina described plot as the following

---

[74]White, *Metahistory*, pp. x, 7–27.

[75]Malina, *Christian Origins*, p. 167. The narrative, as White confirmed the suspicion, deals with legitimacy and authority; a story teller wants to reinforce a particular cultural view (White, "Value of Narrativity," p. 17). Hence, the "historian" can be either a gossip, a gospel writer, or an apocalyptic visionary.

[76]Ibid., pp. 166–184, which parallels the somewhat briefer form found in *Gospel of John*, pp. 2–7.

[77]Ibid., pp. 168–169.

[78]Ibid., p. 169.

[79]Ibid., p. 169.

series of events: an initial state of equilibrium; disequilibrium; counter element; a second state of equilibrium. What brings about the disequilibrium and restoration of equilibrium is a reaction to and then a compliance with some "Generalized Symbolic Media" (commitment, influence, power, or inducement).[80] The mode of emplotment explains the kind of story that is being told.

White posited four basic stories: romance, satire, comedy, and tragedy. Romance focuses on the individual and his or her struggle with and eventual triumph over opposing forces in the world. Malina assigned this mode to the weak group quadrant because of its emphasis on the individual and his or her social transcendence. The gospel of John as representative of the romance, according to Malina, this depicts the Christian excluded members of the synagogue, who struggle to overcome the darkness that is the world; the mode of emplotment entails a heightened sense of the individual.[81]

Satire, which is opposite of the romance, points downward for the character (not upwards as in the romance) and implies the following: "that the individual is ultimately a captive of the world rather than its master, that the individual simply cannot break out of the constraints of his or her social world and indeed should not."[82] The opposing forces of the world are unconquerable. Malina assigned this mode to the strong group quadrant because the individual as captive (rather than master) can survive only embedded in a group. Thus the Apocalypse of John shows the satiric strategy, for the followers of Jesus are captives in the world who will be saved as they remain embedded in the Lamb's group.

Comedy, according to Malina, matches well with the high grid quadrant with its high match of societal values and personal experiences. The comic strategy points ultimately to harmony; the encounter between opposing forces yields a better state. Comedy's opposite, tragedy, points ultimately to the resulting state of

---

[80]Ibid., pp. 74–87, 169–170.

[81]Malina, *Gospel of John*, pp. 8–9. Herman C. Waetjen, in a critique of Malina's thesis (in Malina's *Gospel of John*), objected to the notion that the gospel of John represented a romantic strategy (the emphasis, Waetjen contended, is on "the One [Jesus] and the Many [the community]" not on individuality (pp. 31–32)); Malina countered, nevertheless, that in using a social science model (White and Douglas) one does not specify ". . . an individual person but the collectivity, the author–audience called John," which then realigns the definition of romance into a social sphere (p. 40).

[82]Malina, *Christian Origins*, p. 170.

disharmony that an encounter yields. The tragic emplotment is not to be equated with despair: "Tragedy implies that the human person cannot change conditions but must either work within them or look beyond himself or herself for rescue, salvation, or liberation."[83] Malina assigned tragedy to the low grid quadrant with its low match between societal values and personal experience. The Apocalypse of John has a tragic emplotment; this world cannot be changed by persons, but the followers of the Lamb receive a vision of what they can do in the tragic state: witness and hope.

The strong group, low grid quadrant then is characterized (in terms of mode of emplotment) as satiric tragedy. As satire the story explains the condition of captivity in the world and reinforces the notion that one cannot survive alone (hence, strong group). As tragedy the story explains the ultimate negative results of opposition with the world yet opens options for salvific action. The historian (visionary storyteller) of the Apocalypse tells his story with a satiric tragedy strategy.

Malina added that in the satiric tragedy emplotment (indicative of strong group/low grid) "universal elements serve to explain the sorry condition of humankind and to clarify why experience and social values simply never match as they might have been intended to."[84] Some of the universal elements were identified above (pp. 36-37) in connection with the cosmology of strong group, low grid script features. The symbols of God versus Satan, Jesus versus Beasts, holy versus unholy angels, holy versus unholy women, holy versus unholy cities, saints versus idolaters, are cast in a satiric tragedy plot line in order to explain terror of past, present, and future events and to reinforce how socially embedded individuals might respond to the explanation.

---

[83] Ibid., p. 171–172. The question of the New Testament writings as comedy versus tragedy is answered by Malina, who emphasized tragedy; Malina denied Dan Via, who emphasized comedy (p. 172). Via, in his structuralist–literary analysis of certain Pauline texts and the gospel of Mark, maintained that comic (or perhaps tragicomic) motifs were employed, in particular the motif of death and resurrection, which, Via rightly asserted, gave birth to classical Greek comedy. See Via's *Kerygma and Comedy in the New Testament* (Philadelphia: Fortress Press, 1975), pp. xi, 15, 39. Malina's contention that the gospels, including Mark, evince tragic emplotment is still tenable in view of the fact that within the ultimate tragic state of entrapment ensues "a revelation yielding some higher order explanatory principle," that is, the character realizes what are his or her options for rescue or liberation (Malina, *Christian Origins*, p. 171).

[84] Ibid., p. 172.

Mode of Formal Argument. A second strategy that enters in as the historian (storyteller) constructs a narrative is the mode of formal argument. While the mode of emplotment explained just how a story would progress, the mode of formal argument explains the "'point–of–it–all'" of the story.[85] This "'point–of–it–all'" derives from the social system and thus has a culturally reinforcing effect (the culture of those who tell the story).[86] Following culturally explanative categories of Stephen Pepper, White listed four modes of formal argument: the formist, the contextualist, the organicist, and the mechanistic. The mechanistic strategy is the strategy one finds in the Apocalypse of John.

Briefly, the first three modes are defined as follows. The formist mode of argument "aims at the identification of the unique characteristics of objects inhabiting the historical field, the unprocessed historical field."[87] Malina thus places the formist mode of formal argument into the weak group/low grid quadrant because of the focus on "the individual, the particular."[88] The gospel of John, according to Malina, is an excellent example of the formist mode, with its focus on the individual.

The contextualist mode of formal argument aims at identifying the context within which events occur in order to explain them.[89] Malina placed the contextualist in the weak group/high grid quadrant. The contextualist mode of formal argument is weak group because it focuses on individual events (to explain how event effects event). The contextualist looks to efficiency in context; the formist looks to the unique, the particular without context.

The organicist mode of formal argument, as the adjective leads one to assume, aims at explaining the biotic movement within the historical field.[90] The story in the organicist mode shows how persons and events worked together to produce circumstances as they are. Malina placed the contextualist mode of formal argument in the strong group/high grid quadrant because the focus is no longer on

---

[85]Ibid., p. 172–173.

[86]Malina, *Gospel of John*, p. 3.

[87]Ibid., *Christian Origins*, p. 173.

[88]Ibid., p. 174.

[89]Ibid.

[90]Ibid., p. 175–176.

the particular but on the aggregative process (strong group) and the purpose of organicist mode is to show the match between events and some "purposive laws governing the historical process."[91]

The mechanistic mode of formal argument "seeks out recurrent causes that determine the outcomes of acts in the historical field."[92] One is not surprised to find this mode in the strong group/low grid quadrant, for the satiric tragedy (mode of emplotment; see above, p. 38) attempts to explain why life is as it is. White, employing the categories of the semantic analysis of Kenneth Burke, described the mechanistic mode of the formal argument as focusing essentially on the narrative elements of location, agency, act.[93]

Location is the stage or plane, whether the physical or social environment, on which a story is played.[94] In the Apocalypse of John location is of great importance. The revelation that Jesus gives to John encompasses and concerns the entire physical cosmos, which is conceived either as tripartite (heaven, on the earth, under the earth [5:13]) or quadrapartite (heaven, on the earth, under the earth, in the sea (5:13).[95] The writer is always careful to tell his hearers the physical position or, at least, the direction of his gaze relative to a given vision. Again, location is emphasized in the mechanistic mode of formal argument because the historian (storyteller) attempts to uncover the causative principles behind events that occur in a specific physical or social location.

Agency refers to agents "of an extrahistorical sort" that control the actions of persons on the historical (story) level.[96] The Apocalypse of John, in attempting to explain the past, present, and future course of events, puts its finger on the extrahistorical agencies behind every human action. The agents of good are God,

---

[91]Ibid., p. 176.

[92]Ibid., pp. 176–177.

[93]Ibid., pp. 173, 176–177.

[94]Ibid.

[95]The three– and four–part divisions of creation are not in conflict; the quadrapartite division simply seems to make explicit the "four great fields of life," for the sea is implicitly included in 5:3 (Swete, *Revelation*, p. 83). "Under the earth" (5:3, 13) assuredly refers to Hades (see also Phil. 2:10) (Charles, *Revelation*, pp. 139, 150; Prigent, *L'Apocalypse*, pp. 96, 105).

[96]Malina, *Gospel of John*, pp. 6–7; *Christian Origins*, pp. 176–177.

Jesus, their angels, and a holy woman; the agents of evil are Satan, his angels, two beasts, and an unholy woman.

Act refers to the "acts of agents within the historical field as manifestations of extrahistorical agencies."[97] There is certainly the note of determinism in the mechanistic mode of formal argument.[98] Because the extrahistorical realities (God versus Satan) allow their mutual antagonism to spread beyond the skies, terrestrial inhabitants are necessarily affected.

The Apocalypse of John describes the acts of earthly agents in terms of how their actions evince supernatural forces. The narrative about God's "two witnesses" (11:3–13), for example, displays how John's vision is told with an emphasis on act. The two witnesses are emissaries of the Lord (11:4), who has given them supernatural powers to cause drought, turn water to blood, and send plagues upon the earth as often as they wish (11:6). The two witnesses in a real sense display a direct manifestation of the divine extrahistorical agency.

The two prophets are killed by "the beast which rises from the abyss" (11:7), which most likely refers not only to an evil supernatural entity but to its representative agent (or agents) on the terrestrial plane (although no agent is expressly stated in the text). Charles viewed the beast as a demonic Antichrist (drawn primarily from Dan. 7) that symbolized the Roman Empire, perhaps implicitly referring to the Nero *redivivus* myth or, at least, serving as a proleptic scene of similar evil beasts in chapters 13 and 17.[99] The notion of act, that is, the acts of agents as manifestations of extrahistorical agencies, is brought forward in the description of the beast as rising from the "abyss" (11:7; see also 17:8), which is a region of the demonic over which the heavens exert at least some control (9:1).[100] Satan himself, the chief evil extrahistorical agent, is thrown back down

---

[97]Ibid., pp. 176–177.

[98]Malina noted, *Christian Origins*, p. 178, "These extrahistorical agencies and their regular control of the flow of the action are clearly constraints to human action, unconcerned as they are with human decisions, sealing human beings in a fate beyond human control."

[99]Charles, *Revelation*, p. 286; and Ford, *Revelation*, p. 180, who also maintained that the beast could refer to "a political (domestic or foreign) enemy who attacks the civil and religious leaders of the faithful."

[100]Prigent, *L'Apocalypse*, p. 168, noted that this narrative continued along the lines of the prophecy of Daniel, which announced persecution against the faithful planned by demonic powers and carried out by temporal powers: "Ici nous

into this hole for a thousand years (so that the demonic principality becomes the demonic prison).

Mode of Ideological Implication. The third, and final, mode (or strategy) that the storyteller employs White called the mode of ideological implication. The mode of emplotment concerned the flow of the action, or the plot. The mode of formal argument concerned the explanatory effect of the story, that is, ability to discern the extrahistorical forces at work in society. The mode of ideological implication is concerned with the effect of the story upon the reader or hearer.[101] What actions are urged upon the audience as a consequence of the story? Malina defined ideology as "an assessment of the world along with a set of prescriptions for taking a position in the world and for acting upon that position."[102] Malina, following White, lists four ideological implications: anarchist, liberal, conservative, and radical. The fourth implication will be of greatest interest for the Apocalypse of John, but the first three will be briefly defined here.

The anarchist ideological implication, as the name implies, calls for the abolishment of society so that a new order may be established that is based on "fundamental humanity."[103] The phrase that best captures this ideology is, "The best of times is in the remote past that is immediately recoverable."[104] Malina argued that the gospel of John is the only New Testament writing to fit this category. The anarchist ideological position, Malina noted, fitted the weak group/low grid locus of the Gospel. The "best of times," according to John's gospel, lies in the past, when the Word, Jesus, lived among people (John 1:14), and will be established in the future ("right around the corner"), when Jesus' rule of love (based on values of fundamental humanity) emerges as persons believe in Jesus.[105]

---

apprenons seulement que cette puissance démoniaque doit être regardée comme l'origine réelle de l'hostilité que le monde manifeste aux temoins."

[101]Malina, *Christian Origins*, p. 178.

[102]Ibid., pp. 178–179.

[103]Ibid., pp. 179–180.

[104]Ibid., p. 183.

[105]Malina, *Gospel of John*, pp. 10–11.

The liberal ideological implication calls for social rearrangement: "the best option for the present is to 'fine tune' existing social arrangements, to adjust them for maximum efficiency, and thereby to maximize the current social scheme."[106] The phrase that best captures this ideological position is, "The best times of humankind are in the remote future."[107] Here the theme is the progress of humanity. The weak group/high grid script fits here because progress comes about as individuals (thus weak group) "achieve their maximum," which fixes the liberal ideological position (Malina maintained) as the current mainstream U.S. view.[108]

The conservative ideological implication asserts that "The best of times of humankind are in the present, right now."[109] Society ought to proceed and develop at its own pace; its members, as befitting strong group/high grid, must necessarily follow conformity. Malina used the metaphor of natural growth, and for the natural growth of the society to take place "the present must be maintained at all costs."[110]

The fourth ideological implication is the radical. Radicalism does not call simply for the abolishment of society (as in the anarchist position) but for its restructuring.[111] The phrase that best captures the radical position is, "The best of times is imminent, right around the corner."[112] Malina situated this ideology in the strong group/low grid quadrant, to which he assigned all the New Testament writings except the gospel of John. Even though the twentieth–century reader stands nearly two millennia from the New Testament writings, he or she must remember that the latter were written from a radical ideological position that expected restructuring of the world imminently ("right around the corner"!). Gager, referring specifically to the Apocalypse of John, noted that this New Testament document "was not written for posterity nor as a permanent contribution to Christian worship. For it was the fervent hope of writer and hearer alike that

---

[106]Malina, *Christian Origins*, p. 180.

[107]Ibid.

[108]Ibid.

[109]Ibid., pp. 180–181.

[110]Ibid., p. 181.

[111]Ibid.

[112]Ibid.

there would be no need to hear these words on more than one or two occasions."[113]

The radical then is the ideological position of the Apocalypse of John. Low grid implies a mismatch between values and experience; some people have it better in society than others. Strong group implies a high degree of embeddedness in a group, membership in which provides self–definition. Given this social location (strong group/low grid) and ideological position (radical), the communities behind the Apocalypse of John thus advocate the complete restructuring of society on the basis of the rule of God and his Christ (12:10). David L. Barr analyzed the "symbolic transformation of the world" that takes place in the text and found the following radical restructuring ("transvaluations"): the sufferer is the conqueror (the Lamb becomes the Lion); the victim is the victor (the martyr becomes the ruler).[114] As described earlier (p. 22), the communities of the Apocalypse of John are millenarian sects that, because of experiences of oppression, expect and prepare for a new age.[115] The radical ideological implication is the metahistorical strategy that shapes the telling of John's vision in order to call all believers in Jesus "to follow the Lamb wherever he goes" (14:4), even to death (12:11).

Social Location of Thought and the Apocalypse of John

Social location of thought described, according to Rohrbaugh, (1) "a common structural position occupied by a number of individuals in relation to a larger whole," (2) "the limited range of experience a position implies," and (3) "the process by which that position comes to be occupied."[116] This chapter first analyzed the latter process, that is, the synergy of the social facts of the case, the *realia*, that brought about the social location of the communities of the Apocalypse

---

[113]Gager, *Kingdom and Community*, p. 57.

[114]David L. Barr, "The Apocalypse as a Symbolic Transformation of the World: A Literary Analysis," *Interpretation*, 38 (1984), 41–42. Barr believed the Apocalypse of John is designed to change its audience decisively so that the radical restructuring of society begins within the community: "They [witnesses of Jesus] no longer suffer helplessly at the hands of Rome; they are now in charge of their own destiny and by their voluntary suffering they participate in the overthrow of evil and the establishment of God's kingdom" (p. 50).

[115]Stanley, "Use of Symbol," p. 197.

[116]Rohrbaugh, "'Social Location,'" p. 115.

of John. The writer John, who certainly viewed himself as a prophet to the churches of Asia Minor, writes about A.D. 90–96 to encourage fellow believers in the face of mounting deprivation, both relative and actual.[117] The categories of contemporary sect analysis of Bryan Wilson, as employed by John Stanley, also helped to further define the kind of communities that the prophet John addressed in his vision, particularly, millennial, adventist sects, which declared a new age and prepared for it.

Next, to move beyond the description of "the common structural position" of the communities of the Apocalypse of John as sect and to analyze as well "the limited range of experience [such] a position implies" (again Rohrbaugh), I made use of Malina's kitbashed model of Mary Douglas and Hayden White. The Apocalypse of John, in terms of Douglas's cultural anthropological theory, was viewed as strong group/low grid. As strong group, the text evokes communities with a strong emphasis on belonging to and being defined by the group (salvation comes by membership in the right group). As low grid, the text evokes a high degree of mismatch between socially held values and experience (some people have it better off than others).

Strong group/low grid communities follow their own "cultural scripts" (Malina): purity, rite, personal identity, body, sin, cosmology, and suffering and misfortune. The Apocalypse of John showed a strong concern for maintaining strict boundary lines to mark off the "we" against the "them" (purity). There is emphasis also upon keeping Christians focused on the boundary lines, either to cross over into the group (rituals) or to strengthen group identity (ceremonies). Individual members will define themselves in terms of belonging to the group (otherwise known as the dyadic personality), since there is no salvation outside of it (personal identity). As a "faction in crisis," a key perception in these groups is the transformation of the physical as well as the social body (body).[118] While there is an emphasis on group boundaries, the boundaries are felt to be porous, allowing deviants to enter who cause impurity (sin). The events in the world are perceived

---

[117]The present writer does not feel he has to choose either for a "relative deprivation" (Collins) or for a wholly physical persecution. The textual evidence seems to leave room for both, and one would suspect that such also is the cruel nature of persecution.

[118]Malina preferred this term (or even "fictive kin group facing dire social straits") rather than what he called the anachronistic "millennial sect"; see "Normative Dissonance," pp. 35–37.

by the group to be the work of personal agents, both good and bad (cosmology). Finally, suffering and misfortune are perceived to be the direct result of personal agents.

The Apocalypse of John was then analyzed in terms of Hayden White's metahistory model, which Malina superimposed on the group and grid model. The three modes or strategies of this model are mode of emplotment, mode of formal argument, and mode of ideological implication. The Apocalypse of John was described as satiric tragedy (mode of emplotment), that is, a story that explains the condition of captivity in the world (one cannot survive alone) and the ultimate negative results of opposition with the world.

The mode of formal argument (the "'point–of–it–all'") is mechanistic, which seeks to explain why life is as it is, and focuses on the narrative elements of location, agency, and act. Location, the physical or social stage on which the vision takes place, in the Apocalypse of John is universal, including heaven, the earth, and under the earth. Agency, the extrahistorical agents that control the action on the historical level, refers to the dualistic agents, for example, God versus Satan, Jesus versus Beasts, Holy Woman versus Prostitute. Act, which focuses on the acts of historical agents as manifestations of extrahistorical agents, is found, for example, in the narrative of the two witnesses (11:3–13). The two witnesses manifest divine extrahistorical agency (God); the beast from the abyss manifests evil extrahistorical agency.

The mode of ideological implication in the Apocalypse of John is radical, which calls upon the reader or hearer of the story to seek the restructuring of the present social order. As "factions in crisis," the communities behind the visions hope and prepare for a new age. The radical ideological position urges the hearers to resist the evil age and to follow the Lamb wherever he goes.

Social Location of Thought and Anti–language in the Apocalypse of John

Given the above understanding of the social location of the Apocalypse of John as communities evincing strong group/low grid features and the corresponding metahistorical modes (or strategies) of emplotment (satiric tragedy), formal argument (mechanistic), and ideological implication (radical), one can then proceed to ask the more specific question concerning the kind of language employed in the text. How does one characterize the linguistic usage of a group occupying the social location above? The answer to follow in the next chapter is that the language of the Apocalypse of John is, in sociolinguistic terms, "antilanguage." Anti–language, according to M. A. K. Halliday, is language that is antithetical to the norm society and is used by groups to provide secrecy, verbal play, solidarity, and an alternative social and conceptual reality.[119] Though the word "Anti-Christ" (as in 1 John 2:18, 22, 43; 2 John 7) is not part of John's lexical inventory, his language bears the stamp of antithesis.

---

[119]Malina, *Gospel of John*, pp. 11-17; Halliday, *Language as Social Semiotic* (Baltimore, Maryland: University Park Press, 1978), pp. 164-182; Roger Fowler, *Language as Social Discourse* (Bloomington, Indiana: Indiana University Press, 1981), pp. 142-161.

Chapter 3

ANTI-LANGUAGE

Social location of thought places the Apocalypse of John in the strong group/low grid quadrant of Mary Douglas's cultural anthropological model, which evinces a high concern for belonging to a community as well as a high mismatch between socially perceived values and experiences. Hayden White's metahistorical model confirmed the former identification by specifying the kind of story such a group, or person representing such a group, would tell, namely, a story with a satiric tragic emplotment (serving to explain the mismatch between perception and experience), mechanistic formal argument (focusing on location, agency, and act), and a radical ideological implication (urging the restructuring of society).

The notion of anti–language does not imply a turning away from social location of thought. Anti–language, arising as it does from a sociolinguistic perspective, complements the previous chapter on social location of thought and allows one to delve deeper into the relationship between historical setting and ideas. Language encodes and maintains the cultural system. As one uses language, one conveys meaning as well as indicates one's place in the cultural web. The sociolinguistic notion of anti–language, as well as social location of thought, attempts to explicate the active, social role of language in human interaction.

Anti–language is the language of social resistance. It is a language like any other language, that is, it functions to express and maintain the social structure. There need not be a radical suspension, or "reclassification" (Kress), of syntactical rules in the anti–language, though this can and does occur.[1] For groups who

---

[1] Gunther R. Kress, "Poetry as Anti–language: A Reconsideration of Donne's 'Nocturnall Upon S. Lucies Day,'" *PTL*, 3 (1978), 327–332. While a radical suspension of syntactical rules need not occur, Kress emphasized that "reclassification" constitutes a fundamental element in language: "Classification, and, hence, reclassification are fundamental processes in language, affecting not simply specific areas of language under certain restricted conditions. Classification is seen as a major link between culture and language, providing the specific input to the syntax of a language" (p. 331).

perceive themselves as relegated to the outer margins of society (the Apocalypse of John fits here), anti–language offers one form of protest against the standard society to which it stands opposed. No other means of power or influence may be available to oppressed groups, but they can "talk back." In this "back talk," old words will find new meaning and new words will arise to cover adequately the concerns of the group.

Malina turned to the sociolinguistic theory of Michael Halliday—in particular his notion of "antilanguage"—as a final step in his exercise of kitbashing (selective model building). Having analyzed the Gospel of John as weak group/low grid (Douglas) and romantic–tragic, formist, anarchist (White), Malina found in Halliday's theory a means for further analyzing the specific form that the language of the Gospel of John took as a result of its social placement. I have earlier stated my objections to Malina's reasons for placing anti–language solely in the weak group/low grid quadrant.[2] He stated that anti–language is found among people "forming antisocial groups," and one certainly cannot leave out the communities of the Apocalypse of John when speaking of antisocial groups.[3]

Before turning to an analysis of anti–language itself, this chapter will begin with a brief overview of the elements of Michael Halliday's sociolinguistic theory. A look at four theorists of anti–language will follow, which will provide examples and indicate the functions of anti–language. The four theorists are Michael Halliday, Gunther Kress, Roger Fowler, and Bruce Malina. Next I will compare anti–language and certain aspects of orality or oral culture, employing the works of Ong and Kelber. We tend to think of literature solely in terms of written works and forget—especially as regards the New Testament—the power of orality that underlies such a work as the Apocalypse of John.[4] In many ways anti–language may be seen as a manifestation of what Ong called "primary oral cultures," in which

---

[2]See p. 6 of this dissertation.

[3]Malina, *The Gospel of John in Sociolinguistic Perspective*, Center for Hermeneutical Studies in Hellenistic and Modern Culture Colloquy 48, H. Waetjen, ed. (Berkley: Center for Hermeneutical Studies, 1985), p. 11.

[4]Werner H. Kelber, *The Oral and the Written Gospel* (Philadelphia: Fortress Press, 1983), p. 1, quoted Lou H. Silberman's description: "We still march along the straight black line of the Gutenberg galaxy."

"sounded word" is experienced "as power and action."[5] Finally, I will return to social location of thought and make pertinent comments about social location of thought, anti–language, and the Apocalypse of John. This chapter will then serve as a preparation to investigate anti–language in the Apocalypse of John 11:19–15:3.

The Sociolinguistic Perspective

Language is the primary symbolic resource which humans share.[6] Ferdinand de Saussure, who laid much of the foundation for modern linguistics, recognized a social dimension to *langue*, that is, to language as a system.[7] Halliday noted, however, that when Saussure asserted that 'Language is a social fact,' he was attempting to account for "the special character of linguistics in relation to other sciences."[8] Language possessed (in Saussure's thought) a more visible, social, character; all people use language. Sociolinguistic theory, on the other hand, attempts to explicate the relation between the "social" phenomenon that is language and all levels of human cultural interaction.

The appearance of sociolinguistics may be viewed as a corrective to the emphasis in the early part of this century in structural linguistics with what Halliday

---

[5]Michael A. Harris suggested to me the connection between anti–language and certain aspects of orality. Walter J. Ong, *Orality and Literacy: The Technologizing of the Word*, NA, Terence Hawkes, ed. (London: Methuen, 1982), pp. 31–33.

[6]Bruce Malina, *Christian Origins and Cultural Anthropology: Practical Models for Biblical Interpretation* (Atlanta: John Knox Press, 1986), pp. 1–2; Halliday, *Language as Social Semiotic* (London: University Park Press, 1978), p. 4. Body language comes most readily to mind as a non–linguistic form of communication; however, body language may be more dependent on verbal expression than one first realizes. See also the chapter entitled "Nonverbal Communication" by George A. Miller in *Language: Introductory Readings*, Virginia P. Clark et al., eds. (New York: St. Martin's Press, 1985), pp. 633–641.

[7]Halliday is careful to place in context Saussure's maxim, which "Firth glossed as 'the language of the community, a function of *la masse parlante*, stored and residing in the *conscience collective*'" (*Language as Social Semiotic* [Baltimore, Maryland: University Park Press, 1978], p. 1). See Ferdinand de Saussure, *Course in General Linguistics*, trans. W. Baskin (1916; London: Fontana, 1974), pp. 7–15: "But what is language [*langue*]? It is not to be confused with human speech [*langage*], of which it is only a definite part, though certainly an essential one. It is both a social product of the faculty and a collection of necessary conventions that have been adopted by a social body to permit individuals to exercise that faculty.
. . . .
[Language] exists only by virtue of a sort of contract signed by the members of a community" (pp. 9, 14).

[8]Halliday, *Language*, p. 1.

called "intra–organism" studies, which focused on the individual and his or her language competence.[9] Halliday viewed language as a "social semiotic," that is, as a signalling or information system that is embedded within an encompassing cultural matrix. The initial focus is not on the individual (or the individual's performance or ability)—this is "intra–organism"—but on the languaging that takes place "inter–organism," person to person, in the social context.[10] The sociolinguistic perspective that Malina employed in his analysis of the Gospel of John has this twofold concern: (1) to begin its analysis with the society and not the individual and (2) to show the role language plays inactively symbolizing and maintaining social structures.[11] Language becomes a "resource, a meaning potential, which generates meaning that may be encoded on at least three linguistic levels: semantics (content), lexicogrammar (form), and phonology (expression)."[12]

Sociolinguistics, as the term indicates, is the application of the discipline of sociology to the discipline of linguistics. One often finds difficulty distinguishing between the disciplines since they share many perspectives and methodologies. Sociological method, for example, helped William Labov to bring greater precision in the collection and analysis of speech data in order to demonstrate a segment of linguistic change in New York City, which led to a better understanding of language in its social context.[13] Labov's study of "the social stratification of [the

---

[9]Ibid., pp. 11, 12–15. Examples of "intra–organism" linguistics would be Bloomfield's *Language* (New York: Henry Holt and Co., 1933), where there is a decided absence of the semantic component of language; Zellig Harris's *Methods in Structural Linguistics* (Chicago: University of Chicago, 1951); and Chomsky's revolutionary *Syntactic Structures*, Janua Linguarum Series Minor 4 (The Hague: Mouton, 1957) and *Aspects of the Theory of Syntax* (Cambridge, Massachusetts: The M.I.T. Press, 1965).

[10]Halliday, *Language*, pp. 12–16.

[11]Malina, *Gospel of John*, pp. 1, 12–13; also *Christian Origins*, pp. 1–3, 8–9.

[12]Halliday, *Language*, pp. 21, 187.

[13]William Labov, *The Social Stratification of English in New York City* (Washington, D.C.: Center for Applied Linguistics, 1966); but see the more comprehensive report of the methods and findings of the study in *Sociolinguistic Patterns* (Philadelphia: University of Pennsylvania Press, 1972), pp. 43–159. Labov aimed to record and analyze, in the informal department store setting, the utterance of both preconsonantal and final "r" (as in "fourth floor"). Interviewers would unknowingly (to the informant) record the store, floor within the store, sex, age (estimated in units of five years), occupation, race, foreign or regional accent, if any. The responses were then stratified according to these variables. While Labov noted room for improvement in his method, he concluded, "We see rapid and anonymous observations as the most important experimental method in a linguistic program

phoneme] (r) in New York City department stores" led him to posit that linguistic change is not only observable but that it is triggered by social interaction.[14] He discovered, for example, that lower middle class informants as a whole tended to hyper–correct their speech, that is, shift from casual "r" (not pronounced = "r–0") to prestige "r" (pronounced = "r–1"), as a result of "linguistic insecurity."[15]

Malina drew upon the theories of sociolinguists Joshua Fishman, M. A. K. Halliday, Roger Fowler, and Richard Hudson.[16] The following analysis will focus on Halliday's "language as social semiotic." I will work with this theory in particular since it is within his sociolinguistic framework that the notion of anti–language derives.

Halliday's Sociosemiotic Theory of Language. Michael Halliday studied under John R. Firth, who is often referred to as the founder of the so–called London School of linguistics, with its emphasis on language as a "functionalist 'system and structure.'"[17] Halliday's sociosemiotic theory of language consists of

---

which takes as its primary object the language used by ordinary people in their everyday affairs" (*Sociolinguistic Patterns*, p. 69).

[14]Ibid., pp. 122–123.

[15]Ibid., pp. 64–65: Labov explained the chief factor behind this phenomenon as a lack of formal education in the above group, in which the process of "linguistic socialization" is slower; consequently, when there is an effort to approximate "prestige speech", "the lower–middle–class speakers go beyond the highest–status group in their tendency to use the forms considered correct and appropriate for formal styles" (p. 127).

[16]Joshua Fishman, *Sociolinguistics: A Brief Introduction* (Rowley, Massachusetts: Newbury House Publishers, 1972); Roger Fowler, *Literature as Social Discourse: The Practice of Linguistic Criticism* (Bloomington: Indiana University Press, 1981) and *Linguistic Criticism* (Oxford: Oxford University Press, 1986); R. A. Hudson, *Sociolinguistics* (Cambridge: Cambridge University Press, 1980). Other excellent introductions to the field include Dell Hymes, ed., *Language in Culture and Society* (New York: Harper & Row, 1964); Stanley Lieberson, ed., *Explorations in Sociolinguistics* (Bloomington: Indiana University Press, 1973); Peter Trudgill, *Sociolinguistics: An Introduction* (New York: Pelican Books, 1974); Roger T. Bell, *Sociolinguistics: Goals, Approaches, and Problems* (London: Batsford, 1976); Gerhard Nickel, ed., *Applied Linguistics: Sociolinguistics* (Stuttgart: Hochschul-Verlag, 1978; Brigitte Schlieben–Lange, *Soziolinguistic: Eine Einführung* (2nd ed. Stuttgart: Verlag W. Kohlhammer, 1978); Christian Bachmann, Jacqueline Lindenfeld, Jacky Simonin, eds., *Langage et Communications Sociales* (Paris: Hatier–Credif, 1981).

[17]John R. Firth and his followers, often referred to as the London School, display a functionalist perspective within the European structural linguistic tradition. For an overall history and analysis of structural linguistics and of the London School see G. C. Lepschy, ed., *A Survey of Structural Linguistics* (1970; rpt. London: André

the following six elements: text, situation, register, code, the linguistic system, and the social structure.[18] The above elements form an interrelated theoretical web that attempts to make clear for the sociolinguist, among other things, how people decode and contextualize day to day speech; how they move from what they could say ("meaning potential") to what they actually do say ("actual semantic exchanges"); how they develop dialectal differences.[19]

Text. The first element of Halliday's sociosemiotic theory is the "text." Halliday's theory is derived from actual utterances, given his "inter–organism" perspective, from what people actually say in a given social context. Since the culture is viewed as an information system (semiotic), the text, that is, the language people use in an "operational context" (as opposed to a random "citational context"), represents "'what is meant'" out of the possible meanings available to a given culture.[20] Text, for Halliday, is simply, "actualized meaning potential."[21]

Situation. The text arises from a context or social environment, which is the "situation." People involved in any given linguistic interaction know what to say— and what is going to be said in return—given the particular social situation, of which they are part. Halliday represents the situation three dimensionally as "field," "tenor," and "mode."

> The field is the social action in which the text is embedded; it
> includes the subject–matter, as one special manifestation. The tenor is

---

Deutsche, 1982), pp. 21–73, 110–125; Geoffrey Sampson, *Schools of Linguistics* (Stanford, California: Stanford University Press, 1908), 34–56, 103–129, 212–235; D. Terrence Langendoen, *The London School of Linguistics: A Study of the Linguistic Theories of B. Malinowski and J. R. Firth*, Research Monograph 46 (Cambridge, Massachusetts: The M.I.T. Press, 1968). For background on John R. Firth see his two works *The Tongues of Men* [1937] *and Speech* [1930] (London: Oxford University Press, 1964); *Papers in Linguistics 1934–1951* (London: Oxford University Press, 1957); F. R. Palmer, ed., *Selected Papers of J. R. Firth 1952–59* (Bloomington: Indiana University Press, 1968); and T. F. Mitchell, *Principles of Firthian Linguistics* (London: Longman, 1975).

    Halliday's *Language as Social Semiotic* is fundamentally concerned with the "meaning potential" in language. He has recently extended his functional perspective to grammatical analysis in *An Introduction to Functional Grammar* (London: Edwin Arnold, 1985) and, Halliday and Robin P. Fawcett, ed., *New Developments in Systemic Linguistics* (London: Frances Pinter, 1987).

[18]Halliday, *Language*, pp. 108–114.

[19]Ibid., pp. 108, 126.

[20]Ibid., pp. 108–109.

[21]Ibid., p. 109.

the set of role relationships among the relevant participants; it includes levels of formality as one particular instance. The mode is the channel or wavelength selected, which is essentially the function that is assigned to language in the total structure of the situation; it includes the medium (spoken or written), which is explained as a functional variable.[22]

The three dimensional situation of a text, stated in simpler terms, involves the social activity (field), the role relationships involved (tenor), and the kind of language (spoken or written) employed (mode).[23]

Register. Just as text is an "actualized meaning potential," that is, what is meant as opposed to what could be meant, so "register" deals with the notion of text variety: "[Register] refers to the fact that the language we speak or write varies according to the type of situation."[24] Thus Halliday sees register as linguistic "variety according to use," "the meaning potential that is accessible in a given social context."[25]

Code. A "Code" (here Halliday follows Bernstein's code theory), or regulating process, determines the type of text that is actualized in a given situation (field, tenor, mode).[26] Halliday also referred to code as a "fashion of speaking." Register deals with linguistic variety. Code stands above this process, ordering the kinds of *meaning* a person will choose. Code is thus one of the "symbolic orders of meaning generated by the social system."[27]

As outlined by Bernstein himself, a code is a way of speaking that is generated by the myriad social structures of one's culture; through speech one learns social roles.[28] The code is generated by culture and the role relationships

---

[22]Ibid., p. 110.

[23]Ibid.

[24]Ibid., pp. 31–32, 110–111.

[25]Ibid., p. 111.

[26]Ibid.

[27]Ibid.

[28]Basil Bernstein, "Elaborated and Restricted Codes: An Outline," in *Explorations in Sociolinguistics*, ed. by Stanley Lieberson (Bloomington: Indiana University Press, 1967), pp. 126–127; and *Class, Codes, and Control*, vol. III, (Rev. London: Routledge & Kegan Paul, 1977). See also more recently "Codes, modalities, and the process of cultural reproduction: A model," *LS*, 10 (1981), 327–363: "Thus if code is the regulator of the relationships *between* contexts *and*, through that, the regulator of the relationships *within* contexts, then code must

that obtain within it. A person's choice of one set of meanings over another is regulated by a code, which in turn becomes a "fashion of speaking."

The linguistic system. Halliday emphasized the tri–level structure of the linguistic system by referring to the following "folk linguistic terminology": "'meaning' is represented as 'wording'—which in turn is expressed as 'sound' ('pronouncing') or as 'spelling.'"[29] Meaning, wording, sound or spelling may be glossed as semantics, lexicogrammar, phonology. Of special concern to the sociolinguist is the semantic system. Halliday recognized three functional components of the semantic system: ideational, interpersonal, and textual.[30]

The ideational function represents the "content function of language": people use language to express their experiences of the world that is outside and inside of them. The interpersonal component represents the "participatory function of language": people language with others, usually to some effect, and the relationships that obtain between the conversants determine largely the content and the manner of what is spoken, which is the textual function. The textual function thus represents "the speaker's text–forming potential."

Social Structure. The social structure is an obvious part of sociolinguistic theory, and the theoretical implications that the latter holds for the linguistic system are inexhaustible. Halliday stressed three key points at which the social structure is pronounced in his sociolinguistic theory.[31] First, the social structure shapes and gives meaning to what Halliday called the situation, that is, the social context or environment. The three components of Halliday's theoretical "situation" (field, tenor, and mode) ably demonstrate this. Tenor, which denotes status and role relationships, is a product of the social structure, as is field, which denotes kinds of social activity. Mode, which denotes kinds of linguistic or rhetorical strategies, is a product of the social structure.

Second, the social structure affects the way people express meaning. Bernstein's code theory attempts to take seriously the effect of various social relationships (familial, school, work, and so on) on the "meaning styles" that are

---

generate principles for the *creation and production* of the specialized relationships within a context" (p. 328).

[29]Halliday, *Language*, p. 122.

[30]Ibid., pp. 112–113.

[31]Ibid., pp. 113–114.

open to persons. Role relationships are transformed into fashions of speaking; the social structure is primary in code theory.

Third, the social structure, specifically in the form of social hierarchy (caste or class), is directly related to the forming and maintenance of dialects (linguistic variations according to the user) and registers (linguistic variations according to the use). The changes and incongruities of language, which Halliday termed the "'fuzziness' in language," is generated by the social structure:

> The 'fuzziness' of language is in part an expression of the dynamics and the tensions of the social system. It is not only the text (what people mean) but also the semantic system (what they can mean) that embodies the ambiguity, antagonism, imperfection, inequality and change that characterize the social system and social structure.[32]

An excellent example of this "fuzziness" of language, which is generated by the social structure, is Halliday's concept of anti–language. Anti–language is not linguistic verbal play, secrecy, and construction of an alternate social reality for its own sake.

Anti–language is a language of opposition—opposition which resides in social structures—a language whose mode, in turn, takes the form of secrecy, verbal play, and the creation of an alternate social and conceptual reality.

Theorists of Anti–language

Halliday initially introduced the notion of "antilanguages" in 1976. Since then three other scholars have fruitfully applied his concept. Halliday placed "antilanguages" within his *Language as Social Semiotic* in a section entitled "Language and social structure," in which he dealt with language in urban society and the functional relationship between language and social structure.[33] He illustrated the origin and function of anti–language using examples from Elizabethan England, modern Calcutta, and the subculture of Polish prisons and reform schools. Halliday was careful to correlate anti–language with his overall sociolinguistic theory (the components of which were outlined above).

Gunther Kress, also a British linguist, applied anti–language to poetry, and found that, in the crafted verse of John Donne ("Nocturnall Upon S. Lucies Day"),

---

[32]Ibid., p. 114.

[33]Ibid., pp. 154–193.

60

"every syntactic process and every syntactic classification functions to create and maintain (the world of) the anti–language."[34]

Roger Fowler, in his practice of "linguistic criticism," applied anti–language to prose fiction, and he found in Burgess's *A Clockwork Orange* a stark example of "the dialectical thinking which underlies anti–language, and its basis in social ideologies."[35] Fowler thus stressed, as Halliday did not, the anti–language as process, as well as varietal language.[36]

Bruce Malina applied anti–language as a final aspect of his kitbashed, sociolinguistic analysis of the Gospel of John. Malina wanted particularly to account for the uniqueness of the Fourth Gospel in contrast to the other three, that is, the way in which John highlights the interpersonal mode of language, which, Malina noted, is the linguistic component that is foregrounded in the anti–language.[37]

In the present section I will examine the four preceding theorists of anti–language in order to acquire a better understanding of the notion itself and of its application. I will examine common characteristics of anti–language and the speech of oral cultures and then return to social location of thought (particularly the models of Douglas and White) in order to make clear its relationship to anti–language. Thus one will be prepared to analyze anti–language in the Apocalypse of John.

---

[34]Kress, "Poetry as Anti–language," p. 340. Kress is professor of English and American Studies, University of East Anglia, and has sought to build upon Halliday's theory; see Kress, ed., *Halliday: System and Function in Language* (London: Oxford University Press, 1977).

[35]Fowler, *Literature as Social Discourse* (Bloomington: Indiana University Press, 1981), p. 142. By "linguistic criticism" Fowler denoted "a careful analytic interrogation of the ideological categories, and the roles and institutions and so on, through which a society constitutes and maintains itself and the consciousness of its members. As we have seen, all knowledge, all objects, are constructs: criticism analyzes the processes of construction and, acknowledging the artificial quality of the categories concerned, offers the possibility that we might profitably conceive of the world in some alternative way" (p. 25).

[36]Ibid., p. 150: "I have offered a view of anti–language as relational, contextualized: language sensitive to and working on its relationship with some norm of 'official', 'institutional' language."

[37]Malina, *Gospel of John*, pp. 1, 13–15.

Michael A. K. Halliday. Halliday's first treatment of "anti–languages" appeared in 1976.[38] The summary below follows the chapter on "Antilanguages" in *Language as Social Semiotic.* Studying anti–language is like studying not the ear but the earache, not the tympanum but otitis media.[39] Halliday made it clear that anti–language is pathological in nature:

> It has commonly been found with other aspects of the human condition—the social structure, or the individual psyche—that there is much to be learnt from pathological manifestations, which are seldom as clearly set off from the normal as they at first appear. In the same way a study of sociolinguistic pathology may lead to additional insight into the social semiotic.[40]

The metaphor of ear versus earache cannot be stretched too far; a knowledge of the structures of the ear is understandably essential when earache is indicated. The important difference is that the ear is looked at under certain *pathological* conditions: an inflamed tympanum traceable to such causative pathogens as viruses or hemolytic streptococci. Likewise, according to Halliday, one may study 'inflamed,' pathological, language, that is, anti–language, in order to achieve further understanding of language as a social semiotic, that is, language as an cultural information system.

Language is a reality–generating system. Anti–language is a reality–generating system as well but the "reality" it generates is an alternative reality. Halliday, working from the perspective of Berger and Luckmann, advanced the notion that an anti–language "exists solely in the context of *re*socialization, and the reality it creates is inherently an alternative reality, one that is constructed precisely in order to function in alternation. It is the language of an antisociety."[41] Recalling the ear–earache metaphor, there is the presence in the social system of some causative agent—some tension—that comes to exist between two social realities that manifests itself in the linguistic reconstruction of reality.

Tension in a culture may most readily be seen between a dominant culture and a particular subculture. Halliday gives three examples of this kind of tension:

---

[38]Halliday, "Anti–languages," *AA*, 78 (1976), 570–584.

[39]See p. 12 of this dissertation.

[40]Halliday, *Language*, p. 164.

[41]Ibid., p. 171.

62

the counterculture of vagabonds in Elizabethan England, antisociety in modern Calcutta, and the subculture of Polish prisons and reform schools.[42]

Halliday presented two categories for discerning the presence of anti–language: *re*lexicalization (that is, new words for old) and *over*lexicalization (that is, multiple words for the same concept).[43] The underlying principle in both cases is that, in the process of *re*socialization and *re*construction of the language, alternative and multiple ways of speaking enunciate the specific areas of concern to the speakers, "typically those that are central to the activities of the subculture and that set it off most sharply from the established society."[44]

The anti–language is the language relexicalized. Halliday noted that in Elizabethan England antisociety there were some twenty words used for those who fell into the class of vagabond: "upright man, rogue, wild rogue, prigger of prancers (= horse thief), counterfeit crand, jarkman, bawdy basket, walking mort, kinchin mort, doxy and dell."[45] Now each of these titles involves a relexicalization, that is, a new definition in the anti–lexicon. The first example is striking: upright man = vagabond! Another example involves the description of vagabond criminal activity:

> [N]ames for the strategies themselves, which are known collectively as *laws*—for example *lifting law* (stealing packages) which involves a *lift*, a *marker* and a *santer* (the one who steals the package, the one to whom it is handed, and the one who waits to carry it off.[46]

The above terms constitute the "professional jargon" of the vagabonds. They understand their own language, and often help to create it.

Anti–language is also language overlexicalized. The above examples demonstrate this well; while shifts in meaning (relexicalizations) have taken place in the terms *lift*, *marker*, and *santer*, the fact that three terms evolved to cover the roles involved in the *lifting law* indicates purposeful verbal recreation. Halliday also

---

[42]Ibid., pp. 164–178.

[43]Ibid., pp. 165–166.

[44]Ibid., p. 165.

[45]Ibid.

[46]Ibid.

noted that in the underworld of modern Calcutta there were twenty–one words for 'bomb,' forty–one for 'police,' and twenty–four for 'girl.'[47]

Anti–language may be realized on all three linguistic levels, that is, phonology, lexicogrammar, and semantics. Thus the metaphorical nature of anti–language may be seen phonologically and morphologically, as well as semantically, in the underworld language of Calcutta. Halliday listed a few of Mallik's examples:

> In phonology, Mallik distinguishes some thirty different processes: for example metathesis (e.g. *kodan* 'shop', from *dodan*; *karca* 'servant', from cakar), back formation (e.g. *khum* 'mouth', from *mukh*), consonantal change (e.g. *kona* 'gold', from *sona*), syllabic insertion (e.g. *bituri* 'old woman', from *buri*) . . . .
> In morphology also, Mallik identifies a number of derivational processes: for example suffixing (e.g. *kotni* 'cotton bag', from English *cotton*; *dharan* 'kidnapper', from *dhara* 'hold'); compounding (e.g. *bilakhana* 'brothel', from *bila*, general derogatory term, + *khana* '–orium, place for'); simplifying; shift of word class; lexical borrowing (e.g. *khalas* 'murder', from Arabic *xalas* 'end', replacing *khun*.[48]

Kress spoke of phonological and morphological metaphors as instances of "reclassification."[49] In the anti–language metaphor, or reclassification, has one consistent direction, namely, away from the norm usage. There is verbal play at every level of language.

Referring to his own sociosemiotic theory, Halliday noted that what produced relexicalization and overlexicalization is an orientation away from the experiential mode of meaning towards the interpersonal and the textual functions of the semantic system.[50] The interpersonal mode ("the speaker's meaning potential as intruder") generates re– and overlexicalization because of the speaker's attitude towards the social structure and the persons who represent it; the textual mode ("the speaker's text–forming potential") generates re– and overlexicalization because the speaker's ability to create and recreate language has value in that it sets him or her apart from the dominant social structures and allows him or her to create an alternative social reality.[51]

---

[47]Ibid., pp. 165–166.

[48]Ibid., p. 172.

[49]Kress, "Poetry as Anti–language," pp. 330–331.

[50]Ibid., p. 166.

[51]Ibid.

Halliday emphasized that anti–languages are not simply instances of verbal play for verbal play's sake. The anti–language is language; as such it is a reality–generating and –maintaining device that is marked by its stance toward the dominant social structure.[52] Employing the example of *grypserka*, the language of inmates in Polish prisons, Halliday explored the chief functions that the anti–language serves: to provide an alternative social structure and an alternative identity for those who find themselves "under pressure from the established world."[53] Podgórecki, upon whose study Halliday relies, found that inmates had made a division within the prison world between 'people' and 'suckers.' The anti–language revealed two classes of 'people' and three of 'suckers,' each with its own system of rewards and punishments.[54] Halliday noted that in the creation of this "'caste system'" emerges a distinct social structure based metaphorically on unincarcerated society, which he formulated as follows[55].

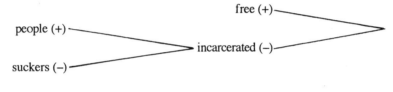

Antisociety   *Society*

Grypserka, or the language of the 'second life,' is the (anti–)language of persons who have become things as far as the dominant society is concerned. The response of inmates is to create, by means of language, an alternative social structure which confers upon some the status of person ('people') and on others the status of things ('suckers').

The creation of the alternative social structure within the prison functions, in turn, to give identity to those who know the anti–language. 'Suckers' will break the rules of verbal contest or, if privy to the language, will sell the secret language

---

[52]Ibid., p. 167: "It [anti–language] is the acting out of a distinct social structure; and this social structure is, in turn, the bearer of an alternative social reality."

[53]Ibid., pp. 166–169, 180.

[54]Ibid., p. 167.

[55]Ibid., p. 168.

to the police.[56] 'People' scorn the latter and, often in a position to do so, prescribe appropriate punishments for them. The final goal of anti–language is "to maintain inner solidarity under pressure."[57] To summarize, Halliday denoted anti–language as pathological language, the limiting case of a social dialect, which functions to create, express, and maintain an alternative social reality and identity for those who stand in tension from the dominant culture.[58] Anti–languages consist in liberal use of verbal contest and display and, sometimes, secrecy. Just as the anti–language is a metaphor for the language of the society as a whole, the anti–language is indicated by metaphorical modes of expression. The two chief characteristics of anti–language are relexicalization (new words for old) and overlexicalization (multiple words for one idea). Halliday considered anti–languages functionally. For him the anti–language emphasized the interpersonal (relational) and textual (expressive) functions of the semantic system as opposed to the experiential function: social relations between persons and the manner in which people speak or write to each other are foregrounded.

The language of inmates and countercultures provide clear examples of pathological language, anti–language. The latter are specimens drawn from real situations. A work of fiction, whether prose or poetry, while generally not a word for word repetition of actual utterances, is, according to Halliday, a speaker's (writer's) "contribution to the reality–generating conversation of society— irrespective of whether it offers an alternative reality or reinforces the received model—and its language reflects this status that it has in the sociosemiotic scheme."[59] The language an author chooses to employ for his or her voice, or the voice of other characters, may be anti–language as well as its opposite, language.

Gunther Kress. The next theorist of anti–language, Gunther Kress, applied Halliday's notion to John Donne's poem entitled "A Nocturnall upon S. Lucies Day." Kress investigated the thoroughgoing syntactic and semantic reclassification of language by the English metaphysical poet, who describes his alienation in a

---

[56]Ibid., p. 166.

[57]Ibid., p. 168.

[58]Ibid., pp. 178–179.

[59]Ibid., p. 182.

66

'frozen' world of negation.[60] The reclassification with which Kress dealt included straightforward negation (total reversal of classification), relexicalization, semantic reclassification of words, and the syntactic categories of tense, modality, voice, and transitivity. Kress took the lead from J. P. Thorne, who referred to the "systematic syntactic reclassification" in Donne's poem, but went a step further by discussing the idea of reclassification in terms of Halliday's anti–language. Reclassification, according to Kress, is exploited in the poem in the direction of negation, and negation (vis–à–vis the perceived norm language) is what anti–language is all about.[61] Kress worked from a solid sociolinguistic understanding of language: "the meanings originate with specific communities and are closely related to the economic and social and cultural organization of that community."[62] The relating of meaning with social structure forms the basis of Halliday's sociosemiotic view of language with its notion of a culturally resident "meaning potential."

Kress displayed the problem of "reclassification" in the poem as set forth by J. P. Thorne, who referred to the negation involved in the bipolar features animate/inanimate, human/nonhuman.[63] His initial examples are found in ll. 8 and 9 (for the complete poem see Appendix C). The first nine lines of the poem are as follows:

Tis the yeares midnight, and it is the dayes.
Lucies, who scarce seaven houres herself unmaskes,

---

[60]Gunther Kress, "Poetry as Anti–language," pp. 330–331. The full title of the poem is "A Nocturnall upon S. Lucies Day, Being the Shortest Day," and was written for the occasion of the onset of the winter solstice (December 12, according to the calendar Donne used) as well as the day to honor Saint Lucy, the patron saint of sight, whose name is the feminine derivative of the Latin "light." For an excellent introduction to Donne's life and writings see C. A. Patrides, ed., *The Complete Works of John Donne* (London: J. M. Dent & Sons, 1985) and Dwight Cathcart, *Doubting Conscience* (Ann Arbor, Michigan: The University of Michigan Press, 1975). Patrides, who quoted T. S. Eliot's poetic description of Donne:

He knew the anguish of the marrow
The ague of the skeleton;
No contact possible to flesh
Allayed the fever of the bone;

noted also "the imagery of decay, decomposition, dissolution" that one finds throughout Donne's secular and sacred poems (pp. 14, 33). For further background to "A Nocturnall upon S. Lucies Day" see Cathcart, *Doubting Conscience*, pp. 41, 177–178.

[61]Ibid., p. 340.

[62]Ibid., p. 329.

[63]Ibid., pp. 327–328.

> The Sunne is spent, and now his flasks
> Send forth light squibs, no constant rayes;
> The worlds whole sap is sunke:
> The generall balme th'hydroptique earth hath drunk,
> Whither, as to the beds–feet, life is shrunke,
> Dead and enterr'd; yet all these seeme to laugh,
> Compar'd with mee, who am their Epitaph.

In line 9 the human/animate pronoun "who" is equated with the nonhuman/inanimate "epitaph." In line 8 there is a similar reclassification: "all these [sun, his flasks, th'hydroptique earth = nonhuman/inanimate] seem to laugh [human quality]. Thorne argued that the shift in bi–polar features resulted simply in a "'breaking of rules'" (in a "counter grammar"), but Kress interpreted the examples not as an instance of the breaking of rules but as a change in the "input to the rule system."[64] Kress viewed Halliday's anti–language as "precisely the framework within which a motivated analysis of the syntactic processes at work in the poem may be carried out."[65]

Kress then viewed the anti–language of the poem, with its anti–grammar, as consisting primarily as negation, which serves to indicate the "total inversion of the world."[66] He demonstrated negation in terms of straightforward negation, relexicalization, semantic reclassification of words; and the syntactic reclassification of voice, tense, modality, and transitivity. Straightforward negation is not difficult to uncover.[67] There are the negative particles (*no, none, not, nor*) and affixes (for example, *un–*). There are words which are opposites of words generally thought as positive; Kress provided the following examples:[68]

dead (not alive)   *hydroptique* (not saturated)
emptiness   *flasks* (not the original source of light)
bed's feet (not head)   *sunk*
epitaph   *interred*
spent   *quintessence*
shrunk   *ruined*
nothingness   *darkness*
privations
absence

---

[64]Ibid., p. 328.

[65]Ibid., p. 329.

[66]Ibid., p. 330.

[67]Ibid., pp. 330–331.

[68]Ibid.

Finally, straightforward negation is indicated by words which carry negative associations but do not possess the antonyms as in the above list of examples (*scarce, dull privations, lean, wept, drowned, chaosses, withdrew, aught else, carcasses*).

Relexicalization, the process of substituting new words for old words, takes the following shape. Instead of replacing the "terms" in the larger community, the poet has relegated all terms denoting negation to his anti–language but terms which do not move in this direction belong to another, "possible world," which is not the world of the poet.[69] Thus the lists above involving straightforward negation constitute the concern of the poet, that is, form the poet's relexicalized interpretation of his own world as opposed to some other world.

The semantic reclassification of words is then clearly understood as "being in the direction of inanimacy, death."[70] This process is seen in the poem in the first few lines, as in the examples above from ll. 8 and 9. *Who* becomes inanimate; *laugh* is the action word for an inanimate, not an animate, agent. Kress poignantly describes the result of such semantic reclassification: "The effect of the poem rests on the eeriness of the 'reality' of the world in which dead things laugh and presumably living things do not."[71]

An anti–language extends to both the semantic and syntactic levels. Kress displayed the poem's anti–grammar on the syntactic level by examining voice, tense, mood (or, modality), and transitivity. Voice is affected by the negation of Donne's anti–language in a process of "passivization and agent deletion," in which an agent subject becomes an affected subject.[72] Kress noted that the process of passivization and agent deletion amounts to the height of negation in the anti–language: "The agent(s) are not specified, and an irrecoverable deletion amounts to a denial/negation of their existence (p. 333)."

Kress provided the following two examples from ll. 3 and 7–8.

---

[69]Ibid., p. 331.

[70]Ibid.

[71]Ibid., pp. 328–329.

[72]Ibid., pp. 332–333.

The sun is spent, and now his flasks [l. 3]

Wither, as to the bed's–feet, life is shrunk,
Dead and interred; [ll. 7–8]

First, "the sun is spent" (l. 3), although translated by some as an active expression (noun + is + adjective), is taken by Kress as the end process in which an underlying active form—"*some agent spends the sun*" (p. 332)—becomes passive and the unknown agent is deleted. The syntactic process facilitates that at the semantic level, which moves in the direction of inanimacy and death. At the syntactic level, however, the direction is from process (or, non–state) to state. The same process is at work, according to Kress, in ll. 7–8. Underlying the forms "life is shrunk . . . and interred," which Kress viewed as two passive constructions ("life is dead" was viewed as adjectival, are the active expressions 'some agent shrinks life' and 'some agent inters life.' Again the passive voice brings with it agent deletion; an active process is thus turned to state.

Passivization affects the tense of the verbs. Kress indicated that, while in the above examples the underlying verbal forms ('spends,' 'inters,' 'shrinks') are present tense, in the passive (agent–deleted) forms one finds the conjunction of present tense ("is") and non–present tense ("spent," "interred," "shrunk").[73] The effect that the poem realizes, according to Kress, is that while the poet writes in the present tense he describes actions that are "'not now but a prior time,'" which adds to the feeling of a static and negated world in which the poet resides (p. 333). Moreover, Donne, so Kress, "uses 'tense' to point to a major distinction between the world of *is* and *not is*" (p. 333). The poet inhabits the world of "not is," that is, the negated world.

Modality, which affirms the relation of a speaker to an action (actual, command, possibility, or wish, for example), finds syntactic expression in the anti–language of the poem.[74] Kress provided the three examples in ll. 10, 30, and 31 (p. 334). The future tense of l. 10 ("Study me then, you who shall lovers bee") points to a possible world, but it is a world from which the poet presumably excluded himself ("*you* who shall lovers bee") and which cannot occur now. The hypothetical "were" of l. 30 ("Were I a man, that I were one") and "should" of ll. 31–32 ("I should preferre, If I were any beast") raises the possibility of a world

---

[73]Ibid., pp. 333–334.

[74]Ibid., pp. 334–335.

"where men are men" and "one in which men are merely animate, *any* beast" (p. 335). Kress argues that the poet distances himself, by means of modality, from the three possible worlds above; he is neither lover, nor man, nor beast (p. 335).

Transitivity is the final syntactic element Kress addressed in his construction of the anti–language of Donne's poem. Transitivity deals with the notion of the presence or absence of a direct object following a verb. Kress first noted the passivization (and agent deletion) in the first stanza of the poem. He found in the second stanza a few examples of verbs with direct objects (p. 337).

l. 10 Study me then, you who shall lovers be
l. 13 In whom love wrought new alchemy
l. 14 For his art did express a quintessence
l. 17 He ruined me, and I am rebegot of absence, darkness,
         death

While "me" is the direct object of "study" (l. 10), Kress noted that the command ("study") belongs to only a future world, from which the poet presumably excluded himself. In the remaining lines Kress argued that the poet is never "a directly affected participant" in the present (p. 337). "Love" did its alchemical work in the poet, but he is merely the locus of the action not the affected object. Again, even though love's "art" performed its highest and purest work ("a quintessence," l. 14) for the poet, l. 17 explains the result: "He ruined me, and I am rebegot of absence, darkness, and death." Kress noted that the third and the fourth stanzas alike repeat the theme of the poet as "a nothing" (p. 338). The multiplication of terms for "poet = a nothing" may correctly be understood in Halliday's term "overlexicalization" (multiple words for one concept). Kress has adequately described what happens in overlexicalization but has not used the terminology as initially set forth by Halliday.

The conclusion of Kress's analysis of the syntax of the poem is that the poet is either indirectly affected as an object or is a negatively affected object, both of which lead to the poet as no lover, no man, nothing. Semantically the process of negation (through straightforward negation, relexicalization, and semantic reclassification) serves to paint the world where all life is dead yet has the ability to "laugh" at the nothing poet. Kress was correct in applying the term anti–language to Donne's "Nocturnall Upon S. Lucies Day," for, according to Kress's argument, the language of one world is set up over against the language of another in conscience opposition to it. The anti–language is a language which is determinedly relexicalized to focus on the interpretation of existence offered by one person (or by one person who speaks for others).[75] Donne's poetic experience may indicate the harsh world of lovers, or, as Kress suggested, Donne's creation of anti–language may indicate his "despair at being 'nothing,' living in a waste, unable to act, unable to create" (p. 342).

Whatever may be the background to the poem, as anti–language it evinces, in Halliday's terms, a foregrounding of the interpersonal and textual functions of the semantic system of language.[76] The ideational function, which Kress denoted as the expression of "the external world" (Halliday: "the content function of language"), is displaced by the semantic functions of language that deal with "the self [interpersonal function], and its appropriate expression [textual function]" (p.342). Simply, what counts in the anti–language is the relation of tension between speaker and addressee (in this case, the social structure) and how that relation is expressed (relexicalization, overlexicalization, and, for Kress, reclassifications at other linguistic levels). While one is not dealing here with a language of tension and the verbal play of an anti–language.

Roger Fowler. A third theorist of anti–language is Roger Fowler, who, like Kress, is professor of English and American studies at the University of Anglia. Fowler has been instrumental in forging a new path in literary studies, which he has termed "linguistic criticism." Linguistic criticism, in contradistinction to 'literary criticism,' attempts to analyze literary texts employing "an analytic method drawn from linguistics."[77] The functional sociolinguistic theory of Halliday provided a

---

[75]Kress made a careful distinction between personal and community anti–language: "To restate, the anti–language may be a personal one, specific to the relation between two lovers; it may be a personal one, but more generally about the poet and the world in which he finds himself; or it may be the language of a community, of which the poet is one member, albeit the creator or articulator of the values, meanings, and (anti)language of the community" (p.340).
The Apocalypse of John evinces both a personal and a community anti–language. As persecuted prophet John is expressing personal anti–language; yet, viewing the communities which John addressed as apocalyptic sect, one can see John's anti–language as spoken for the community, that is, he is the "articulator."

[76]Ibid., pp. 341–342; and see the explanation of Halliday's ideational, interpersonal, and textual functions above (p. 58).

[77]Fowler, *Linguistic Criticism* (Oxford: Oxford University Press, 1986), pp. 1–12; *Literature*, p. 245.

major basis for Fowler's linguistic criticism. The language of linguistics, according to Fowler, is both comprehensive and systematic enough to explicate "the relationships between textual construction and the social, institutional, and ideological conditions of its production and reception."[78]

Fowler examined two works of prose fiction, Anthony Burgess's *A Clockwork Orange* and William S. Burrough's *Naked Lunch.* He found in both works the "dialectical semantics" of anti–language at work.[79] I shall focus only on Fowler's investigation of Burgess's *A Clockwork Orange*, which constitutes a more overt example of the processes of an anti–language.

Two important hypotheses about language constituted Fowler's approach to anti–languages, both of which are rooted in Halliday's sociosemiotic theory.[80] First, the semantic level of a language is essentially a "product of the social/cultural/economic/technological structure" (p. 145). What people can mean is determined to a large extent by their cultural landscape. Second, "Linguistic varieties encode. . . different semantic potentials" (p. 146). For example, dialects (regional varieties of language) are not simply different ways of saying the same thing but (as the first hypothesis indicates) are referents to different "social/cultural/economic/technological structure[s]." An important ramification of the second hypothesis is that a linguistic variety—an anti–language, in particular— is not only a "variety" but also a "process," which constitutes Fowler's modification to Halliday's theory about anti-languages.[81]

Fowler characterized Halliday's depiction of anti-language as too static a term. Halliday viewed anti-language as an instance of pathological linguistic variety but, according to Fowler, did not make explicit the more active process that is involved in its use.

> While I accept the varietal status of anti–language, I also want to say that anti–language is a *process* as well as a *variety.* Emphasizing the 'secret language' aspect of anti–language, one might regard it as isolated variety, cut off from the norm just as its

---

[78]Fowler, *Linguistic Criticism*, p. 12.

[79]Ibid., p. 146: "Because they are antithetical to the norm society, Halliday argued, their language structure will involve systematic inversion and negation of the structures and semantics of the norm language."

[80]Ibid., pp. 145–146.

[81]Ibid., p. 150.

speakers are segregated from the mass of the population. . . . Similarly, it is not satisfactory to regard anti–language as creating a completely autonomous alternative reality (which might be *any* ideology); the alternative is most fruitfully seen as provoked by, and a creative critique of, the norm. It is in this sense of dialogue between ideologies, reflected in linguistic transformations, that I am going to apply the concept of anti–language to literature.[82]

I think this criticism might better be viewed as clarification by Fowler, for Halliday is not completely lacking in at least the mention of most of these elements. Fowler's modified understanding of anti–language certainly makes more explicit that the anti–language is active dialogue between society and anti–society.

Fowler worked with the same dual symptoms of anti–language, namely, relexicalization and overlexicalization. His modification (clarification) to Halliday's initial theory enabled him to expand the gloss of each term. Relexicalization, for Fowler, was still essentially "new words for old": "'Relexicalization' is the provision of new vocabulary item for a new concept peculiar to the deviant group, in adaptation of an existing item in such a way as to make it clear that a shift of values has occurred" (p. 147).

Fowler commented that relexicalized language is "a technical necessity," for every language will have its own jargon. Overlexicalization, according to Fowler, is "the provision of a large number of alternatives for the important concepts of the counter culture" (p. 147). Where relexicalization and overlexicalization occur, a dialogue is taking place between a norm society and an anti–society.

The anti–language is more than verbal play for its own sake. One must always keep in view the meanings residing in the norm society, to which the anti–language becomes open confrontation and challenge. The notion of dialogue—anti–language as process, not stasis—is central for Fowler because he is investigating here one particular literary form, the novel. Within the novel an author can present the "negotiation" that obtains between characters in terms of language and anti–language, ideology and anti–ideology, in which process of negotiation the reader enters as well (at least vicariously).[83]

---

[82]Ibid. Fowler's criticism of Halliday extends in the right direction yet may reach a little further than necessary. Halliday, while listing anti–languages as the limiting cases of a social dialect, nevertheless described their function as the expression, symbolization, and maintenance of a social order, which connote not only process but process engaged over against a standard community and its language (see Halliday, *Language*, pp. 172, 179). Fowler's criticism (perhaps better, clarification) is helpful as he introduced the notions of "transaction" and "negotiation" (Fowler, *Literature*, p. 150).

[83]Ibid., p. 157.

Fowler found the perfect paradigm for an anti–language in Anthony Burgess's early novella, *A Clockwork Orange*.[84] The story is set in a future where violent gangs rule the streets by night. One of the gangs is headed by the fifteen year old Alex, who narrates the entire story. The novella consists of three sections (of seven chapters each). In Part One, Alex recounts the cruel antics of his own marauding group, which climax in his unfortunate (for him) capture by the police. In Part Two, Alex tells of his life in prison and the chemical–hypnotic cure ("Lodovico Technique") that not only brings about his release but also transforms him into an unresponsive, albeit moral, person. In Part Three, Alex painfully narrates the results of his cured life back in society and of the reversal of his cure, after which it slowly dawns on him that life would be better spent in more positive pursuits.

Alex is the speaker of anti–language in the novel. Members of the norm society (middle–class, for example, his parents and some of his victims; upper–class, for example, doctors and prison officials) speak standard English, which Alex, as first–person narrator, faithfully quotes. His own language, invented by Burgess, is called "Nadsat" and is a Russified version of English, which makes it stand out as an example of anti–language. Burgess indicated that Alex's "invented lingo" was meant to "muffle the raw response we expect from pornography"; the shocking deeds that are described in the novel are rendered in a speech that the reader has to learn, adds to the distance (or tension) that the anti–language creates.[85] Fowler queried that the anti–language was "presumably designed to connect [it] . . . with the modern London underworld."[86]

---

[84]I have used the following edition: *A Clockwork Orange* (1962; rpt. New York: Norton & Co., 1987); hereafter abbreviated as *CO*. As a British scholar Fowler naturally used the edition that contained twenty–one chapters. There were twenty in the original edition published in the United States. In a forward to the "restored" (twenty–one chapter) American edition, Burgess commented that, although *A Clockwork Orange* is not the writing for which he would like most to be remembered, the novel as he wrote it contained twenty–one chapters. The twentieth chapter is important to the story, he stated, because in it the main character, the young Alex, "grows bored with violence and recognises the human energy is better expended on creation than destruction" (p. vii). Such "moral transformation," missing from the first American edition that Stanley Kubrick translated into a popular film, is the *sina qua non* of novel writing (p.viii). Of course, it is interesting that the publisher for the restored American edition, Eric Swenson, noted that he and Burgess "differ in their memories as to whether or not the dropping of the last chapter, which changed the book's impact dramatically, was a condition of publishing or merely a suggestion form conceptual reasons" (p. xiii).

[85]Burgess, *CO*, p. x.

Nadsat, Alex's language, is a highly descriptive criminal language, abounding in relexicalization and overlexicalization. With respect to relexicalization, I quoted Fowler's examples of "peet" (= drink), "britva" (= razor, knife), and "droog" (= friend) earlier (see above, p. 5). Anatomical terms are nearly all relexicalized: "rooker" (= hand), "rot" (= mouth), "glazzies" (= eyes), "gulliver" (= head), "litso" (= face), "zoobies" (= teeth). These terms are used descriptively as Alex narrates violence inflicted on others, as here, for example, an elderly professor who is walking home from the library (*CO*, pp. 6–7):

> "You naughty old veck [man], you," I [Alex] said, and then we began to filly about with him. Pete held his rookers and Georgie sort of hooked his rotwide open for him and Tim yanked out his false zoobies, upper and lower. He threw these down on the pavement and then I treated them to the old bootcrush, though they were hard bastards like, being made of some new horrorshow plastic stuff. The old veck began to make sort of chumbling shooms—"wuf waf wof"––so Georgie let go of holding his goobers apart and just let him have one in the toothless rot with his ringy fist, and that made the old veck start moaning a lot then, then out comes the blood, my brothers, real beautiful.

"Veck" (= man) is a relexicalized term for middle– or upper–class person, and thus a derisive term (as is "chelloveck").[87] Alex and his gang are able to beat up the old man without fear of getting caught by "millicents," that is, the police.

In the above quote, "horrowshow" provides an excellent example of a form of relexicalization that Fowler termed "semantic inversion."[88] "Horrowshow" becomes a cognate of the Russian adjective *xorosho* (= good). While Alex intends a positive meaning (a cup of tea ["chai"] as well as giving someone a violent blow to the head ["gulliver"] can both be very "horrowshow," that is 'great'), the English word has a negative primary meaning.

Two overlexicalized areas of concern for Alex and gang, as indicated in the story, are terms connected with violence (and the instruments used to inflict it) and terms denoting females. As for violence, Alex's *raison d'etre*, there are

---

[86]Fowler, *Literature*, p. 152.

[87]Chelloveck is not a derisive term in Russian per se, since it is the ordinary word for "human being." It can be derisive in certain contexts; it functions like "Mensch" in Yiddish, e.g. a real Mensch applied to a jerk or hobo is derisive.

[88]Ibid.

overlexicalized terms for gangs: "bandas or gruppas or shaikas" (p. 31).[89] Instruments of violence include "britva" (= razor, knife), "nozh," "oozy" (= chain). "To do the ultraviolent" is a general term for committing a crime. There are more specific terms, as in robbery, for example: to "smeck off with the till's guts" is to empty the contents of a cash register.

Terms for females are as varied as the terms for violence. The words Alex uses to denote his mother are not all that unrecognizable: "mum" and "em" (initial letter of the word "mum"). Besides the general term for a woman, "devotchka," there are "baboochka," "cheena," "ptitsa," and "little sister."

Next to relexicalization and overlexicalization there is verbal play of many kinds. Halliday initially noted that anti–languages manifest open verbal contest, which is important in that it allows the (anti–language) speaker to identify herself as a member of the anti–society by means of her knowledge and use of the language of the anti–society. Fowler's list included puns, alliteration, onomatopoeia, rhyme, chiasmus, hyperbole, and parallelism. Verbal play, Fowler presumed, is employed in the anti–language "to signify energy, confidence, creativity: to emphasize their [Alex and company's] freedom from the patterns of the language and so their freedom from the norms of the society."[90]

Alex's language, as well as his violence, is directed against the "norm" society, particularly, the middle class.[91] As stated above, the narrator Alex is careful to quote the language of the norm society as he hears it; his language, anti–language, creates a sharp tension between him (and his droogs [= friends]) and nearly every one else. The middle–class is seen as hard–working but otherwise impotent. They hide, afraid, in their houses and apartments by night, gluing themselves to the television.

---

[89]Ibid. Fowler noted that he was unsure whether the words are synonymous or of distinct gloss.

[90]Ibid., p. 153. Of course Fowler suggested that the "dialogic openness" between language and anti–language is closed by Burgess himself, who has Alex narrating not in a substandard English dialect but in one manifesting a "high literariness," which would in turn indicate "socialization into the aesthetic norms of the (for the reader) dominant society" (p. 154). One might question Fowler's contention, however, that "urban delinquency and violence" and "high literariness" were mutually exclusive, particularly in a (hypothetical) future society.

[91]Ibid., pp. 151–152.

> It [the alley] was like resting between the feet of two terrific and very enormous mountains, these being the flat–blocks, and in the windows of all of the flats you could viddy [= see] like blue dancing light. "This would be the telly. Tonight was what they called a worldcast, meaning that the same programme was being viddied by everybody in the world that wanted to, that being mostly the middle–aged and middle–class lewdies [= people] (*CO*, p. 17).

The "implicit addressee" of the story, as Fowler noted, happens to be largely the "book–reading" middle–class, for whom Alex often provides translations for words and terms: "a rooker [a hand, that is]," "litso [face, that is]," "nagoy [bare, that is].[92] Fowler concluded that anti–language, more than a mere "representation" of the language of an extreme segment of society, is a process of negotiation between two segments of society. The latter process allows the reader of the novel to experience vicariously the "life–experience, or world–view" of the anti–society, particularly where the world–view is "presented as a troubling challenge to the norms encoded in middle language."[93]

For Fowler, the "logic" of the anti–language is more important than its "content."[94] By "logic" Fowler meant the very "essence" of anti–language:

> The essential feature is the antithetical logic of the relationship between an official and an unofficial voice: an unresolved, unmediated, antithesis which preserves a critical, dialogic openness in the novel's examination of its central ethical or social or psychological (or whatever) concerns.[95]

In *A Clockwork Orange* the "unofficial voice" of Alex becomes the locus of the challenge and the tension between the "official voice." Throughout the novella the tension is unresolved. Even to the end, when Alex begins to experience his "moral transformation," his language is anti–language:

> But where I itty [= go] now, O my brothers, is all on my oddy knocky [= own], where you cannot go. Tomorrow is all like sweet flowers and the turning vonny earth and the stars and the old Luna [= moon] up there and your old droog Alex all on his oddy knocky seeking like a mate [presumably a wife] . . . . But you, O my brothers, remember sometimes thy little Alex that was. Amen. And all that cal [stuff] (*CO*, pp. 191–192).

---

[92]Ibid., p. 153.

[93]Ibid., p. 157.

[94]Ibid., p. 158.

[95]Ibid.

78

Alex is on his own, seeking his own devotchka (a middle–class pursuit as well), yet maintaining the antithesis that is indicated by his anti–language.

Bruce Malina. The final theorist of anti–language is Bruce Malina, whose kitbashed theory (social location of thought and sociolinguistics) I am following in this dissertation, examined the Fourth Gospel as anti–language in order to account for the uniqueness of the gospel as over against Matthew, Mark, and Luke. In terms of Halliday's sociosemiotic theory, Malina found that the interpersonal and textual components of the text were foregrounded (the ideational component moves to the background) as is typical of anti–languages.[96] In other words, the writer of the gospel emphasized relation, that is, "of whom and to whom Jesus speaks" (interpersonal component) as well as linguistic form, that is, "how Jesus speaks, how others speak to Jesus" (textual component). In the anti–language emphasis on the interpersonal and the textual translates into relexicalization, overlexicalization, various kinds of verbal play, and a conversational mode of discourse.[97] Johannine anti–language is the communication of a weak group/low grid group as it "talks back" to strong group/low grid groups, both Christian and non–Christian.[98]

Relexicalization took the following shape in the Gospel of John, according to Malina. Relexicalization, basically, new words for old, shows the fundamental concerns of a group lexically, that is, at the word level. In the Fourth Gospel Malina pointed to the pre–epilogue climax of 20:31 as the fundamental message that becomes relexicalized: "'that you may continue to believe that Jesus is the Messiah, the Son of God, and that believing you may have life in his name.'"[99] "Jesus," as

---

[96]Malina, *Gospel of John*, p. 13.

[97]Ibid., p. 14. While Halliday, *Language*, pp. 169–170, stressed the resocialization function of conversation (à la Burger and Luckmann), Malina is the only other of the anti–language theorists that I am analyzing who emphasized the place of conversation in the anti–language.

[98]Ibid., p. 12. Malina noted the following groups as targeted by John's gospel: "the world," "the Jews," and, referring to Raymond Brown's list, "the adherents of John the Baptist who do not as yet believe in Jesus, and three groups which claim to believe in Jesus: crypto–Christians, Jewish Christians and Christians of the apostolic churches."

[99]Ibid. Otto Böcher, "Das Verhältnis der Apokalypse des Johannes zum Evangelium des Johannes," in *L'Apocalypse johannique et l'Apocalyptique dans le Nouveau Testament*, BETL 53, ed. J. Lambrecht (Leuven: Leuven University Press, 1980), pp. 295–301, has an excellent list of the central categories of concern in the gospel of John (Christology, pneumatology, angelology, satanology, ecclesiology,

"Messiah," as "Son of God," and the new life available through faith in him, become the lexical foci of the Johannine community.

Overlexicalization, multiple words for one concept, is foreseeably large in the Gospel of John. Malina listed the following "contrasts":[100]

spirit	flesh
the above	the below
life	death
light	darkness
not of the/this world	of the/this world
freedom	slavery
truth	lie
love	hate

The above words constitute contrasting overlexicalizations of "modes of living and being." One other example given by Malina is synonymous expressions involving a believer's response to Jesus:[101]

> believing into Jesus
> following him
> abiding in him
> loving him
> keeping his word
> receiving him
> having him
> seeing him

Malina's conclusion is that the above kind of language is "quite predictable" as anti-language.

All kinds of verbal play are readily observed by the hearer of the Gospel. This is a function of the textual component in the semantic system of language. Malina gave examples of passages involving movement from ambiguity to misunderstanding and finally to clarification.[102] A fine example of this device of misunderstanding is in the story of the raising of Lazarus (John 11:1–46).[103] One

---

eschatology, and the sacraments) as well as a list of literary forms (*Formales*) (dualism and antonyms; metaphors; numeric symbolism; formation of the material; quotes from the Old Testament).

[100]Malina, *Gospel of John*, p. 12.

[101]Ibid.

[102]Ibid., p. 13. Passages cited are John 2:19ff.; 3:3ff.; 4:32ff.; 6:33ff.; 8:31ff.; 8:38ff.; 11:11ff.; 11:23ff.; 13:8ff.; 14:7ff.; 14:21ff.; 16:16ff.

[103]For a fine introduction of "misunderstanding" in the Gospel of John see R. Alan Culpepper, *Anatomy of the Fourth Gospel* (Philadelphia: Fortress Press, 1983), pp. 152–165. See also Jacob Kremer, *Lazarus: Die Geschichte einer Auferstehung* (Stuttgart: Verlag Katholisches Bibelwerk, 1985), for a thorough

notes ambiguity in Jesus' declaration, "'Our friend Lazarus has fallen asleep, but I go to wake him out of sleep'" (John 11:11); misunderstanding in the disciples' reaction, "'Lord, if he has fallen asleep, he will recover'" (John 11:12); and clarification in Jesus' response, "'Lazarus is dead; and for your sake I am glad that I was not there, so that you may believe. But let us go to him'" (John 11:15). Malina referred to the verbal play in the word "sleep." The use of irony is also indicative of the tendency of an anti–language to foreground the textual dimension of language.[104]

Anti–language not only places the textual function in the foreground but also the interpersonal function of language. The interpersonal component focuses on relation and is translated into overlexicalization in the following ways, according to Malina.[105] The two lists above of the "two contrasting realms" and "activities of discipleship" (above, p. 79) indicate an interpersonal direction. The "I am" sayings of Jesus overlexicalize "various, real world objects" (bread, light, door, life, way, vine) as interpersonal metaphors for Jesus.[106]

Conversation is a distinctive mark of Johannine discourse and, according to Malina, evidence of the foregrounding of the interpersonal component in the anti–language.[107] As a bearer of an alternative social reality in the Gospel, anti–language is an agent of resocialization. The several conversations in John indicated for Malina the process of resocialization with a "heavy foregrounding of interpersonal meanings directed to individuals."[108] For example, the conversations between Jesus and the ruler Nicodemus (John 3:1–21) and between Jesus and the

---

investigation of the text, historical representation in art and literature, and contemporary message of the pericope; for John 11:11–16 in particular see pp. 61–63.

[104]Malina listed John 2:9–10; 4:12; 7:27; 7:42; 7:52; 11:16; 11:36; 12:19; 13:37; 18:31; 18:38; 19:5; 19:14; 19:19ff (p. 13). For an introduction to the use of irony in the Gospel of John see Culpepper, *Anatomy*, pp. 165–180; and, particularly, Paul Duke, *Irony in the Fourth Gospel* (Atlanta: John Knox Press, 1985), pp. 1–42, 117–135.

[105]Malina, *Gospel of John*, p. 13.

[106]Ibid.

[107]Ibid., p. 14. Malina listed John 3:1–4:42; 5:10ff.; 6:22ff.; 9:13–10:42; 11:1–44; 11:45–12:36a; 13–17.

[108]Ibid.

woman from Samaria (John 4:1–26) have the function of instructing the Johannine anti–society about believing in Jesus.

Malina followed Halliday in the functions to which he put anti–language. An obvious omission, however, regards the notion of secrecy, which Halliday found as a functional component in the various criminal languages he used as examples of anti–language. Malina presumably did not find evidence of this function in John. Malina suggested the following uses of anti–language.

The anti–language is a medium for "an alternative social reality" and, thus, "resocialization."[109] Malina clearly showed the social location of thought of the Fourth Gospel and its placement in (Douglas's) weak group/low grid, which shows a great concern for group boundaries ("we" versus "they"). The "we," the Johannine Christians, through their use of anti–language, successfully constructed and became bearers of an alternative reality where Jesus was the true manna (John 6:41), which directly contradicted "the Jews'" (strong group/low grid) perception. Malina noted the function of conversation in the resocialization process.

As weak group/low grid, the Gospel of John represents a community that "talks back" to the strong group/low grid communities among which it resided.[110] If, for example, the Johannine community was feeling the pressure of synagogue expulsion (John 9:22 (34); 12:42; 16:2), then its use of anti–language serves the function of maintaining "inner solidarity under pressure."[111] The ability of

---

[109]Ibid., pp. 13–14.

[110]Ibid., p. 15.

[111]I find ample support for the theory of an expulsion from the synagogue suffered by the early church (and reflected in the Fourth Gospel). J. L. Martyn's "two level drama" attempted to account for the expulsion from the synagogue and its effects in his *History and Theology in the Fourth Gospel* (New York: Harper & Row, 1968), pp. 3–40. See also Robert Kysar, "The Gospel of John in Current Research," *RSR*, 9 (1983), 316; D. M. Smith, *Johannine Christianity: Essays on its Settings, Sources, and Theology* (Columbia: University of South Carolina, 1984), pp. 23–24; and Klaus Wengst's intriguing attempt at localization of the Johannine synagogue expulsion in *Bedrängte Gemeinde und verherrlichter Christus: Der historische Ort des Johannesevangelium als Schlüssel zu seiner Interpretation* (2nd ed. Neukirchen–Vluyn: Neukirchener Verlag, 1983), pp. 32–96.
  One must be careful not to equate every reference to "the Jews" with 'archenemy.' There is abundant critical analysis of the description and function of the Johannine "Jews": see in particular Urban C. von Wahlde, "The Johannine 'Jews': A Critical Survey," *NTS*, 28 (1982), 33–60; John Ashton, "The Identity of the ΙΟΥΔΑΙΟΙ in the Fourth Gospel," *NovT*, 27 (1985), 40–75; and, most recently, Michael Cook, "The Gospel of John and the Jews," *RE*, 84 (1987), 259–271; and R. Alan Culpepper, "The Gospel of John and the Jews," *RE*, 84 (1987), 273–288.

members of the weak group/low grid community to speak as well as understand the anti–language strengthened their perception of belonging to the group.

Anti–language and Aspects of Oral Culture

The anti–language is the language of one group that sees itself as opposed to another group. Relexicalization, overlexicalization, and verbal contest of all sorts indicate the presence of anti–language. Malina, following Halliday, observed that an anti–language is no one's "mother tongue," that is, it is a language that exists "solely in a context of resocialization."[112] Nevertheless, one notes striking similarities between anti–language and certain characteristics of orality or oral cultures, in which 'language play' is handed down from mouth to ear, as it were. Walter J. Ong and Werner H. Kelber are two scholars who have examined orality and its impact on written texts. One may look to them to understand primarily oral cultures.

Walter J. Ong: Aspects of Oral Culture. Walter J. Ong has recently analyzed the profound changes that occur in the shift from oral to literate cultures. By primary oral cultures Ong denoted oral cultures untouched by writing.[113] Upon taking up the subject of literate culture, Ong delineated what is essentially at heart of the latter shift: literacy becomes "the new world of autonomous discourse," that is, "discourse which cannot be directly questioned or contested as oral speech can because written discourse has been detached from its author."[114] What are the characteristics that anti–language shares with the oral speech of primary oral cultures?

---

[112]Malina, *Gospel of John*, p. 14; also Halliday, *Language*, p. 171.

[113]Ibid., p. 31.

[114]Walter J. Ong, *Orality and Literacy: The Technologizing of the Word*, NA, ed. Terence Hawkes (New York: Methuen, 1982), p. 78. The following quote indicates the extent to which writing has pervaded "human consciousness" (p. 78):
A deeper understanding of pristine or primary orality enables us better to understand the new world of writing, what it truly is, and what functionally literate human beings really are: beings whose thought processes do not grow out of simply natural powers but out of these powers as structured, directly or indirectly, by the technology of writing. Without writing, the literate mind would not and could not think as it does, not only when engaged in writing but normally even when it is composing its thoughts in oral form. More than any other single invention, writing has transformed human consciousness.

The following characteristics comprise those "psychodynamics of orality" that correspond to anti–language.[115]

(1) Additive rather than subordinate (pp. 37–38): oral discourse tends to connect utterances with "and" (Gen. 1:1–5, for example, where "and" occurs nine times) not "then," "when," or "if." Fowler noted that the anti–language syntax of Alex was often paratactic (as well as hypotactic).[116]

(2) Redundant or 'copious' (pp. 39–41): redundancy, that is, "repetition of the just said," allows both the speaker and the hearer to keep in focus what is being said. Similarly, overlexicalization supplies multiple words for one concept to focus the hearer's (or reader's) attention on the concept involved, as in the examples of the numerous Johannine terms for discipleship.

(3) Close to the human lifeworld (pp. 42–43): genealogical lists, for example, do not contain neutral facts but describe human relations in an oral culture. The anti–language emphasizes the interpersonal function of language and is therefore concerned to stress relation between persons.

(4) Agonistically toned (pp. 43–45): Ong noted that "writing fosters abstractions that disengage knowledge from the arena where human beings struggle with one another" (pp. 43–44). Oral culture is characterized by a more vituperative, "name–calling," stance. Antagonism strikes at the heart of anti–language. Halliday viewed anti–language as the extreme case of a social dialect not because of the distance between society and anti–society but because of the tension between the two.

(5) Empathetic and participatory rather than objectively distanced (pp. 45–46): here the emphasis is "close, empathetic, communal identification with the known" (p. 45). Ong spoke of the "objectivity" of the literate culture. Anti–language is no one's mother tongue; it is subjective in that the speaker of the anti–language consciously identifies himself or herself with the core values of the group. Anti–speech indicates subjective choice and participation in anti–society.

(6) Homeostatic (pp. 46–49): the meaning of words in an oral culture are generated by contemporary usage (there are no dictionaries). In the same manner, "oral societies live very much in a present which keeps itself in equilibrium or homeostasis by sloughing off memories which no longer have present relevance"

---

[115]Ibid., pp. 37–57.

[116]Fowler, *Literature*, p. 153.

(p. 46). Relexicalized and overlexicalized words in anti–language have direct referents to the (present) situations that gave rise to them.

(7) Situational rather than abstract (pp. 49–57): the situational aspect of an oral culture is similar to homeostasis, for both concepts are directly related to "the living human lifeworld" (p. 49). An oral culture is "situational" in that it "tend[s] to use concepts in situational, operational frames of reference that are minimally abstract" (p. 49). Halliday's examples of Elizabethan England criminal anti–language demonstrated the situational function of language. Lexical items involved in the "lifting law," that is, how to go about stealing packages, indicate the contextualized nature of anti–language.[117]

Werner H. Kelber: Orality in the Gospel of Mark. Werner H. Kelber applied the insights of Ong's investigation into oral versus literate cultures to the field of Biblical studies, which, according to Kelber, evinced "a disproportionately print–oriented hermeneutic," especially in form critical studies.[118] He analyzed the synoptic tradition, Mark, Paul, and the Q source in terms of orality and textuality. An example of aspects that anti–language shares with speech in oral cultures may be found in Kelber's examination of "oral syntax and story" in the Gospel of Mark.[119]

Kelber listed the following elements in Markan narrative (Mark 1–13) that possess a heightened "oral profile."

(1) "The many stories are linked together by stereotypical connective devices" (p. 65), among them the adverbial "immediately" and "and immediately" (1:29; 3:6; 6:54; etc.); the iterative "again" and "and again" (2:1; 7:31; 14:40; etc.); the formulaic "and it happens" or "and it happened" (1:9; 2:15, 23; etc.); and abundant use of paratactic "and" (9:2; 11:20; 15:42; etc.). Ong used the term "additive" to denote the highly paratactic style of orality.

---

[117]Halliday, *Language*, p. 165. The following elements of the "lifting law" are relexicalizations of the norm language that cover the "technical and semitechnical features" of the contextually generated anti–language: "*lifting law* (stealing packages) which involves a *lifter*, a *marker*, and a *santer* (the one who steals the package, the one to whom it is handed, and the one who waits outside to carry it off); names for the tools, e.g. *wresters* (for picking locks), and for the spoils, e.g. *snappings*, or *garbage*; and names for various penalties that may be suffered, such as *clying the jerk* (being whipped) or *tyining on the chats* (getting hanged)" (p. 165).

[118]Kelber, *Oral and Written*, p. xv.

[119]Ibid., pp. 64–70.

(2) "Interchangability of actions and words" (p. 65), by which Kelber explained what he called "the gospel's *activist syntax*" (p. 66), which is seen, for example, in Jesus' first exorcism (1:21–28). Jesus' 'new teaching with authority' (word) is equated with the account of the exorcism (action). Anti–language possesses an "activist syntax," where "words carry the force of action, and actions speak as loud as words" (p. 66).

(3) "A number of stylistic and rhetorical features contribute to the gospel's oral flavor" (p. 66), including folkloristic triads, prolific use of the third person, use of historical present, and preference for direct speech. The above devices create an impression of vividness, and this tendency is at work in anti–language in the form of all kinds of verbal play.

(4) Duality of duplication consists in "[t]he reiteration of words, clauses, and themes and allows the hearer to return and link up with what was said before" (p. 67). Kelber drew from Neirynck's investigation of "Markan pleonasms, redundancies, and repetitions" (p. 66): for example, compound verbs followed by the same preposition (1:16; 10:25; 15:32; etc.), multiplication of cognate verbs (2:15; 8:6–7; 14:45; etc.), double imperatives (4:39; 14:38; 15:36; etc.), double negatives (1:44; 13:32; 16:8; etc.), local and temporal redundancies (1:32; 11:15; 15:42; etc.), repetition of motifs (3:21, 22; 10:32; 14:41, 42; etc.), double questions (2:7; 8:17; 14:37; etc.). The anti–language manifests such multiplication or duality.

(5) "Narration in the form of actions is where the oral interest lies" (p. 69). Characters in the Gospel story are not portrayed in any detail, but their actions (in the form of dialogues, controversies, and confrontations) tell the audience all he or she needs to know. Anti–language reflects the antagonistic as well as the action–centered aspects of oral speech.

The comparison above shows a striking similarity between elements of orality and anti–language. The primary reason for this is the grounding of the former and the latter in concrete, human events. There is a natural and lively quality to interpersonal communication. I have referred to anti–language as "back talk," which indicates not only the tension between person and anti–person but also, in Fowler's terms, the transaction that takes place between them. The speech of oral cultures, the similarities notwithstanding, is not ipso facto anti–language. The distinguishing marks of anti–language are (1) a social situation that generates confrontation and negotiation between two communities, (2) relexicalization, (3) overlexicalization, and (4) verbal play of all kinds. Anti–language thus serves to promote solidarity, verbal play, an alternative social and conceptual reality, and sometimes secrecy, as the anti–group "talks back" to the norm group to which it stands opposed.

Bruce Malina and Social Location of Thought

Bruce Malina is to be credited with bringing Mary Douglas, Hayden White, and Michael Halliday together in his kitbashed theory for investigating the Gospel of John. One theory builds upon the next. Douglas's group and grid model delineated the social placement of a group as well as the cultural scripts it will follow. White's metahistorical model, which is superimposed onto Douglas's group and grid model, delineated the kind of story that one may expect to hear from a group (or person representing a group) residing in a social location. Finally, Halliday's theory of anti–language delineated the particular form that a group's language will take whenever a group is characterized as existing in a state (and process) of tension with the dominant society.

It is outside the scope of this dissertation to examine the social location of thought of each example given by the four preceding theorists of anti–language. Malina, however, has provided a most useful paradigm in his sociolinguistic analysis of the Gospel of John. Malina placed the Gospel of John in Douglas's weak group/low grid quadrant: the transitional weak group corresponds to the experience of the Johannine community as an expelled community; the low grid indicates the mismatch between culturally shared values and actual experience of the group.[120] Johannine Christians gave evidence of following the cultural scripts for this social location (purity, rite, personal identity, body, sin, cosmology, suffering and misfortune).[121]

Malina employed White's metahistory model to indicate the kind of story the weak group/low grid community would tell.[122] Finally, Malina employed Halliday's notion of anti–language to show how a language relexicalized and overlexicalized functioned to encompass and express the group's social location (group and grid) and story (metahistory). Malina was careful to point out that the

---

[120]Malina, *Gospel of John*, pp. 11–12.

[121]Ibid., p. 2. For Malina's sketch of the cultural script for weak group/low grid see see his *Gospel of John* (Figure 1, unnumbered page).

[122]Ibid., pp. 2–11.

components of the kitbashed theory (Douglas/White/Halliday) cannot determine the exact form that an anti–language will take (no more than one can determine who will become a sinner and who a saint); the theoretical components do, however, "determine and define the limits within which an author's selection process can take place."[123]

In the next chapter I will attempt to follow the above paradigm in order to analyze anti–language in the Apocalypse of John. In Chapter Two I described the social location of the Apocalypse (strong group/low grid) and corresponding story (satiric tragedy). In this chapter I have examined the form as well as the function of anti–language as criminal speech (Halliday), as poetry (Kress), as prose fiction (Fowler), and as gospel (Malina). In Chapter Four I will look for relexicalization, overlexicalization, and all kinds of verbal play in the Apocalypse of John 11:19–15:4 as an expression of strong group/low grid concerns and a satiric tragic (meta)perspective.

---

[123]Ibid., p. 11.

Chapter 4

ANTI-LANGUAGE IN THE APOCALYPSE OF JOHN 11:19-15:4

The next task for one who attempts to analyse anti-language in the Apocalypse of John is to delimit a section of the prophecy for particular focus. I have chosen Apocalypse of John 11:19-15:4, which consists of a series of what James Blevins called "tableaux."[1] One form of the tableau, the French *tableau vivant*, is the depiction of a scene usually presented by silent and motionless costumed participants.[2] While the participants often do not speak in the tableaux of the Apocalypse of John, their voices resound nevertheless with "the sound of a trumpet" (Rev. 4:1).

As John views and describes one tableaux after the other, he betrays the perception dominant in the first-century world that unseen, heavenly forces controlled all events in the cosmos, forces which divine revelation could expose to a prophet.[3] Since life was controlled by what was transpiring in the heavens, people

---

[1]Blevins, *Revelation as Drama* (Nashville: Broadman Press, 1984), p. 79, defined tableau as "a short dramatic piece with two or three main actors." Adela Collins, *The Apocalypse*, NTM, vol. 22 (Wilmington, Delaware: Michael Glazier, 1979), p. xiii, referred to the section simply as seven unnumbered visions, which speak of the triad of persecution, judgment, and triumph.

[2]Emile Mâle, *Religious Art in France: The Late Middle Ages*, trans. Marthiel Mathew (Princeton: Princeton University Press, 1986), pp. 171-172, described how the "'confrères of the garden'" at the cathedral of Rouen in the early sixteenth century "transformed their chapel into a garden, and dressed as apostles, performed the funeral and miraculous resurrection of the mother of God." The confrères were discouraged from performing *tableaux vivantes* for the reason that money might be better spent on an ornamental window.

[3]Walter Wink, *Naming the Powers: The Language of Power in the New Testament*, vol. 1 (Philadelphia: Fortress Press, 1984), pp. 13-96, has assembled an impressive description of the New Testament "powers," which--contrary to a modern understanding--pervaded both the physical and metaphysical: "For the ancients, heaven and earth were a seamless robe, a single interacting and continuous reality" (p. 16). Wink, in his account of the "imprecise, liquid, interchangeable, and

paid close attention to horoscopes and constellations. The seer John, perhaps seeing what no other person could see, was told to record what was going on in the sky. Messages in the stars were also translatable. While ancient Israel was forbidden to worship stars (Deut. 4:19), the New Testament story opens, according to Matthew, with astrologers following a star. According to the closing story of the New Testament canon, what was happening in the sky would very soon affect the earth.

Anti-language emphasizes the interpersonal function of language, and one finds in the seven tableaux such a dialogical thrust, though the interpersonal relations are often of the most antagonistic sort. There is a woman, her child, and a dragon (12:1-17); a beast from the sea and the people of the earth (13:1-10); a beast from the land and the people of the earth (13:11-18); the Lamb and his 144,000 followers (14:1-5); the Son of Man and the earth (14:14-16); and angel and the earth (14:17-20); and the Lamb and an innumerable host of conquerors (15:1-4).

The language of the seven tableaux evinces an emphasis on the textual function of language, which is another indication of the presence of anti-language. The person spoken to (interpersonal) as well as how one speaks (textual) is of concern. Thus the language of the Apocalypse of John is a language employing verbal play of all kinds that incessantly marks the tension between the Lamb and his followers and the Beast and his followers.

I will analyze each tableau using the following categories.

(1) Setting and Content of the Tableau
(2) Relexicalization in the Tableau
(3) Overlexicalization in the Tableau
(4) Verbal Play in the Tableau
(5) Anti-language and Strong Grid/Low Group

First, I will examine the setting and content of the tableau in order to describe the essential components of each dramatic scene. I will examine the essential components to see how they fit a satiric tragic mode of emplotment, mechanistic mode of formal argument, and radical ideological implication (Hayden White's metahistorical model). I will then investigate the text for overt signs of relexicalization, overlexicalization, and various forms of verbal play. The

---

unsystematic" vocabulary of power in the new Testament (p. 9), described the following categories: the powers; angels; fallen angels, evil spirits, demons; and angels of the nations (pp. 13-35). John's visions of divine and anti-divine forces shift in location from sky to earth and back to sky with great ease, which is indicative of the all-pervasive presence of "the powers."

investigation aims to be functional as well as descriptive, that is, to answer the following questions: What purpose is the anti-language serving in its particular setting? How is this use of anti-language indicative of strong group/low grid concerns (purity, rite, personal identity, body, sin, cosmology, and suffering and misfortune)? As a prologue to the investigation, however, I will defend the selection of Apocalypse of John 11:19-15:4 as the focus of my analysis of anti-language in the Apocalypse of John.

Structure of the Apocalypse of John

The thesis of this dissertation is that the language of the Apocalypse of John is anti-language. I have singled out one section for a test case. Apocalypse of John 11:19-15:4 suggests itself as a pivotal section because it serves as part of the climactic center of the revelation to John.[4] The thesis can be tested without reference to the overall structure of the book, yet I have referred to Apocalypse of John 11:19-15:4 as a part of the climactic center, which betrays my presuppositions about the outline. How does 11:19-15:4 fit in the flow of John's prophecy?

Realistically the answer to the latter question is "It all depends on whom you ask." The outlines of no two scholars will coincide (or coincide at all). Just as each approach to structure has its attractiveness (as well as shortcomings), so too each approach entails the methodological and exegetical presuppositions of the user. Yet, as Prigent has suggested, the Apocalypse of John itself encourages attempts at structuration.[5]

Wayne Kempson has extensively investigated the numerous external and internal approaches to the structure of the book and concluded that external methods, while they stressed the unity of the text, imposed a foreign framework to construct an outline, and that internal methods, since they attempt to follow the text

---

[4]Here I am following Elisabeth Schüssler Fiorenza, *The Book of Revelation: Justice and Judgement* (Philadelphia: Fortress Press, 1985), pp. 176-177. The center of the book, according to Fiorenza, is Rev. 10:1-15:4, which involves the prophetic scroll (10:1-11) and "the prophetic interpretation of the political and religious situation of the community."

[5]Pierre Prigent, *L'Apocalypse de Saint Jean*, CNT, vol. 14 (Lausanne: Delachaux & Niestlé, 1981), p. 364, is encouraging: "Mais on ne se décourage pas: en effet le livre offre des invitations, il signale liu-même des structures numérique par exemple, et l'on se désespère de ne pas pouvoir les suivre jusqu'à leur aboutissement."

92

exclusively, were "more reliable in determining the shape of the Apocalypse."[6] He based his own outline on a literary and content analysis, which contained the valuable elements of both the external and internal approaches.[7]

The key phrase (an internal approach) indicating structural division, according to Kempson, is "in the Spirit" (1:10; 4:2; 17:3; 21:10).[8] Richard Jeske's analysis of the phrase "in the Spirit" as a "code-symbol" for John's "identification" as a true prophet, his "reception" as a fellow hearer of the Spirit, his "prophetic responsibility" to, as well as his "participation" with, the fellow sufferers strengthens Kempson's argument that the phrase "in the Spirit" serves as a sign of "topical structuring of the writing."[9] Kempson then divided the prophecy into four "visions" (p. 119):

Vision I	1:9-3:22
Vision II	4:1-16:21
Vision III	17:1-21:8
Vision IV	21:9-22:5

---

[6]Wayne Kempson, "Theology in the Revelation of John" (Ph.D., dissertation, The Southern Baptist Theological Seminary, 1982), p. 95.

Kempson listed the following external approaches to viewing the structure of the Apocalypse of John: (1) as a reflection of prior literature (Ezekiel, e.g.); (2) as based on liturgical patterns; (3) as a Greek drama; (4) as revolving around the imperial games; (5) as using symbols (following the signs of the zodiac, e.g.); and (6) as a text exhibiting a deep structure at the actantial level (following the work of Greimas) pp. 45-70).

Internal approaches to the structure of Revelation are as follows: (1) the septenary approach; (2) content analysis approach (following, e.g., the trichotomy [things which you saw/which are/ which are about to happen] derived from Rev. 1;19); (3) the phrase approach; (4) the recapitulation approach; (5) the transposition approach (pp 72-95).

Besides the analysis of Fiorenza and Kempson, other systematic approaches to the structure of the Apocalypse of John include the following: U. Vanni, *La Struttura letteraria dell' Apocalypse* (Rome: Herder, 1971); Adela Collins, *The Combat Myth in the Book of Revelation*, HDR, 9 (Missoula, Mt.: Scholars Press, 1976); Ferdinand Hahn, "Zum Aufbau der Johannesoffenbarung," in *Kirche und Bibel. Festgabe für Bischof Eduard Schick* (Paderborn: Ferdinand Schöningh, 1979), pp. 145-154; Jan Lambrecht, "A Structuration of Revelation 4:1-22:5," in *L'Apocalypse johannique et l'Apocalyptique dans le Nouveau Testament*, BETL 53 (Leuven: Leuven University Press, 1980), pp. 11-18.

[7]Ibid., pp. 95-142.

[8]Ibid., pp. 103-112 (also pp. 83-86).

[9]Richard Jeske, "Spirit and Community in the Johannine Apocalypse," *NTS*, 31 (1985), 463-464. Jeske reacted against the consensus view of the phrase as denoting exclusively the prophet's "ecstatic condition" (pp. 452-453). Kempson, following the consensus view, understood the phrase as the "special condition of the Seer in which he was especially open to divine inspiration" (p. 111).

He placed within Vision II The Seven Seals (5:1-8:1), The Seven Trumpets (8:2-11:19), The Three Signs (12:1-16:21), which nearly correspond to Blevins's Act IV (11:19-15:4).[10] Moreover, The Three Signs (12:1-16:21) constitute, for Kempson, the climax to the development of Vision II.[11]

While the phrase approach is appealing as a signal to overall structure ("in the Spirit" handily provides an overt structural marker), Fiorenza has rightly criticized the latter approach for the simple reason that one should look for the "joints of the structure" and not the "'dividing marks'":

> However, these "dividing marks" do no occupy such a clear position in the outline of Rev. that the author could have intended to indicate the structure of his work with them. The author does not divide the text into separate sections or parts, but joins units together by interweaving them with each other through the method of intercalation. It is therefore more crucial to discern the joints of the structure which interlace the different parts than to discover "dividing marks."[12]

Fiorenza's proposal (look for joints not dividing marks) seems, in the final analysis, to be the better criterion for discerning an outline concerning which, as Kempson himself noted, John "left no explicit indications."

Fiorenza allowed the following three "structural patterns and compositional techniques" to determine the plan of the Apocalypse of John:

1. The pattern of seven.
2. The two scroll visions and the christological inaugural visions in 1:12-20 and 19:11-16.
3. The method of intercalation and interlocking, of joining."[13]

The "surface structure" of the Apocalypse of John then finds an outline consisting of a concentric A B C D C' B' A' pattern.[14]

---

[10]Ibid.

[11]Ibid., p. 131.

[12]Fiorenza, *Revelation*, p. 172.

[13]Ibid., p. 174. Her resulting 'deep structure' outline consisted, like Kempson's, of four parts:
  I. The inaugural vision and the letter septet (1:9-3:22);
  II. The seven sealed scroll (4:1-9:21; 11:15-19; 15:1, 5-16:21; 17:1-19:10);
  III. the small prophetic scroll (10:1-15:4);
  IV. The visions of judgment and salvation (19:11-22:9).

[14]Ibid., p. 175. Fiorenza presented a different albeit concentric outline in her earlier article, "The Eschatology and Composition of the Apocalypse," *CBQ*, 30 (1968), 561. The concentric pattern above is the deliberate result, according to

```
A    1:1-8
B    1:9-3:22
C    4:1-9:21;  11:15-19
D    10:1-15:4
C'   15:1, 5-19:10
B'   19:11-22:9
A'   22:10-22:21
```

While Kempson's Three Signs section (12:1-16:21) represented the climax of Vision II (the Scroll unsealed; heralded and summarized; opened and executed; culminating in seven bowls of wrath), Fiorenza's chiastic structure placed the climax of the whole apocalypse at the introduction of the small scroll of prophecy and its subsequent visions.[15]

Kempson's Vision II (4:1-16:21) covered Fiorenza's C, D, and a small part of C', which points to the unevenness of employing phrases (such as "in the Spirit") to account for the structure of the Apocalypse of John. One finds, however, that 11:19-15:4 is common climactic material for Kempson and Fiorenza. I concur with Kempson that one finds a climactic section for his Vision II in the above section; but I find Fiorenza more convincing that Apocalypse of John 10:1-15:4 serves as "the climactic center of the action," for the section of early Christian

---

Fiorenza, of the writer's attempt to structure his prophecy "after the authoritative Pauline letter form" (p. 76). Such a concentric structuration is not without its problems, as Jan Lambrecht, "Structuration," p. 84, has shown: "It is extremely hard to admit for BB' and CC' a clearly concentric structure intended by the author." Also Strand, "Chiastic Structure and Some Motifs in the Book of Revelation," *AUSS*, 16 (1978), 401-408, wondered how Fiorenza concluded that D (10:1-15:4) was the center of the book simply because it was a prophetic interpretation of the community (p. 406). Strand felt that the entire Apocalypse was prophetic interpretation.

Fiorenza's concentric structural theory cannot be so easily dismissed. BB' and CC' are not as dissimilar as Lambrecht charged. B and B' both deal with the people of God, troubling evil, and the divine promises; C and C' both contain two septets of judgment. While it appears that Fiorenza posited Rev. 10:1-15:4 as the climactic center of the book because this section corresponded to D in her concentric outline, one can claim the section as climactic center on the following basis. First, beginning in chapter 10, John presents his credentials as prophet to the community and to the world most solemnly (10:1-11). This is followed by the measuring of the place of prophecy and the worshiping community (11:1-2); the description of two other prophets (11:3-14), which contains a proleptic reference to the beast (11:7) that dominates much of the prophetic interpretation of the prophet in the rest of the section (D). Second, the "compositional rules" (Fiorenza) underlying the Apocalypse of John call for a central climax. Regardless of the extent to which one applies the genre of Greek drama to the Apocalypse, one can at least acknowledge an affinity in structure between the former and the latter. Fiorenza noted that in Greek drama, "the climax falls near the center of the action, and the denouement comes near the end" (p. 176). Thus Fiorenza's section D may rightly be referred to as the climactic center of the book.

[15]Ibid., pp. 175-177.

prophecy presents the "prophetic interpretation of the political and religious situation of the community."[16]

James Blevins, like Fiorenza, viewed the structure of the Apocalypse with a structuralist pattern of A B C D C' B' A' and likened the core section (D) to the climactic center of Greek tragic drama.[17] In this dissertation I will follow the terminology of Blevins's Act II with its Seven Tableaux. My investigation will also include the "interlude" of the announcement of the three angels (14:6-13) that comes between the fourth and fifth tableaux. Apocalypse of John 11:19-15:4 is part of the climactic center of the prophecy and, as I contend, comprises an excellent paradigm of anti-language for the whole book.[18]

---

[16]Ibid., p. 175.

[17]Blevins, *Revelation*, KPG (Atlanta: John Knox Press, 1984), p. 8; Fiorenza, *Revelation*, p. 176. Blevins has constructed an outline of the Apocalypse based on Greek tragic drama, particularly the seven-windowed theater at Ephesus. See his essay "The Genre of Revelation," *RE*, 77 (1980), 393-408; and *Revelation as Drama*, pp. 16-22.
Act IV (The Seven Tableaux--11:19-15:4) is the climactic center of his seven-act drama and has the following outline:

	Stage setting--11:19
Scene 1	The first tableau--woman, child dragon (12)
Scene 2	The second tableau--the beast from the sea (13:1-10)
Scene 3	The third tableau--the beast from the land (13:11-18)
Scene 4	The fourth tableau--the lamb with the 144,000 (14:1-5)
Scene 5	The fifth tableau--the son of man on a cloud (14:14-16)
Scene 6	The sixth tableau--the harvest of grapes (14:17-20)
Scene 7	The seventh tableau--the hymn of the lamb (15:1-4)

Blevins's overall approach, which evinces an excellent pedagogical method, has not gone without negative criticism. Kempson, "Theology in Revelation," pp. 59-62, was doubtful in his analysis of Blevins's 'Revelation as Greek drama' of even the existence of a seven-windowed theater in Ephesus at the time of John; he noted the declining function of the chorus in later Greek tragedies (John, according to Blevins, makes great use of the chorus). Kempson did not consult, however, the archaeological evidence within the first century; see Wilhelm Alzinger, *Die Stadt des siebenten Weltwunders* (Wien: Wollzeilen, 1962), pp. 70-75. More recently Michael Harris, "The Literary Function of Hymns in the Apocalypse of John (Ph.D. dissertation, The Southern Baptist Theological Seminary, 1988), pp. 8-12, has demonstrated essential problems with making the hymns of the Apocalypse of John dependent on Greek tragic dramatic form.

[18]Fiorenza's structural conclusion as to the importance of this section tends to support the contentions of others about the centrality of at least parts of the section above; see, e.g., George Beasley-Murray, *Revelation*, NCB (Grand Rapids, Michigan: Wm. B. Eerdmans, 1978), p. 191; and Pierre Prigent, *Apocalypse 12: Histoire de l'éxègese* (Tübingen: J. C. B. Mohr, 1959), p. 1.

Anti-language in the Apocalypse of John 11:19-15:4

The opening of the temple of God that is in heaven and the appearance of the ark of his covenant in the Apocalypse of John 11:19 serve as a prologue to the seven tableaux. Their appearance is attended by a great geophysical disturbance (lightnings, voices, thunders, earthquake, and large hail). The kind of story John tells is satiric tragic (Hayden White) and the mode of formal argument is mechanistic, emphasizing location, agency, and act. The Seven Tableaux evince thoroughly a mechanistic mode of formal argument, and one is not surprised to find the preface (Rev. 11:19) so described. The location of events involves heaven and earth, in that order. God's heavenly temple and covenant box become visible. God is indirectly posited as the agent, that is, the extrahistorical agent, involved in the story. While the actions of persons are not here the direct results of the acts of the extrahistorical agent, the physical cosmos is directly affected by the divine extrahistorical agent. The bringing forward of the temple shakes heaven and earth. The Apocalypse of John, as satiric tragedy, calls for the restructuring of society. It is fitting then that the preface to the Seven Tableaux begins the shaking process.

The prefacing section of the tableaux (Rev. 11:19) begins with abundant evidence of anti-language, that is, relexicalization, overlexicalization, and verbal play. God's protection and presence is relexicalized in the Apocalypse of John as "the temple" (ὁ ναός: 3:12; 7:15; 11:1, 19; 14:15, 17; 15:5, 6, 8; 16:1, 17; 21:22). "The ark of his covenant in his temple" (ἡ κιβωτὸς τῆς διαθήκης αὐτοῦ ἐν τῷ ναῷ αὐτοῦ) is an overlexicalized item which also indicates divine presence. Overlexicalization serves to reinforce the divine role as well as the solemnity of the situation. With the revealing of God's temple and covenant box there is disturbance overlexicalized: "and there were lightnings and voices and thunders and an earthquake and large hail." The latter overlexicalization occurs elsewhere in the book (4:4; 8:5; 16:18).

The First Tableau--Woman, Child, and Dragon (12:1-18). The Seven Trumpets of the judgment of God (8:5-11:18) have passed before John's eyes. The trumpet judgments were partial judgments (by one thirds); the seven bowls of wrath (15:5-16:21) will cover nearly identical judgments but will be more complete in their destruction. Thus the seven tableaux come between a vision of incomplete and complete judgment, serving to clarify how the battle started in the first place and how it will end.[19] The battle between good and evil begins in heaven and, consequently, spreads to the earth. The language in which the description is clothed bespeaks the tension that exists between the prophet John (and the community he represents) and opposing social forces, especially Roman.

Setting and Content. The first tableau consists of the following characters: a woman, her child, and a dragon. As the highly mythological tableau unfolds it shows a resplendent yet suffering woman, who most likely represents the faithful yet suffering people of God about to give birth to the savior (12:1-2).[20] She is joined by a ferocious dragon, who, we are told, is none other than Satan himself and who maliciously waits to devour the woman's child the moment it is born (12:3-4).[21] The woman gives birth to a male child, but the child is taken safely up

---

[19]Robert Mounce, *The Book of Revelation*, NICNT (Grand Rapids, Michigan: Wm. B. Eerdmans, 1977), p. 234: "John turns aside to explain the underlying cause for the hostility about to break upon the church."

[20]The prophet John understands the people of God, whether composed of tribes or apostles, as one. Here the woman represents the ideal Israel, but in 12:17 she represents the followers of Jesus Christ. Mounce, *Revelation*, p. 236, and Prigent, *L'Apocalypse*, p. 177, both pointed to John's fluid understanding of the faithful community. Prigent saw the twelve stars above the woman's head (12:1) as well as the twenty four elders around the throne (4:4) as indicative of John's understanding that "[t]he people of God are one throughout redemptive history" (Mounce, p. 236). Even Larry Hurtado's analysis of the "Christological elements" of the throne vision (particularly Rev. 4) revealed John's reorientation of Jewish apocalyptic as well as the continuity between Israel and the church; see "Revelation 4-5 in the Light of Jewish Apocalyptic Analogies," *JSNT*, 25 (1985), 105-124.

For a history of interpretation of the biblical, extra-biblical, and mythological elements of the woman clothed with the sun and the dragon see R. H. Charles, *The Revelation of St. John*, vol. 1, ICC (Edinburgh: T. & T. Clark, 1920) pp. 310-320; L. Cerfaux, "La Vision de la Femme et du Dragon," *ETL* 61 (1955), 7-33; Prigent, *L'Apocalypse 12: Historie de l'exégèse*; A. Feuillet, *The Apocalypse*, trans. Thomas E. Crane (Staten Island, New York: Alba House, 1965), pp. 109-117; John Court, *Myth and History in the Book of Revelation* (London: SPCK, 1979), pp. 106-121; Prigent, *L'Apocalypse de Saint Jean*, pp. 176-188; George Beasley-Murray, *Revelation*, pp. 191-199; Roland Bergmeier, "Altes und Neues zur 'Sonnenfrau am Himmel (Apk 12)' Religionsgeschichtliche und quellenkritische Beobachtungen zu Apk 12 1-17," *ZNW*, 73 (1982), 97-109.

Bergmeier, "Altes und Neues," p. 99, who here quoted Böcher, seemed correct in his understanding of the presence of mythological elements in the Apocalypse of John: 'Nach dem weitgehenden Verlust der nichtpharisäischen jüdischen Literatur infolge der Katastrophe von 70 n. Chr. ist die Johannes-offenbarung auch zu werten als ein Zeugnis für die Rezeption mythischer Stoffe durch das antike Judentum.' With the loss of non-pharisaic literature prophets were more open to other sources of truth.

[21]The dragon as a symbol for evil is an international myth. See the literature in the footnote above for the history of interpretation. In light of the freedom with which the prophet John draws upon biblical and non-biblical sources, the dragon (as well as the woman) can be understood as a targum of the Old Testament or a

to heaven and the woman is taken safely to the desert before the dragon can harm either one (12:5-6). The dragon turns his thwarted desires for devouring upon the good angels who watch over the woman and her child, but the devil is again unsuccessful and is subsequently thrown down to earth (12:7-9). A song of victory is sung over the angels' and the community's defeat of the dragon (12:10-12). Finally, the dragon renews the hunt for the woman on earth, but the earth comes to her rescue, leaving the dragon standing on the seashore awaiting his next move in order to kill, if not the woman, her remaining children (12:13-18).

The action begins in the sky (the seer is not transported to "heaven" but is reading what he sees in the sky); the enmity is essentially a heavenly war between God and Satan. The dragon's war in the sky is thwarted and the action shifts to land, specifically the land where Zion is found, that is, the Holy Land. With the struggle between God and Satan shifted to earth, humankind--both sinner and saint--feels the effects of the dragon's maliciousness. The language used to describe this scene of heavenly and (the beginnings of) earthly struggle is characterized by relexicalization, overlexicalization, and all kinds of verbal play to register the community's opposition to satanic oppression, which is pointed ultimately to real social structures, not simply the dragon.

The astronomical implications of the text are clear. Since John is looking at the sky, what particular constellations might he have seen as he began to describe a woman, a dragon, a sea beast, and a land beast? The dragon could correspond to Draco, who entwines the two great heavenly beasts, The Great Bear and the Little Bear (while Heracles the Kneeler has his right foot on Draco's head). The woman could be identified with Demeter, Athena, Isis, Atargatis, or Tyche.[22] As communicator of anti-language, the seer "reads" the common constellations against the norm society: Draco is the dragon called Satan and devil, the two beasts are not

---

reference to another cultural and mythological base. As a targum of the Old Testament the dragon may stand for the encapsulation of the divine enemy (the sea monster) or the serpent of Genesis 3; see Michèle Morgen, "Apocalypse 12, un targum de l'Ancien Testament," *FV*, 20 (1982), 63-67, in which targums of the Pentateuch shed light on Apocalypse of John 12 (pp. 68-72). Ford, *Revelation*, p. 199, while affirming the impossibility of determining precisely which mythologies may have influenced John's use of the dragon, commented that "it is significant that the color of the dragon is red like the Babylonian snake and the Egyptian typhon."

[22]See "Constellations," in *The Oxford Classical Dictionary* (Oxford: Clarendon Press, 1949), pp. 228-231.

bears but a sea being and a land being, the woman is the Christian community giving birth to the Messiah.

Relexicalization. The community of the faithful is relexicalized as a resplendent and pregnant woman (γυνή). The laboring woman is a relexicalization which persecuted Jews had used before, but the image is not a mere borrowing, as is attested by the wide range of mythical as well as scriptural allusions the word evokes. The prophet, given his particular setting, responds uniquely to anti-societal pressure. Anti-Christian pressure has its source in God's chief spiritual enemy, who takes the form of a big red dragon (δράκων μέγας πυρρός). Again, this is not the first time evil has been given a face, but John's linguistic response is meant to indicate the distance as well as the tension between him and spiritual and social evil. Jesus is relexicalized as "a male child" (υἱὸν ἄρσεν) and as the one "who is about to tend all nations with an iron rod" (ὃς μέλλει ποιμαίνειν πάντα τὰ ἔθνη ἐν ῥάβδῳ σιδηρᾷ) (12:5).[23] Once the spiritual warfare moves to the geophysical plane, the faithful community, previously represented by the woman, is referred to as the rest of the woman's offspring (οἱ λοιποὶ τοῦ σπέρματος αὐτῆς) (12:17). The woman's offspring are faithful followers and witnesses of her previously born son.

Overlexicalization. The first of the seven signs (σημεῖον) in the Apocalypse of John (12:1, 3; 13:13, 14; 15:1; 16:14; 19:20) is replete with multiple words to express the concerns of the community, that is, overlexicalization.[24] The description of each of the relexicalized items above also contain overlexicalized elements that underscore the essential notion involved. The description of the

---

[23]While the phrase "male child" is peculiar (υἱον [masc.] + ἄρσεν [neut.]), it is found in Tobias 6:12 (ℵ) and probably emphasizes the sex of the child; see Charles, *Revelation*, p. 320; Mounce, *Revelation*, p. 238; Prigent, *L'Apocalypse*, pp. 188-189. Ford interpreted the phrase as a sign of "manliness," the baby boy possessing "characteristics of a warrior," since the reference from Psalm 2:7 follows (*Revelation*, pp. 200-201). Ford likened the male child Jesus to other "spiritually precocious infants" of Jewish tradition (she referred to an example in 1QapGen 6-15 of the birth of Noah [p. 201]). The "manliness" of the male child is not so much in view in 12:5 as is his destiny as a "manly" ruler of nations. At his birth he had to be snatched up to his God for the simple reason that a dragon was about to eat him up; so Fiorenza, *Priester für Gott: Studien zum Herrschafts- und Priestermotiv in der Apocalypse* (Münster: Verlag Aschendorff, 1972), p. 365.

[24]Ford, *Revelation*, AB, vol. 38 (Garden City, New York: Doubleday & Company, 1975), p. 195, noted that the sign at 12:1 is the only "felicitous" sign among the seven. Ford also noted that the word "woman" or "women" occurs nineteen times in the Apocalypse of John: "It might be said, therefore, that the woman symbol is almost as important as the Lamb" (p 188).

woman has the overlexicalized elements of sun, moon, stars to underscore her glory, while "(she) cries out . . . to give birth" (κράζει . . . τεκεῖν), "being in pain" (ὠδίνουσα), and "being tormented" (βασανιζομένη) underscore her role as sufferer.

The dragon is the foremost example of overlexicalization in the passage. There is almost no end to the 'name calling' of the chief adversary. The dragon is introduced as the "great red dragon" (12:3), which is followed (12:3-4) by the overlexicalized elements of "seven heads" (κεφαλὰς ἑπτά), "ten horns" (κέρατα δέκα), "seven diadems on his heads" (ἐπὶ τὰς κεφαλὰς αὐτοῦ ἑπτὰ διαδήματα) and "his tail" (ἡ οὐρὰ αὐτοῦ), which is capable of great destruction.

Beginning with the dragon's oust from heaven, one finds multiple terms for the dragon. The terms are connected in the Apocalypse of John ultimately to concrete social institutions. In Apocalypse of John 12:9 one finds the following list.

> ὁ δράκων ὁ μέγας
> ὁ ὄφις ὁ ἀρχαῖος
> ὁ καλούμενος Διάβολος καὶ ὁ Σατανᾶς
> ὁ πλανῶν τὴν οἰκουμένην ὅλην

> The Great Dragon
> The Old Snake
> The one who is called the Devil and Satan
> The one who deceives the whole world

The names do not stop. The hymn which follows the above scene contains the epithet "the accuser" (ὁ κατήγωρ) (12:20).

> ὁ κατήγωρ τῶν ἀδελφῶν ἡμῶν
> ὁ κατηγωρῶν αὐτοὺς ἐνώπιον τοῦ θεοῦ ἡμῶν ἡμέρας καὶ νυκτός

> The accuser of our brothers
> The one who accuses them before our God day and night

Satan thus has some six epithets in the first tableau, the title "dragon" alone used eight times, "snake" thrice, and "devil" twice.

In the anti-language of the Apocalypse of John the concepts "woman" and her antithesis "dragon" are central, for they encapsulate the community's understanding of itself and of external social realities and events. While "woman" is not overlexicalized in the first tableau, the word is used eight times.

Verbal Play. Verbal play in the first tableau takes the following form: irony, repeated use of the passive voice, alliteration, secrecy. The anti-language as verbal play is indicated first of all by the ironic battle between a glorious though pregnant woman and a big, fiery red dragon. John sees the dragon poised over the woman ready to strike (12:4). Ironically both the woman and her son escape. The use of irony underscores the prophet's perception of his own predicament; he senses the dragon ready to strike again but clearly presages the doom of all ungodly powers that attempt to devour the faithful community.

Just as the dragon is ready to devour (καταφάγῃ) the newborn child, he is snatched up to God and his throne, places of safety and, more Christologically important, places of Messianic authority (12:5).[25] The child makes the trip through the sky and its seven heavens, generally inhabited by anti-human beings, and arrives at the very throne of God unscathed.[26] The Messianic authority of God's child Jesus consists, in part, of enabling others to make the same journey to God without getting stuck by the various beings who populate the heavens.

The irony escalates: the woman escapes from the dragon twice (12:6, 13-16).[27] Although the dragon's logic is questionable (pursue the child first, the

---

[25]Henry Swete, *Commentary on Revelation* (1911; Grand Rapids, Michigan: Kregal Publications, 1977), p. 151, underscored position over place: "The Ascension involves the Session of the Sacred Humanity at the Right Hand of the Father . . . , and not merely an elevation of spirit into the Divine Presence, which was never wanting to the Divine Son of Man." The paucity of detail of the life of Jesus has led many, like J. Wellhausen, to exclaim, "'Was wäre das für ein Resümé des Lebens Jesu: geboren und entrückt!'" (Bergmeier, "Altes und Neues," p. 98). The seer John believed in the death of Jesus and its saving effects for the church, yet there is no reference to the death of the child only to his being caught up (ἡρπάσθη). The focus seems to be on "John's vivid way of asserting the victory of God's anointed over every satanic effort to destroy him" (George Ladd, *A Commentary on the Revelation of John* [Grand Rapids, Michigan: Wm. B. Eerdmans, 1972], p. 170). It is most likely, moreover, that the underlying mythological elements, which speak only of a child's birth and its removal, have precluded reference to other aspects of Jesus' ministry; see Charles, *Revelation*, pp. 320-321; also Traugott Holtz, *Die Christologie der Apokalypse des Johannes* (Berlin: Akademie Verlag, 1962), pp. 98-99.

[26]Below God's dwelling place in heaven is the habitation of Satan and his demons in the air (ἀήρ; see Eph. 2:22). The intermediate structure of the cosmos, while it is the locus of "an organized kingdom under the single ruler Satan" (Foerster), becomes at the eschatological return of Christ the meeting place for Savior and saint (1 Thess. 4:17). The initial journey of the infant Jesus (Rev. 12:5) dethrones the powers in the air (and earth; see Col. 2:15). Jesus will journey there again to summon believers to be with him in his kingdom. See W. Foerster, "ἀήρ," *Theological Dictionary of the New Testament*, vol. 1, ed. Gerhard Kittel and trans. G. W. Bromiley (Grand Rapids: Wm. B. Eerdmans, 1964), pp. 165-166.
The Apocalypse points the hearer skyward, where the struggle begins. One must agree with Wink, however, that "the spiritual hosts (*pneumatika*) of wickedness in the heavenly places" (Eph. 6:12) are not restricted to an intermediary position in the cosmos. Rather, the principalities, powers, world rulers, and spiritual hosts of wickedness in the heavenly places refer to "the ineffable, invisible world-enveloping reach of a spiritual network of powers inimical to life" both human and nonhuman, earthly and heavenly; see Wink, *Naming the Powers*, pp. 84-85.

[27]Note the antithesis: Jesus the child is caught up; the dragon is thrown down.

woman second), the woman finds herself now the target of the dragon's malice. She finds in the desert "a place prepared by God" (τόπον ἡτοιμασμένον ἀπὸ τοῦ θεοῦ) (12:6). After Michael and his angels cast the dragon and his angels down to the earth, the dragon attempts to kill the woman again (12:13-16). The earth comes to the aid of the woman personally, by swallowing the flood that the dragon sent to sweep the woman away (12:16). Irony is descriptively focused on the word "mouth" (στόμα): the snake's mouth in v. 15 stands agape and in contrast to the earth's mouth in v. 16.

The verbal play of anti-language is seen in the repeated use of the passive voice. The impersonal passive is not common in the New Testament, but Aramaic generally used the passive voice to indicate the actions of a celestial being.[28] The impersonal passive is common in apocalyptic literature.[29] Jeremias indicated that in apocalyptic literature the "divine passive" found frequent use not only out of reverence ("to avoid uttering the name of God") but also "as a way of describing in veiled terms God's mysterious activity in the end-time."[30] One function of anti-language is to provide secrecy, and the repeated use of the passive voice in the first tableau is the means John employs to present his visions with an air of secrecy.[31]

---

[28]BDF, pp. 72, 164-165.

[29]Joachim Jeremias, Theology of the New Testament, trans. John Bowden (New York: Charles Scribner's Sons, 1971), pp. 9-14; Steven Thompson, The Apocalypse and Semitic Syntax (Cambridge: Cambridge University Press, 1985), pp. 21-22.

[30]Jeremias, Theology, p. 13. "It is significant," Jeremias also noted, "that the Revelation of John always has God acting through messengers or uses the 'divine passive'. Only in Rev. 21.5-8, which speaks of the final consummation, is there a direct mention of God's speaking and acting."
The impersonal (or, divine) passive differs here from the passivization (and agent deletion) that Kress analyzed in Donne's "Nocturnall" (see pp. 68-69 of this dissertation). Passivization, according to Kress, is the process whereby an agent subject becomes an affected subject and the agent becomes irrecoverable, constituting the height of negation in the anti-language. Here the anti-language uses the passive voice for secrecy; the divine agent, though veiled in mystery, is not negated but rather veiled (so Jeremias) by the passive voice.

[31]For the social functions of secrecy, see Stanton Tefft (ed.), Secrecy: A Cross-Cultural Perspective (New York: Human Sciences Press, 1980). Tefft defined secrecy as a "social resource (or adaptive strategy) used by individuals, groups, and organization to attain certain ends in the course of social interaction" (p. 35). Tefft viewed secrecy from a conflict theory model and concluded that a social group employs secrecy in order, among other things, to "maintain . . . social boundaries and contribute to group cohesiveness" (p. 51).

The passive voice occurs twelve times in the first tableau, and all but four of these may be categorized as divine passives:

12:1   καὶ σημεῖον μέγα ὤφθη ἐν τῷ οὐρανῷ
12:3   καὶ ὤφθη ἄλλο σημεῖον ἐν τῷ οὐρανῷ
12:5   καὶ ἡρπάσθη τὸ τέκνον αὐτῆς πρὸς τὸν θεὸν
         καὶ πρὸς τὸν θρόνον αὐτοῦ
12:8   οὐδὲ τόπος εὑρέθη αὐτῶν ἔτι ἐν τῷ οὐρανῷ
12:9   ἐβλήθη εἰς τὴν γῆν
12:9   καὶ οἱ ἄγγελοι αὐτοῦ μετ᾽ αὐτοῦ ἐβλήθησαν
12:10   ὅτι ἐβλήθη ὁ κατήγωρ τῶν ἀδελφῶν ἡμῶν
12:13   ὅτι ἐβλήθη εἰς τὴν γῆν
12:14   καὶ ἐδόθησαν τῇ γυναικὶ αἱ δύο πτέρυγες
         τοῦ ἀετοῦ τοῦ μεγάλου
12:14   ὅπου τρέφεται ἐκεῖ καιρὸν καὶ καιροὺς καὶ
         ἥμισυ καιροῦ ἀπὸ προσώπου τοῦ ὄφεως
12:17   καὶ ὠργίσθη ὁ δράκων ἐπὶ τῇ γυναικί
12:18   καὶ ἐστάθη ἐπὶ τὴν ἄμμον τῆς θαλάσσης

The four passives that may be excluded as divine passives are 12:1, 3, 17, 18. The first two have the passive of the verb ὁράω: a sign became visible, appeared. The last two (12:7, 8) are deponent forms: ὠργίσθη (from ὀργίζομαι) = he was angry; ἐστάθη (from ἵστημι) = he stood.

The remaining eight passives function in the anti-language to veil the divine extrahistorical agent in mystery. The woman's child is caught up (12:6) *by God* to heaven; no place was found (12:8) *by God* in heaven for the dragon; the dragon (and his armies) was thrown down (12:9, 10, 13) *by God* to earth; the woman was given (12:14) *by God* the two wings of the great eagle; and she was nourished (12:14) *by God* for a time, times, and half a time. The anti-language has employed the passive voice to play with the language in order to veil in secrecy the acts of the extrahistorical agent as the language registers its opposition to the dominant social structures.

Secrecy is also evinced in the first tableau by the two temporal expressions "1,260 days" (ἡμέρας χιλίας διακοσίας ἑξήκοντα) (12:6) and "for a time, times, and half a time" (καιρὸν καὶ καιροὺς καὶ ἥμισυ καιροῦ) (12:14).[32] the

_____

[32]The former phrase interprets the latter, and the two are joined by a third in the Apocalypse of John 11:12 and 13:5 (μῆνας τεσσαράκοντα καὶ δύο = forty-two months). All three temporal descriptions appear to be derived from Daniel 7:25, 12:7 (ἕως καιροῦ καὶ καιρῶν καὶ ἕως ἡμίσους καιροῦ = for a time and times and for half a time), which was the period of Jewish oppression under the Syrian tyrant Antiochus Epiphanes. Here the expressions indicate the length of the dragon's persecution of the woman. See Charles *Revelation*, p. 279; Prigent, *L'Apocalypse*, p. 191; and Mounce, *Revelation*, p. 246.

repeated use of the passive and the above temporal phrases function in the anti-language of the Apocalypse to inject the notion of secrecy.

A final form of verbal play in the first tableau consists of various forms of word play.[33]

(1) Initial alliteration: ποταμοφόρητον ποιήσῃ (12:15); ποιῆσαι πόλεμος (12:17).

(2) Pun (Paronomasia: recurrence of same word or word stem): τέκῃ τὸ τέκνον (12:4); κατήγωρ . . . κατηγόρων (12:6); καιρὸν καὶ καιροὺς καὶ ἥμισυ καιροῦ (12:14).

(3) Homonym (Parechesis: recurrence of different words of similar sounds): ἔχει ἐκεῖ (12:6).

Alliteration by itself does not indicate anti-language. As one combines verbal play of all kinds, relexicalization, and overlexicalization to form a polemic of one group against another, one is using anti-language.

Anti-language and Strong Group/Low Grid. The kind of language the prophet John employs arises out of a strong group/low grid cultural setting. The anti-language of the first tableau indicates the following strong group/low grid concerns.

(1) Purity. The lines are clearly marked between "us" and "them": the woman, her unique male child, and all her remaining children (and their protective angels) versus the dragon (and his army). While the vision speaks of spiritual realities, it reinforces the purity lines of the community. Note the porous state that exists in spite of clearly delineated boundaries. The heavens are infiltrated by the dragon; the woman is not outside his reach.

(2) Rite. Rites takes the form of a ceremony, a "regular time out" (Malina), in order to focus on the boundary lines. This moment occurs immediately after the dragon's removal from heaven and takes the form of choral ode (12:10-12). The ceremony reinforces boundary lines: God and his Christ do in fact rule (v. 10); the accuser is thrown down (v. 10); they (αὐτοί--the followers of the Lamb) have conquered their accuser (v. 11); the above state of affairs is a cause for rejoicing (in heaven) as well as woe (on earth) (v. 12).

(3) Personal identity. Only by embeddedness in the group can one be saved. The righteous group is the one where persons bear witness to the Lamb, are self-

---

[33]*GNTLHR*, p. 1201; *BDF*, pp. 258-259.

effacing, and keep the commands of God (vv. 11, 17). The witnesses of Jesus (or, the offspring of the woman) become the fictive kin group by which persons will perceive their identity.

(4) Body. The key perception of body--both physical and social--for strong group/low grid is transformation. The body in its present state is not a "symbol for life" (Malina).[34] Although the woman conceives a son, whose destiny is messianic, her male child cannot fulfil his destiny until he has been bodily transferred to a heavenly estate (v. 5). Those who conquer their accuser do not hold their physical selves as ultimate; they are promised a transformed state (v. 11; cf. 2:6, 11, 17, 26; 3:5, 12, 21).

(5) Sin. Sin is deviance in the social order, which lodges itself in individuals and groups. The dragon (one name among many given to the evil that confronts Christians) is the chief deviant who has permeated life in heaven as well on earth.

(6) Cosmology. The strong group/low grid collective views events that happen in the world anthropomorphically, that is, "who" is the causal factor behind them. The first tableau makes clear those who stand behind the events of human history, that is, God and the Dragon, who comprise the positive and negative forces engaged in dualistic struggle.

(7) Suffering and misfortune. Whatever trials face the saints on earth are precisely the result of the latter struggle. In John's view the dualistic struggle between God and the Dragon and between the saints and the Dragon is an intertwined struggle. Note how John dovetails the casting out of the Dragon by Michael and his angels (12:7-10) with the confession that "they" (probably not Michael and his angels but rather godly mortals) defeated the Dragon, implying that "they" helped to bring about his downfall. Yet ultimately malevolent forces are the cause for suffering and misfortune on the part of the Lamb's followers.

The Second Tableau--The Beast from the Sea (13:1-10). The first tableau returned to the beginning of the struggle between Good (the Woman and her children) and Evil (the Dragon) in order to show its descent to the terrestrial plane. The action left off with the dragon posed for further malice, standing on the seashore (12:18), where the action of the second tableau begins. The battle is moved to the earth, and the anti-language will find more explicit aim at real social

---

[34]See p. 33-35 of this dissertation.

structures. The beast from the sea, though multifariously interpreted in particular, most likely represented the world power of Rome in general. Anti-Roman sentiment is drawn with sharp lines.

Setting and Content. The second tableau consists of the following characters: a beast from the sea, the whole world of people, and the saints. As the symbolical tableau unfolds it shows a frightening beast rising from the sea (13:1-3a). The whole world of people is astonished by the beast and worships it (13:3b-8). John hears a solemn pronouncement in the midst of the beast worship that depicts the fate of the saints as patient and faithful witnesses (13:9-10). The first tableau described the dragon's schemes, but these were overshadowed by the divine protection of the woman and the child. In the action that follows, one wonders if the dragon's beast is not the true victor.[35]

In terms of White's metahistorical model, the second tableau evinces a satiric tragic mode of emplotment. It is evident that one cannot escape the worship of the beast, for the whole world (ὅλη ἡ γῆ) will worship the blasphemous beast from the sea (13:3). The most that one can do is to be faithful to God and refuse to join the liturgy. Of course, salvation comes to those who refuse and join the liturgy of the Lamb, who holds the solution to the helpless situation in which believers find themselves.

The mechanistic mode of formal argument, with its emphasis on location, agency, and act, takes the following shape in the second tableau. The location encompasses the whole earth (ὅλη ἡ γῆ), which may be understood both as terra firma and the totality of social groups on the earth. The extrahistorical agent at work in the physical and social location is the dragon of the last tableau. The dragon directly affects the acts of agents: from him the beast from the sea receives authority to deceive humanity (13:2), and humanity's new found zeal for this beast can be traced indirectly to the dragon (13:3b-4). Concerning the ideological implication, that is, the effect of the tableau upon the hearer, the call for the radical restructuring of society is not explicitly stated. All one can do in the present time is exhibit the patience and faith of the saints (ἡ ὑπομονὴ καὶ ἡ πίστις τῶν ἁγίων)

---

[35]So Prigent, *L'Apocalypse*, p. 199: "La pointe du passage est bien cette rivalité: qui a le vrai pouvoir et la véritable victoire? Et en fin de compte qui est Dieu? Le Tout-Puissant ou cette bête qui revendique, en blasphémant, l'élévation suprême (qui est comme la bête?)?"

(13:10). Such behavior corresponds to an ideology that "the best of times is right around the corner"; hold on until the restructuring of society takes place.

Relexicalization. The presence of the chief spiritual enemy, the big red dragon, is only indirectly, although keenly, felt. The dragon gives the beast from the sea its authority to blaspheme and to deceive (13:2, 5, 6). The "beast arising from the sea" (ἐκ τῆς θαλάσσης θηρίον ἀναβαῖνον) (13:1) is the world power of Rome relexicalized.[36] The objects of the beast's deceit are relexicalized as "the whole earth" (ὅλη ἡ γῆ) (13:3), which underscores the widespread faithlessness that will occur at this time.[37] All persons who do not follow the slaughtered Lamb

---

[36]The history of interpretation of the first beast (13:1-10), as well the "other beast" (13:11-18), is long and complex. One certainty is that the beast from the sea is based on Daniel 7:2-7, in which four beasts are described as they ascend from the sea. Note the prophet John's liberal use of the vision in Daniel; he describes one beast, in which the characteristics of all four beasts exist. I have followed the majority of commentators who identify the beast from the sea with the Roman Empire (no consensus exists as to the identification of the wounded and healed head [13:3]); see Swete, *Revelation*, pp. 161-165; Charles, *Revelation*, pp. 345-351; Heinrich Schlier, "Zum Verständnis der Geschichte nach der Offenbarung Johannis," in *Die Zeit der Kirche* (Freiburg: Verlag herder, 1956), pp. 265-274; "Vom Antichrist Zum 13. Kapitel der Offenbarung Johannis," in *Die Zeit der Kirche* (Freiburg: Verlag Herder, 1958), pp. 21-26; Heinrich Kraft, *Die Offenbarung des Johannes*, HNT, vol. 16a (Tübingen: J. C. B. Mohr, 1974), pp. 174-176; Ford, *Revelation*, pp. 217-223; Court, *Myth and History*, pp. 122-139; Beasley-Murray, *Revelation*, pp. 206-211; Adela Collins, *Crisis & Catharsis: The Power of the Apocalypse* (Philadelphia: The Westminster Press, 1984), pp. 58-64, 99-104; Fiorenza, *Revelation*, pp. 181-182; Steven J. Scherrer, "Signs and Wonders in the Imperial Cult: A New Look at a Roman Religious Institution in the Light of Rev 13:13-15," *JBL*, 103 (1984), 599-600.

Collins, *Revelation*, pp. 59-64, has clearly laid out the four basic positions concerning the identity of the wounded and healed head of the beast from the sea and concluded that the latter referred to Nero and the *Nero redivivus* myth; see also Jarl Ulrichsen, "Die sieben Häupter und die zehn Hörner zur Datierung der Offenbarung des Johannes," *ST*, 39 (1985), 11-12. Prigent, *L'Apocalypse*, p. 203, however, stressed the "symbolisme vague," which intends to point only to the satanic character of the Roman Empire that sees itself as "invulnérable et finalement immortel."

Some commentators have emphasized the anonymous face of the Antichrist, as did Ernst Lohmeyer, *Die Offenbarung des Johannes*, HNT, vol. 16 (Tübingen: J. C. B. Mohr, 1926), pp. 110-112, 189-191): "Jüdische Apokalyptiker waren wohl gezwungen, die Zeichen der Zeit zu befragen und in der Geschichte die Antwort auf die Frage zu suchen: 'Wie lang noch die Nacht?' (Js 21 11). Der christliche Seher hat den 'Morgenstern' (22 16) geschaut. So kümmern ihn nicht Zeit und Geschichte, sondern allein die übergeschichtlichen und unterirdischen Mächte, die der Vollendung entgegenstehen" (p. 190). Ulrichsen, "Die sieben Häupter," p. 2, has criticized Lohmeyer's "eschatologisch-*überzeitliche* Auslegung" as too one-sided: "Obwohl man die Johannesapokalypse primär traditions-geschichtlich auslegen soll, muss man immer eventuelle zeitgeschichtlich Anspielungen vor Augen haben."

[37]Swete, *Revelation*, p. 161, noted that "the whole earth" is symbolized already in the sea (θάλασσα), out of which the beast arises: "The Sea is an apt symbol of the agitated surface of unregenerate humanity (cf. Isa. lvii. 20), and especially of the

will blindly follow the slaughtered beast (13:3b-4 describes compactly the world's infatuation with the beast). The faithful are relexicalized simply in the second tableau as "the saints" (τῶν ἁγίων) (13:7, 10). In the anti-language no other word could be more suitable, for the basic notion of the cultic term ἅγιος conveys separation and morally qualitative distinctions between persons.[38]

Overlexicalization. The above terms are overlexicalized in the anti-language of the prophet John. The beast from the sea, like the dragon in the first tableau, is the object of the greatest overlexicalization since the notion of the spiritual and social adversary is of primary concern to John and the community that he represents. The beast from the sea has ten horns (κέρατα δέκα), seven heads (κεφαλὰς ἑπτά), and ten crowns for its ten heads (δέκα διαδήματα) (13:1)[39]; its appearance was like a leopard (ὅμοιον παρδάλει), with the feet of a bear (οἱ πόδες αὐτοῦ ὡς ἄρκου), the mouth of a lion (τὸ στόμα ὡς στόμα λέοντος) (13:2)[40]; the dragon makes his presence indirectly felt because he has given to the beast "his authority (τὴν δύναμιν αὐτοῦ), "his throne (τὸν θρόνον αὐτοῦ), and "a great authority" (ἐξουσίαν μεγάλην) (13:2);[41] one of his heads had been smitten to death, but his death wound had been healed.[42] The overlexicalized beast

---

seething cauldron of national and social life, out of which the great historical movements of the world arise." The sea may very well refer to the Mediterranean Sea as the Roman sea; thus the beast would signify the Roman Empire that comes across the sea from the west (Kraft, *Offenbarung*, p. 175; Prigent, *L'Apocalypse*, p. 201).

[38]BAGD, p. 9-10, glossed ἅγιος "in the cultic sense *dedicated to God, holy, sacred*, i.e., reserved for God and his service" (things) and "*the holy ones*," "*saints* of Christians as consecrated to God" (persons).

[39]The dragon has seven heads, ten horns, seven diadems for its heads, and a large tail (12:3-4). While the appearance of the sea beast is similar to that of the dragon, one notes a difference in tactical ploy: the dragon sought to devour but the beast seeks to delude, through physical violence ("to make war") (13:7) is part of his program.

[40]John, departing from Daniel's vision, focuses on the overall appearance of the beast, its feet, and its mouth. In Daniel's vision (7:2-7) the winged lion represented the Babylonian empire, the bear the Medes, the four-headed winged leopard the Persians, the dragon-like beast the Greeks or Macedonian empire. In the Apocrypha the latter (fourth) beast was relexicalized as the Roman Empire (2 Esdras 12:10-32). See Ford, *Revelation*, p. 220; Mounce, *Revelation*, pp. 251-252.

[41]"His" here probably refers to the beast's, not the dragon's, authority and throne, that is, the authority that the dragon has given to the beast.

[42]John's description of the beast has long been noted as antithetical to the earlier portrait of the Lamb (Rev. 5). Ford stated, *Revelation*, p. 219, "The dragon is

is both fearful and amazing, as is indicated by the response of the world to him (13:3-4).

The whole earth is relexicalized to indicate the extent to which unbelieving humanity will blindly follow the beast. The following terms are used (13:7, 8).

φυλήν	= tribe
λαόν	= people
γλῶσσαν	= tongue (language)
ἔθνος	= nation
πάντες οἱ κατοικοῦντες	= all those who dwell
ἐπὶ τῆς γῆς	upon the earth

In the anti-language the above neutral terms are all negative in this context. The entire world consists of unbelief; it is from the former, however, that the followers of the lamb come: The Lamb "purchased to God by [his] blood from every tribe and tongue and people and nation" (5:9; cf. 7:9; 11:9).

Overlexicalization of the strong group/low grid community that John represents is slight in the second tableau. "The saints" (οἱ ἅγιοι) are shown in the light of persecution: they are the object of the beast's war (13:7); they are pictured as going "into captivity" (εἰς αἰχμαλωσίαν) and being "put to death by the sword" (ἐν μαχαίρῃ ἀποκτανθῆναι) (13:10); and they are encouraged, in spite of dismal circumstances, to be patient and faithful (13:10). Though the overlexicalization is slight, John paints a dark picture for the saints; except for the fact that they--as opposed to all the earth dwellers--do have their names inscribed in the book of life of a slaughtered Lamb (13:8).

Verbal Play. Verbal play is indicated by various forms of word play, repeated use of the passive, and parallelism. Word play occurs in the following verses:

(1) Initial alliteration: θαλάσσης θηρίον (13:1); κέρατα . . . καὶ κεφαλὰς . . . κεράτων . . . κεφαλάς (13:1); δέκα διαδήματα (13:1); ἐθεραπεύθη καὶ ἐθαυμάσθη (13:3); ποιῆσαι πόλεμον (13:7); καταβολῆς κόσμου (13:8).

(2) Pun (Paronomasia: recurrence of same word or word stem): βλασφημίας . . . βλασφημῆσαι (13:6); τὴν σκηνὴν αὐτοῦ, τοὺς ἐν τῷ οὐρανῷ σκηνοῦντας (13:6).

---

the antithesis of God, but the sea beast is the antithesis of the Lamb." See also Charles, *Revelation*, pp. 348-349; Kraft, *Offenbarung*, p. 176; Prigent, *L'Apocalypse*, p. 203.

(3) Homonym (Parechesis: recurrence of different words of similar sounds): *οὗ*
οὐ (13:8).

The passive voice occurs nine times in the second tableau, injecting the
notion of secrecy as well as underscoring the acts of extra-historical agents within
the development of the visions. Of the total passives six may be categorized as
divine (impersonal) passives:

> *ἐθεραπεύθη* (13:3)
> *ἐθαυμάσθη* (13:3)
> *ἐδόθη* (13:5--twice; 13:7--twice)
> *γέγραπται* (13:8)
> *ἀποκτανθῆναι* (13:10--twice)

The three passives that may be excluded as divine passives are 13:3 (*ἐθαυμάσθη*),
10 (*ἀποκτανθῆναι* occurs twice). In verse 3 the passive is deponent: The whole
earth wondered (marvelled) after the beast.[43] In verse 10 the passive occurs in the
phrase "to be put to death by the sword" (*ἐν μαχαίρῃ ἀποκτανθῆναι*). The agent
is most likely a human agent.

The remaining divine (impersonal) passives may be divided into two
categories, which in the anti-language correspond to the dualistic struggle between
God and the divine antithesis, the dragon. The agent of the first category is God,
and the agent of the second is the dragon.

God as Agent	Dragon as Agent
γέγραπται (v. 8)	*ἐθεραπεύθη* (v. 3); *ἐδόθη* (vv. 5, 7)

The Lamb has excluded from the book of life the names of those who worship the
beast (13:8). The passive voice is employed more often in the second tableau to
indicate the work of the anti-divine spirit of the dragon. Note first, however, the
active voice in verses 2 and 4 to describe the transference of power from the dragon
to the beast: "And the dragon gave (*ἔδωκεν*) to him his power and his throne and
his great authority" (13:2). The anti-divine passives in 13:3, 5, 7 contrast with the
explicit use of the active voice. The dragon is allowed the beast's wound to heal
(13:3) and gave the beast his blasphemous mouth (13:5), the power to be active for
forty-two months (13:5), the plan to make war with the saints (13:7), and authority

---

[43]Prigent, following Charles, viewed the unparalleled construction *ἐθαυμάσθη*
. . . *ὀπίσω* as influenced by the use of אחר (= after, behind) in Hebrew, though
Prigent correctly saw no need to infer an underlying Hebrew text; see Prigent,
L'Apocalypse, p. 203; Charles, *Revelation*, pp. 334-335.

over all humanity (13:7). The use of the passive in the second tableau gives the beast a decided advantage over the saints.

There is verbal play in the form of a parallelism at verse 10.

εἴ τις εἰς αἰχμαλωγίαν, εἰς αἰξμαλωσίαν ὑπάγει
εἴ τις ἐν μαχαίρῃ ἀποκτανθῆναι αὐτὸν ἐν μαχαίρῃ ἀποκτανθῆναι
If anyone is destined to captivity, he is going to captivity
If anyone is to be put to death by the sword, he is to be put to death by the sword

The parallelism is based on Jeremiah 15:2, and provides another example of John's intertextuality, that is, (according to Roger Fowler) John's use of "traces and gleanings of earlier texts."[44] The scrap of text that John employs here deals with Jeremiah's insistence of the irrevocability of judgment, which is a relevant scrap in John's anti-language.[45] The verbal play of the anti-language seriously confronts the members of the strong group/low grid community with the consequences of maintaining the tension between worshiper of the beast and worshiper of the Lamb.

Anti-Language and Strong Group/Low Grid. The anti-language of the second tableau indicates the following strong group/low grid concerns.

(1) Purity. The lines are drawn clearly between "us" and "them": the frightening beast and worshipful humanity dominate the tableau; while pictured in cursory

---

[44]Roger Fowler, *Linguistics and the Novel* (London: Methuen and Co., 1977), pp. 69, 145-125.

[45]The passage reads as follows in the LXX:
ὅσοι εἰς θάνατον, εἰς θάνατον·
καὶ ὅσοι εἰς μάχαιραν, εἰς μάχαιραν·
καὶ ὅσοι εἰς λιμόν, εἰς λιμόν·
καὶ ὅσοι εἰς αἰχμαλωσίαν, εἰς αἰχμαλωσίαν.
I have followed the UBS (3rd ed.) Greek text, to which the textual committee gave the readings εἰς αἰχμαλοσίαν, εἰς αἰχμαλωσίαν ὑπάγει and ἀποκτανθῆναι, αὐτόν the {C} rating, which reflects the unsatisfactory, if not divided, nature of the textual variants (Bruce Metzger, *A Textual Commentary on the Greek New Testament* [New York: United Bible Societies, 1975], pp. 747-748). I prefer the above reading, following Prigent, *L'Apocalypse*, p. 207, for the following three reasons:
(1) it is the only reading supported in its entirety by one of the oldest manuscripts (Alexandrinus);
(2) it presents a perfect parallelism between the two propositions, following the model in Jeremiah 15:2; and
(3) it provides the best harmony with the appended saying that concludes the verse ("Here is the patience and faith of the saints").
See also Charles's excellent analysis, *Revelation*, pp. 355-357. A second rendering, which follows the majority text (𝔐) makes the first proposition ("to captivity") refer to the saints but the second ("to be put to death") to refer to the person responsible for the killing, which would introduce the notion of retribution (see Metzger, *Textual Commentary*, 747-748; Mounce, *Revelation*, p. 257; Ford, *Revelation*, p. 213).

fashion is the group that has excluded itself from the worship but thereby included itself in the persecution. Also, porous boundaries are indicated by the impunity with which a water creature moves through the border of the seashore onto land to exercise power there.

(2) Rite. Ritual takes the form of status elevation: the water beast is invested with the authority of the sky dragon. Rite also takes the form of ceremony, which focuses on the boundary lines between two groups. The ceremony is introduced by a solemn clause, part of which John employed in the seven letters to the churches: "If anyone has ears, let him hear" (13:9). The parallelism and wisdom statement of verse 10 serve to reinforce the duty and thus the boundary lines of the group.

(3) Personal Identity. Only by embeddedness in the group can one be saved. While the "if anyone has ears" statement and following parallelism use the singular form of the pronoun $\tau\iota\varsigma$ (= anyone), the strong group/low grid community--not individuals--is in view, which is also indicated by the use of the plural "saints" ($\dot{\alpha}\gamma\dot{\iota}\omega\nu$) in verses 7 and 10.

(4) Body. The key perception of body--the physical and social--for strong group/low grid is transformation. The second tableau presents the social body, that is, "the whole earth," directing itself toward a terrible physical form (the beast = Roman Empire) and in need of transformation. The physical and social body of the saints, which is also in need of transformation, suffers captivity and death.

(5) Sin. Sin is deviance in the social order, which lodges itself in individuals and groups. The anti-language of the second tableau is aimed more at real structures than in the first tableau. The beast that rises from the sea symbolizes the Roman Empire, which in turn is the deviant that has lodged itself in the socio-cultural matrix of late first century Asia Minor. The deviant has infected the whole body, according to John.

(6) Cosmology. The strong group/low grid collective views events that happen in the world anthropomorphically, that is, "who" is the causal factor behind them. The second tableau makes clear who stands behind the human infatuation with the beastly Empire and behind persecution that Christians may face, namely, the dragon (the divine antithesis). John states six times (13:2, 4, 5, 7) explicitly and implicitly the "who" that stands behind events.

(7) Suffering and Misfortune. The saints suffer as a direct result of the dualistic struggle begun in chapter twelve. Patience and faith are necessary in view of the fact that the dragon, having lost the initial struggle between the woman and her child, has set about "to make war with the rest of her [the woman's] offspring, the

ones who keep the commandments of God and have the testimony of Jesus" (12:17).

The Third Tableau--The Beast from the Land (13:11-18). The trinity of evil is complete with the third tableau: dragon, marine beast, terrestrial beast. The two previous tableaux, while not lacking in positive characters (woman, child; saints), have focused more on the evil than on the good. The third tableau is no exception; in fact, the presence of positive characters has diminished while the description of evil has increased.

The Apocalypse of John is not ultimately a pessimistic vision. The first three tableau are balanced, indeed superseded, by the final four tableaux, in which the Lamb takes his place on Mount Zion (14:1-5); one like the Son of Man reaps judgment on the earth (14:17-20); and the song of Moses is sung to God, whose anger has finally subsided (15:1-4). The visions of divine victory must wait, however, until the third tableau has pictured the oppressive regime ("no mark, no market") of the beast from the land. While the first three tableaux are visions of unrestrained evil, one must remember that the language is anti-language, which actively registers its opposition to the dominant and oppressive Roman Empire.

Setting and Content. The second tableau consists of the following characters: a beast from the land, the inhabitants of the earth, and the one who has understanding. As if the beast from the sea needed assistance, the beast arising from the land enters, looking like a lamb but speaking like a dragon, to make all earth dwellers to worship the first beast (13:11-12).[46] The terrestrial beast performs signs (coercive wonders) in order to accomplish his task: fire from heaven for all to see (13:13). One of the 'other signs' the beast carries out involves a statue (13:14-17): he deceives the world into making the statue (v. 14), makes the statue speak (v. 15), commands death to everyone who does not worship the statue (v. 15), and restricts buying and selling to those who possess a special mark on their hand or forehead (vv. 16-17). The third character plays a minor role in the third tableau: the one who has understanding (13:18). This person, while he or she may know the code of the number of the beast, stands under the shadow of the coercive regime of the beast, which, at a minimum, would prohibit them from commerce (13:17), but, at a maximum, would condemn to death (13:15).

---

[46]The marine beast seemed to have no trouble inspiring abandoned praise of himself among humanity; cf. 13:3b-4.

In terms of White's metahistorical model, the third tableau evinces a satiric tragic mode of emplotment. One's entrapped circumstances (satire) are as evident as in the second tableau; here the refusal to worship the beast and his statue spells death. Even the person who has the wisdom necessary to decipher the code number 666 cannot change oppressive circumstances; the most he or she can do is to look for salvation from an outside source.

The mechanistic mode of formal argument attempts to explain why life is as it is, emphasizing location, agency, and act. The physical and social location is the "earth" (ἡ γῆ). The extrahistorical agent at work is still the dragon, for the dragon empowers the sea beast who empowers the land beast. The extrahistorical agent (the dragon) directly affects the acts of historical agents in the tableau: the terrestrial beast deceives the earth dwellers to create a statue of the first beast (13:14).

Concerning the ideological implication, that is, the effect of the tableau upon the hearer, the call for the radical restructuring of society is not explicitly vented. All one can do in the present time is understand who the enemy is and not be fooled by it. The tableaux that follow will explicitly deal with the radical ideological implication of John's prophecy.

Relexicalization. The beast from the sea is the Roman Empire relexicalized. The beast from the land is the Roman Empire relexicalized, though viewed from a different aspect, namely, emperor worship, which to Jew and Christian alike constituted the height of ungodliness.[47] The objects of the beast's regime are

---

[47]The background of the symbol has been variously explained as (1) the second of two primeval monsters, one from the sea and one from the land (Job 40; 1 Enoch 60:7-10; 2 Esdr. 6:49-52; a Apoc. Bar. 29:4); (2) suggested by the phrase "the four kings that shall arise out of the earth" (Dan. 7:17); and (3) unlike the first beast that comes out of the sea, the second beast arises out of Asia Minor itself ("a native of the soil . . . a product of the life of the Asian cities" [Swete, *Revelation*, p. 168]). The latter accords with Prigent's suggestion that "il y a de fortes chances que cette deuxième bête ait été entierèment créée par notre auteur pour complétér ce que le symbolisme de la première avait d'insuffisant" (*L'Apocalypse*, p. 208). Thus, according to Prigent, the second beast completes the symbolism of the first beast by particularizing, localizing, the face of the enemy. For a history of the background see Swete, *Revelation*, pp. 168-169; Charles, *Revelation*, pp. 357-358; Beasley-Murray, pp. 215-216; Ford, *Revelation*, pp. 223-225; Prigent, *L'Apocalypse*, pp. 208; Mounce, pp. 258-259.

The beast from the land likely refers to aspects of the Emperor cult, although there is no evidence that people had to bear marks (χαράγματα) as a part of the cult. Beasley-Murray, *Revelation*, p. 216, quoting Cullmann, delineated the beast as "'the religio-ideological propaganda authority of the totalitarian state'": "In provincial Asia its spear head was the so-called 'Commune of Asia', a council made up of representatives from the chief cities of the province and whose president was called Asiarch. Historically it was the enthusiasm of this Asiatic league for the cult of Rome and the emperor which popularized this particular form of idolatry in the empire."

relexicalized, similarly to the second tableau, as "the ones who inhabit the earth" (τοὺς κατοικοῦντας ἐπὶ τῆς γῆς) (13:14; cf. v. 12). The earth-dwellers symbolize unbelieving humanity. Note how the word "earth" (γῆ) relates the terrestrial beast, whose origin is the earth (that is, Asia Minor), to the actual inhabitants of earth. The faithful are relexicalized by the phrase "the one who has understanding" (ὁ ἔχων νοῦν) (13:18). This term in the anti-language expresses the tension that exists between "the one who has a mark" (ὁ ἔχων τὸ χάραγμα) (13:17) and "the one who has understanding."

Overlexicalization. Since the reign of evil is emphasized in the third tableau, one is not surprised to find overlexicalization with the relexicalized terms of "beast" and "earth-dwellers." The best from the land is described with multiple words to emphasize the spiritual and social adversary of John and the community that he represents. The less threatening, though more deceptive, appearance of the beast is first described: "he had two horns like a lamb and spoke like a dragon" (13:11).[48] Further overlexicalization occurs almost uniformly in a strophic configuration that begins with "and he makes" (καὶ ποιεῖ) (13:12, 13, 16); verse 14 diverges yet maintains an element of verbal play, namely, alliteration ("and he deceives"--καὶ

See also Kraft, *Offenbarung*, p. 180, who rejected the above interpretation as not corresponding to the essential description of the second beast, which Kraft would rather view as an anti-salvific figure (a false prophet) that from time to time appears in human history. Even if Kraft's proposal is correct, one could nevertheless see behind the symbolic beast the workings of the emperor cult. The beast from the land certainly fits the description of the Antichrist; see, e.g., Lohmeyer, *Offenbarung*, pp. 113-114; and the still powerful essay by Schlier, "Vom Antichrist," pp. 16-21, 26-29.

[48]According to Genesis 22:8 and Targums, God's first prophet, Abraham, tells us that God has a lamb; yet when Abraham is ready to sacrifice, God has him use a ram (Gen. 22:13) or sheep, but not a lamb. For this reason it was commonly held in Israelite tradition that God indeed has a lamb, and this from the dawn of creation (as in 1 Pet. 1:19-20). Hence the significance of the lamb of God.

Note the similarity to Matt. 7:15 (οἵτινες [ψευδοπροφῆται] ἔρχονται πρὸς ὑμᾶς ἐν ἐνδύμασιν προβάτων, ἔσωθεν δὲ εἰσιν λύκοι ἅρπαγες). The word "sheep" (προβάτων) in the Apocalypse of John 13:11 is replaced by the Christologically significant "lamb" (ἀρνίῳ). While Matthew 7:15 speaks of false prophets, the beast from the land will, after chapter thirteen, be referred to only with the nonsymbolic term "false prophet" (Rev. 16:13; 19:20; 20:10).

Lohmeyer, *Offenbarung*, p. 113, referred to what he called the Johannine custom (*Gepflogenheit*) of describing persons by their appearance and voice (John 5:37; 20:14ff), which, Lohmeyer claimed, had widespread "religionsgeschichtliche Bedeutung": "Nach ihr ist eine Gestalt dann in der Gesamtheit ihrer Erscheinung dargestellt, wenn ihr εἶδος und ihre φωνή, d. h. ihr Aeußeres und Inneres angegeben ist."

πλανᾷ).[49] The terrestrial beast "makes," that is, exercises, the authority of the first beast (13:12); he makes the earth-dwellers to worship the first beast (13:12); he "makes," that is, performs, great signs (13:13); he deceives the earth-dwellers into making an idol of the first beast (13:14); he "makes," that is, coerces, everyone to receive a mark in order to buy and sell (13:16).

Unbelieving humanity is overlexicalized in order to emphasize the widespread nature of the beast's regime: "people" (ἀνθρώπων) (13:13); "everyone, small and great, both rich and poor, both free and slaves" (13:16). Overlexicalization also serves to emphasize the idolatrous nature of unbelieving humanity: "the one who has the mark, (which consists of) the name of the beast or the number of his name (13:17). In contrast to the unbelieving humanity, the smaller group of the faithful has the bare association with "wisdom," which serves, nonetheless, to emphasize the saints as possessing understanding in contrast to everyone else.

Verbal Play. The anti-language of the Apocalypse of John emanates from a strong group/low grid social location, and the prophet John thus sees and speaks from an inferior position, in which verbal play serves as one form of confrontation and challenge to the dominant culture. Verbal play in the third tableau takes the following form: word plays, repeated use of ποιεῖ ("he makes"); repeated use of the passive voice; and the well-known numeration of the name of the beast. Verbal play functions to underscore the notion of the extent as well as the corruption of the terrestrial beast.

Alliteration takes the following forms in the third tableau:

(1) Initial alliteration, with a preference for the phoneme "p" (π), occurs in the following verses: πᾶσαν ποιεῖ (13:12); πῦρ ποιῇ (13:13); ποιεῖ πάντας (13:16); μικρούς/μεγάλους, πλουσίους/πτωχούς (13:16); χάραγμα/χειρός (13:16).

(2) Other kinds of alliteration: mesial/initial: ἐλευθέρους/δούλους (θ/δ) (13:16); initial-mesial/mesial-initial (ἀριθμὸν/θηρίου, ἀριθμὸς/ἀνθρώπου (ἀρ-θ/θ-ρ, ἀρ-θ/θ-ρ) (13:18).

(3) Pun (Paronomasia: recurrence of same word or word stem) occurs twice: ἐδόθη αὐτῷ δοῦναι (13:15); ἑξακόσιοι ἑξήκοντα ἕξ (13:18).

---

[49]Lohmeyer pointed to the "strophische Gleiderung" of the above verses (p. 112).

The enumeration of the terrestrial beast's activities underscore his personal agency by the use of active forms of the verb ποιέω. Ποιέω occurs seven times in strophic form, which is broken midway with the use of another active verb, πλανάω ("I deceive"), and may be listed as follows.

13:12	καὶ ἐξουσίαν . . . πᾶσαν ποιεῖ
13:12	καὶ ποιεῖ τὴν γῆν . . . ἵνα προσκυνήσουσιν τὸ θηρίον τὸ πρῶτον
13:13	καὶ ποιεῖ σημεῖα μεγάλα
13:14	καὶ πλανᾷ τοὺς κατοικοῦντας ἐπὶ τῆς γῆς
13:14	ποιῆσαι ἐνώπιον τοῦ θηρίου
13:14	ποιῆσαι εἰκόνα τῷ θηρίῳ
13:15	ποιήσῃ ἵνα ὅσοι ἐὰν μὴ προσκυνήσωσιν τῇ εἰκόνι τοῦ θηρίου ἀποκτανθῶσιν
13:16	ποιεῖ πάντας . . . ἵνα δῶσιν αὐτοῖς χάραγμα

The verbal play of anti-language is seen in the repeated use of the passive voice, which occurs three times in the third tableau. The passive voice functions to inject an air of secrecy as well as to emphasize the acts of extra-historical agents in the development of the visions. The passive "was healed" (ἐθεραπεύθη) (13:12) is repeated from the second tableau; the agent would appear to be an anti-causative agent, that is, the dragon. The oft-recurring passive of δίδωμι is found twice: "which [signs] were given (ἐδόθη) him to do before the [first] beast (13:14); "and there was given to him to give" (ἐδόθη αὐτῷ δοῦναι) a spirit to the statue of the beast (13:15).

Finally, anti-language functions to provide a group with its own identity, for only those who know and use the anti-language are privy to the concerns of the group, which are often shrouded in secrecy or code. A clear example of secret, or coded, language is Alex's criminal glossary in A Clockwork Orange (see pp. 74-77) of this dissertation). The third tableau provides a clear example of the kind of language that can be understood only by insiders; indeed, the aim of the Apocalypse of John is to reinforce the boundary lines between insiders and outsiders.

Those who have understanding, that is, those for whom John is writing, will recognize the code: "the number of the beast, for it is the number of a man, and his number is 666" (13:18). No one outside the group can claim certainty of decipherment, as nearly two millennia suggest.[50] Decipherers have largely taken

---

[50]Prigent, L'Apocalypse, p. 214, has summed the problem with deciphering number codes: "transcrire un nom dans tous les codes imaginables est un jeu d'enfant, mais réaliser l'opération inverse sans avoir idée du code, c'est une entreprise qu'un service de contre-espionnage ne peut esperér mener à bien que s'il dispose d'un texte assez long."

one of three paths: (1) 666 as gematria, (2) 666 as triangulation, and (3) 666 as thrice repetition of the number for evil, that is, the number six.[51] Ultimately, whether the number was the enumeration of a person's actual name or merely symbolized the person, one can view the number as the attempt of a strong group/low grid group to express in numerical verbal play the tension between itself and that figure (and the dominant society of which he or she is part).[52]

Anti-language and Strong Group/Low Grid. The anti-language of the third tableau indicates the following strong group/low grid concerns.

(1) Purity. The permeability of boundaries is indicated again by the way the beast rises up out of the earth and does not remain in its subterranean domain. The lines are drawn clearly between "us" and "them": the terrestrial beast and unbelieving humanity dominate the third tableau, in which the faithful are only slightly pictured as the one's who have understanding and do not give worship or receive marks.

(2) Rite. Rite in the third tableau focuses on anti-boundary lines, the "them" lines. The unfaithful group is known by its observance of beast worship and external marks on the hand or forehead; worship and mark ($\chi\acute{\alpha}\rho\alpha\gamma\mu\alpha$) constitute ceremonial reminders of the social group to which one belongs.[53]

---

[51]Decipherment is complicated by the addition of the textual variation of 616, which is attested by C; see Metzger, *Textual Commentary*, pp. 749-750. The majority of manuscripts, however, support the reading 666.

Gematria is the process in which a letter of the alphabet is given a corresponding numeral. Nero has been a major candidate: for example, Metzger, p. 750, "the Greek form Neron Caesar written in Hebrew characters (נרון קסר) is equivalent to 666, whereas the Latin form Nero Caesar (נרו קסר) is equivalent to 616." Triangulation is the process in which an underlying symbolic number is derived from a larger number: 666 = sum of numbers from 1-36 = sum of letters (in Hebrew language) from 1-8; 8 is the underlying symbolic number for the number of the Antichrist (Rev. 17:11). According to the number code in the Apocalypse of John, the number six ($\overset{\prime}{\epsilon}\xi$) implies evil and appears only in the third tableau in triple six form.

For examples of the three modes of decipherment see Oskar Rühle, "$\dot{\alpha}\rho\iota\theta\mu\acute{\epsilon}\omega$, $\dot{\alpha}\rho\iota\theta\mu\acute{o}\varsigma$," *TDNT*, vol. 1, pp. 461-464; John Bowman, Six hundred and sixty-six," *IDB*, vol. 4, pp. 381-382; Prigent, *L'Apocalypse*, pp. 214-217; Ford, *Revelation*, pp. 226-230.

[52]Rühle, "$\dot{\alpha}\rho\iota\theta\mu\acute{\epsilon}\omega$," p. 462, presented an excellent example of gematria from excavations at Pompeii that indicates the position in which the modern interpreter finds him- or herself. On a wall was found the following inscription: $\phi\iota\lambda\hat{\omega}$ $\mathring{\eta}\varsigma$ $\dot{\alpha}\rho\iota\theta\mu\acute{o}\varsigma$ $\phi\mu\epsilon$ ($\phi\mu\epsilon = 545$). The possibilities of names are endless; only the wall inscriber himself (and perhaps $\phi\mu\epsilon$ as well!) knew the secret.

[53]The earth beast serves as a mediator or broker for the first beast, through whom all the earth has access to the first beast, the patron of all.

(3) Personal Identity. Only by embeddedness in the group can one be saved. The slight reference to the faithful group as "the one who has understanding" (13:18) underscores group--not merely individual--identity. With the use of the singular verb in the Apocalypse of John usually the whole community is in view.[54]

(4) Body. The key perception of body--both physical and social--for strong group/low grid is transformation. The body in its present state is not a "symbol of life" (Malina). The physical body becomes further defiled by the marks of the beast upon it; the social body becomes further defiled by unthinking adherence to the deceptive regime of the beast. The body, both physical and social, is need of transformation.

(5) Sin. Sin is deviance in the social order, which lodges itself in individuals and groups. The terrestrial beast, symbolic of social deviance, is the chief deviant, which spreads its infection throughout the social body. The unbelieving world seems most receptive to the infection, although in strong group/low grid perception all boundaries are porous and open to attack.

(6) Cosmology. Events that happen in the world are described anthropomorphically in order to uncover the causal factor (the "who") that stands behind them. The third tableau makes clear that the dragon ultimately stands behind the worship and the marks: the terrestrial beast receives its authority from the marine beast, who received its authority from the dragon, who is the divine antithesis.

(7) Suffering and Misfortune. The hearer of the Apocalypse could only imply from the third tableau that suffering will be a direct result of the beast's regime ("no worship, no life"; "no mark, no market"), which is ultimately the ongoing dualistic struggle between the dragon and God.

The Fourth Tableau--The Lamb with the 144,000 (14:1-5). The first three tableaux indicated the increasing encroachment of evil in the last days. Anti-language drew the tension between saint and unbeliever, God and dragon, in vivid terms. Originating in heaven, the dualistic struggle between the divine and the anti-divine spreads to the earth, where evil--incarnated as the Roman Empire--spells certain doom for the saints. In the second tableau the earth-dwellers pose the rhetorical question of the marine beast: "Who is like the beast and who is able to

---

[54]See pp. 32-33 of this dissertation.

wage war with him?" (13:4b). Such universal awe is repeated in the third tableau, in which the terrestrial beast is able to force all persons, upon threat of death, to worship the first beast (13:12); all persons, that is, except the few who possess "the patience and faith of the saints" (13:10).

In the next four tableaux the anti-language will relexicalize, overlexicalize, and evince all kinds of verbal play in order to stress the final upper hand of God and all saints. The fourth tableau presents the image of saints who though persecuted were ultimately victors like like the slaughtered Lamb before them. I will also examine in the present section the so-called interlude of the announcement of the three angels (14:6-13) that occurs immediately after the fourth tableau. The announcement of the three angels functions to punctuate the scene of the persecuted 144,000: the dragon and the beasts will no longer have the upper hand!

Setting and Content. The fourth tableau consists of the following characters: the Lamb and 144,000 persons who have his name and his Father's name. Evil is only hinted at. The tableau stands in stark contrast to the second and third tableaux, in which the description of the faithful was meager. One notes a strong similarity to an earlier description of torment (6:1-17: "Who is able to stand [in the great day of wrath]?" [v. 17]) that was followed by a vision of 144,000 persons who received God's seal (7:1-8).

The Lamb, who is none other than Jesus (5:6-12), stands upon a symbolically safe place, Mount Zion (14:1).[55] Standing beside the Lamb are 144,000 persons, who describe themselves in some detail by means of a song (14:2-5). The fourth tableau consists of the following structure: (1) vision (14:1), (2) audition (14:2-3), and (3) explanation (14:4-5).[56] The interlude that follows, while not a part of the tableau proper, serves as a fitting conclusion to the tableau

---

[55]The prophet Joel proclaimed Mount Zion and Jerusalem as places immune from God's wrath (Joel 2:32). One should note, however, that geography alone does not insure safety, for in Joel, as well as in the Apocalypse of John, calling on the name of the Lord is prerequisite to deliverance. Mounce, *Revelation*, p. 267, correctly asserted that the Apocalypse of John here refers to "the heavenly Zion," and physical deliverance of the saints is not in view but ultimate bliss beyond death. One may assume that the 144,000 are identical to those in Chapter Seven who "come out of the great tribulation" (7:14).

[56]Fiorenza, *Revelation*, p. 181, listed the "clearly marked composition and structure" above, contrasting it with the "exegetical conundrum" that surrounds the identification of the principal vision of the section, namely, the 144,000.

that marks the shift away from the unhindered movement of evil. The three angels clearly anticipate tableaux five, six, and seven:

> First Angel (14:6-7): Fear and worship God!
> Second Angel (14:8): Babylon the Great has fallen!
> Third Angel (14:9-12): Woe to the one who worships the beast.

In the fourth tableau and in the interlude the prophet John continues to register his opposition to the ungodly, dehumanizing powers of Rome by means of anti-language.

In terms of White's metahistorical model, the fourth tableau evinces a satiric tragic mode of emplotment. While one could not escape the regime of the beast, one could look beyond this world for salvation. John's vision and audition of the Lamb and his followers serves as a sign of extrahistorical deliverance.

The mechanistic mode of formal argument, with its emphasis on location, agency, and act, takes the following shape in the fourth tableau. Location encompasses heaven and earth. Mount Zion (Rev. 14:1) is probably the heavenly entity here. The agent is the Lamb, who functions as the extrahistorical agent that controls the actions of persons. Act, that is, the acts of agents within the historical field, is most poignantly described in verse 4: "these are the ones who follow the Lamb wherever he goes."

Concerning the ideological implication, which is a call to radical restructuring of society, the fourth tableau only hints. The interlude, however, is more vocal. The first angel announces that the "best of times is right around the corner": "Fear God and give him glory, for the hour of judgment has come" (14:7a). The second angel announces the same (14:8): "Fallen, fallen is Babylon the Great!"

Relexicalization. The Lamb is the first of the two characters of the fourth tableau, both of which are presented in verse 1. The Lamb ($\tau \grave{o}$ $\dot{\alpha} \rho \nu \acute{\iota} o \nu$) is the crucified and risen Jesus, who, as the Lamb, is the model of faithful witness to all who would follow him (Rev. 1:5; 3:14).[57] The second set of characters is the 144,000 who stand beside the Lamb.[58] In the anti-language of the Apocalypse of

---

[57]Holtz, *Christologie*, p. 47, noted that "witness" ($\mu \acute{\alpha} \rho \tau \upsilon \varsigma$) denotes one who has lost his or her life for Christ and that, as the Lamb, Jesus symbolizes the paschal lamb that was sacrificed for the church.

[58]The exegetical possibilities take a quantum leap when one deals with the larger number 144,000 (as opposed to the smaller 666). Fiorenza, "Followers of the Lamb," p. 124, listed, following Boechner, some of the more visible interpretations: (1) Jewish-Christians, (2) elect and "saved" Christians, (3) Christian ascetic males, (4)

John this number represents the antithesis of those who worship the beast. The believers described here were only meagerly described in the first three tableaux. The notion of numeration most likely plays a role here: 12 (the number of wholeness; the number of the tribes of Israel) x 12,000 (1,000 is the symbol of a great multitude).[59]

Overlexicalization. Overlexicalization is primarily in the direction of those who stand next to the Lamb (= Jesus relexicalized), that is, the 144,000. This group, which has stood in the shadows until now, suddenly becomes the object of extensive overlexicalization. The subjects of the regime of the beast (the earth-dwellers) were overlexicalized in order to stress their unquestioning unbelief. The 144,000 are overlexicalized in order to stress unquestioning loyalty, discipleship, and purity, which, in the anti-language, stresses the tension between the two.

The 144,000 are overlexicalized in the following manner. Each overlexicalization serves to intensify the fourth tableau as "anti-image" (Fiorenza).

---

the eschatologically saved and protected "holy rest" of Israel (5), the "perfect" victims and sacrifice, (6) the high priestly followers of the Lamb, (7) the military army of the Lamb gathering in Sion for the messianic battle, (8) those who have followed the Lamb into death, and (9) those who follow the Lamb in heaven. These nine, and other, interpretations result from the four-fold explanation given in verses 4-5 (144,000 are virgins, followers of the Lamb, a first fruit, and blameless). One is encouraged by the text to see multivalence in the image; the anti-language by nature encourages such by overlexicalization. See, for example, Swete, *Revelations*, pp. 176-177; Charles, *Revelation*, vol. 2, pp. 5-7; Caird, *The Revelation of St. John the Divine*, New Testament Commentaries (New York: Harper, 1966), pp. 178-181; A. Feuillet, "Les 144.000 Israelites marques d'un sceau," *NovT*, 9 (1967), pp. 191-224; Beasley-Murray, *Revelation*, p. 222; Mounce, *Revelation* pp. 267-268; Kraft, *Offenbarung*, pp. 186-187; Ladd, *Revelation*, pp. 189-190; Ford, *Revelation*, pp. 244-246; Prigent, *L'Apocalypse*, pp. 218-219.

In affirming one image over another one must still be sensitive to the larger issue of the less than adequate images and roles of women in the Apocalypse of John 14:1-5, which, according to Adela Collins, "Women's History and the Book of Revelation," *SBLSP*, 26 (1987), 80-91, is a record to both the oppression and the liberation of women. Collins found in the fourth tableau the one-sided impression that "the model Christian is male" (cf. Rev. 14:4). Viewing the 144,000 virgins in terms of eschatological asceticism does not fully expunge the text of its male orientation.

Fiorenza, "Followers of the Lamb," p. 124, was correct in sensing in the image of the 144,000 primarily the "anti-image of the beast and its followers." Whether one wishes to identify the 144,000 with first century believers or, in a timeless sense, true witnesses of any age, the image still functions in the text as "an antithetical vision of the dragon and the two beasts" (p. 131). I concur with Fiorenza, however, that symbols of the fourth tableau are a "fitting response to the social-historical-political situation faced by the Christians of Asia Minor" (p. 123).

[59]See Ford, *Revelation*, p. 245.

(1) They belong to God not beast: "They have his [the Lamb's] name and the name of his Father written on their foreheads" (14:1).

(2) They worship God not beast: "They sing as it were a new song before the throne and before the four creatures and before the elders" (14:3). This is the new song of salvation (Pss. 144:9; 33:3).

(3) They were in the world but not of it (John 17:5): "The ones who were bought from the earth" (οἱ ἠγορασμένοι ἀπὸ τῆς γῆς) (14:3). The verse refers to liberation from (ἀπό) the tyranny of the earth-dwellers and the beast.[60]

(4) They are separated and pure: "The ones who have not defiled themselves with women, for they are virgins" (14:4). The image most likely refers to the eschatological asceticism of the soldiers of the Lamb.[61]

(5) They follow Lamb not beast: "These are the ones who follow the Lamb wherever he goes" (14:4). The description does not necessarily infer the death of martyrdom (though the notion is in no way external to the text; cf. 13:7, 15-17), but the 144,000 were at least willing to follow their Lord to that point.[62]

(6) They are "a first fruit to God" (ἀπαρχὴ τῷ θεῷ) (14:4). This overlexicalization serves to emphasize the extent of discipleship as does the

---

[60]The indicative verb is used at 14:4: οὗτοι ἠγοράσθησαν ἀπὸ τῶν ἀνθρώπων. Kraft, *Offenbarung*, p. 188, suggested that the verb "buy, purchase" (ἀγοράζω) probably has the sense here of "procure, get" (κτάομαι) since no details are given of the purchase. Thus, Kraft noted, the LXX rendering of Isa. 26:13a is in view: κύριε ὁ θεὸς ἡμῶν κτῆσαι ἡμᾶς ("O Lord our God, purchase us for yourself."). See also Prigent, *L'Apocalypse*, p. 220; Mounce, *Revelation*, p. 269; Ford, *Revelation*, p. 234.

[61]In spite of the best attempts to interpret the images symbolically as abstinence from fornication with the great whore of chapter seventeen (see, e.g., Beasley-Murray, *Revelation*, pp. 222-223), the text becomes problematic in terms of "questions about the underlying definitions of maleness and femaleness" (Collins, "Women's History," p. 90). In the anti-language of the Apocalypse of John the symbols connote purity and holiness, the antithesis of which is the earth-dwellers who devote themselves to the worship of the beast. See also David Sholer, "Feminist Hermeneutics and Evangelical Biblical Interpretation," *JEvTh*, 30 (1987), 407-420.
For background to the images see Collins, "Women's History," pp. 84-91; Swete, *Revelation*, pp. 179-180; Ford, *Revelation*, pp. 234-235, 241-243; Prigent, *L'Apocalypse*, pp. 220-221; Mounce, *Revelation*, pp. 269-271; Gerhard Delling, "παρθένος," *TDNT*, vol. 5, pp. 826-831; Ford, "The Meaning of 'Virgin,'" *NTS*, 12 (1966), pp. 293-299; C. Lindijer, "Die Jungfrauen in der Offenbarung des Johannes XIV 4," in *Studies in John*, ed. A. Geyser, et al. (Leiden: Brill, 1970), pp. 124-142.

[62]See Mitchell Reddish, "The Theme of Martyrdom in the Book of Revelation" (Ph.D. dissertation, The Southern Baptist Theological Seminary, 1982), pp. 170-171; also more recently "Martyr Christology in the Apocalypse," *JSNT*, 33 (1988), 89.

124

preceding image. They present their lives willingly to God, whereas the earth-dwellers unthinkingly devoted themselves to the beast.[63]

(7) They are true prophets not false prophets: "And in their mouth was not found a lie, they are spotless (ἄμωμοι)" (14:5). The second beast is also referred to as "the false prophet" (Rev. 16:13; 19:20; 20:10), which denotes both that he is an inauthentic prophet of God as well as a prophet of falsehood.[64] The 144,000 are an anti-image of the beast, and eschatological witnesses know that pure speech forms one requisite of eternal salvation (cf. Rev. 21:27; 22:14-15).[65]

Verbal Play. Verbal play is indicated by various word plays, repeated use of the passive voice, and another example of numeration. Word plays occur as follows.

(1) Initial and mesial alliteration: ἑστὸς ἐπί (14:1), ἥν ἤκουσα (14:2); οὐδεὶς ἐδύνατο μαθεῖν τὴν ᾠδήν (14:3).

(2) Pun (Paronomasia: recurrence of same word or word stem): εἶδον καὶ ἰδού (14:1); τεσσεράκοντα τέσσαρες (14:1); τὸ ὄνομα . . . τὸ ὄνομα (14:1); φωνή occurs four times (14:2; κιθαρῳδῶν κιθαριζόντων ἐν ταῖς κιθάραις (14:2); ᾄδουσιν ὡς ᾠδήν (14:3); ἐνώπιον . . . ἐνώπιον (14:3); οὗτοι occurs three times (14:4).

---

[63] The notion of the first fruits referred originally to the initial part of a harvest that was offered to God (Num. 15:21; Deut. 18:4) and later signified an offering or gift (Jas. 1:18). The textual variant in 𝔓⁴⁷ and ℵ (ἀπ᾽ ἀρχῆς, "from the beginning") is obviously a scribal error or scribal interpretation.

[64] Prigent, *L'Apocalypse*, p. 222.

[65] Hans Conzelmann, "ψεῦδος κτλ," *TDNT*, vol. 9, pp. 602-603, was correct in viewing truth speaking in an eschatological perspective; Prigent, *L'Apocalypse*, p. 222, noted that the Qumran writings evince the antagonism between truth and falsehood, Baal and God, which is reflected in John 8:44-45. See Community Rule IV (1QS) for the destiny of truth and falsehood in G. Vermes, *The Dead Sea Scrolls in English* (2nd ed. New York: Penguin Books, 1975), pp. 76-78. While truth speaking is an essential ethical quality (see 1 Pet. 2:22), Kraft, *Offenbarung*, pp. 190-191, underscored that the truth-found-mouth as well as spotlessness are both the gift of God (Zeph. 3:13; Isa. 53:9; Ps. 32:2). See also Ford, *Revelation*, p. 235.

For a sociological understanding of lying see Michael Gilsenan, "Lying, Honor and Contradiction," Bruce Kapferer (ed.), *Transactions and Meaning: Directions in the Anthropology of Exchange and Symbolic Behavior* (Philadelphia: Institute for the Study of Human Behavior, 1976), pp. 191-219; Juliet du Boulay, "Lies, mockery and family integrity," in J. G. Peristiany, ed., *Mediterranean Family Structures* (Cambridge: Cambridge University Press, 1976); and John H. Elliott, "The Fear of the Leer: The Evil Eye from the Bible to Li'l Abner," *Forum*, 4 (1988), 42, 71.

The previous tableaux have displayed a repeated use of the passive voice to inject the notion of secrecy as well as stress the acts of extrahistorical agents. The passive voice occurs four times in the fourth tableau, and the second passive (ἐμολύνθησαν) may be categorized as an anti-divine (impersonal passive).

14:1	γεγραμμένον	=	(name) having been written
14:4	ἐμολύνθησαν	=	they were not defiled
14:4	ἠγοράσθησαν	=	they were purchased
14:5	οὐχ εὑρέθη	=	(a lie) was not found

The verb ἐμολύνθησαν is often translated with the middle voice, "they did not defile themselves." The active translation does not convey the full force of the anti-language, for the passive voice is used to emphasize the acts of extrahistorical agents.[66] Thus the beast as implicit anti-divine agent was not able to defile the 144,000 with social and spiritual impurity ("with women").[67]

The remaining three passives are divine passives. God and the Lamb have written their names upon the foreheads of the 144,000 (14:1). The Lamb, as the divine agent, purchased for God a people from among all the earth-dwellers (14:4; cf. 5:9). God found no falsehood in the mouth of his eschatological witnesses (14:5).

A final form of verbal play is the enumeration of the 144,000, which in the anti-language serves to stress the notion of group boundaries: opposed to the earth-dwellers is the much smaller, though providentially complete, group of the followers of the Lamb. The enumeration likely has the following significance: 12 (the number of wholeness; the number of the tribes of Israel) x 12,000 (1,000 is the symbol of a great multitude).[68]

Interlude: Three Angels (14:6-13). Three angels flying in the midst of the sky appear before John, each announcing their "eternal good news" to the whole world. The angels thus are the voice of God relexicalized.[69] The interlude

---

[66]The verb occurs in the active voice in 3:4, which concerns the few Sardinian Christians that did not dirty their clothes, that is, lead an impure unrepentant life, see *EWNT*, vol. 2, p. 1080.

[67]The preposition μετά, here a synonym of σύν + dative, expresses the notion of accompaniment not means or agency; see *GGNTLHR*, pp. 610-612 and *BDF*, pp. 120-121.

[68]See Ford, *Revelation*, p. 245.

[69]A. P. van Schaik, "῎Αλλος ἄγγελος in Apk 14," in *L'Apocalypse johannique et l'Apocalyptique dans le Nouveau Testament*, BETL 53, ed. J. Lambrecht (Leuven: Leuven University Press, 1980), pp. 217-228, made a good case

functions to punctuate the shift away from the upper hand of evil that marked the movement of the first three tableaux.[70] The anti-language of the section functions as well to strengthen group boundaries and perceptions, including an evangelical call.[71] The first angel urges everyone to fear and worship God (14:7); the second angel reports the downfall of Rome relexicalized, that is, Babylon the Great (14:8); the third angel warns against beast worship (14:9-12). The announcements of the three angels are concluded by the second makarism of the Apocalypse of John, which appropriately returns the focus upon the subject of the fourth tableau, namely, the 144,000.[72]

The interlude is indicated by the verbal play of anti-language as it spells the end to the upper hand of evil.

(1) Overlexicalization: ἔθνος, φυλὴν, γλῶσσαν, λαόν (14:6); θεόν, ποιήσαντι τὸν οὐρανόν (14:7); θηρίον, εἰκόνα αὐτου, χάραγμα τοῦ ὀνόματος αὐτοῦ (14:9, 11); ἁγίων, τηροῦντες τὰς ἐντολάς (14:12).

(2) Highly paratactic speech: frequent use of καί.

(3) Initial alliteration: ἄλλος ἄγγελος (14:6, 8, 9); ἔχοντα εὐαγγέλιον αἰώνιον εὐαγγελίσαι ἐπὶ . . . ἐπὶ . . . .ἐπί (14:6); φοβήθητε/θεόν, δότε/δόξαν, προσκυνήσατε/ποιήσαντι (14:7); πεπότικεν πάντα (14:8); ἀγγέλων ἁγίων (14:11).

(4) Pun (Paronomasia): εὐαγγέλιον . . . εὐαγγελίσαι (14:6); αἰῶνας αἰώνων (14:11).

---

for understanding "another angel" (14:6, 8, 9; also 10:1; 14:15, 17; 18:1) as the voice of God personified: ἄλλος ἄγγελος is viewed "als eine geprägte Einleitungsformel zu verstehen, die die dringenden Gottesworte aus dem AT in der anderen Situation der Endzeit erneut verkündigt" (p. 225).

[70]Michael Harris, "Literary Function," pp. 165-168, viewed the section as a series of direct comments directed to the implied reader of the text to encourage faithfulness and endurance. Kraft, *Offenbarung*, p. 191, noted that according to the usual pattern of the Apocalypse of John the gathering of the saints on Zion is followed by judgment.

[71]While the "eternal good news" is addressed to all the earth-dwellers, thus constituting an evangelical call to all persons, one should note also the tendency in the Apocalypse of John to urge the evil to remain evil and the saint to remain saintly (Rev. 22:11, 14; 13:10).

[72]Dan Hatfield, "The Function of the Seven Beatitudes in Revelation" (Ph.D. dissertation, The Southern Baptist Theological Seminary, 1987), p. 153, added that "[u]nlike their persecutors, saints have rest, and their labor is granted eschatological dignity." The following three tableaux delineate the lack of rest accorded to unbelievers.

(5) Epanadiplosis (repetition of an important word for emphasis): ἔπεσεν ἔπεσιν (14:8; also at 18:2).

(6) Concatenation of genitives: ἐκ τοῦ οἴνου τοῦ θυμοῦ τῆς πορνείας αὐτῆς (14:8); ἐκ τοῦ οἴνου τοῦ θυμοῦ τοῦ θεοῦ τοῦ κεκερασμένου ἀκράτου (14:10).

Anti-language and Strong Group/Low Grid. The anti-language of the fourth tableau indicates the following strong group/low grid concerns.

(1) Purity. The location of the 144,000 with the Lamb on Mount Zion, as well as the relatively lengthy song about them, serves as an anti-image to the beast and his followers and clearly draws lines between "us" and "them." The announcement of the three angels enunciates the values of the group and functions as a challenge to keep the purity level high, for boundaries are still porous and insiders are not to trust the unmarked or negatively marked.

(2) Rite. Rite, according to Malina, is of two kinds, ritual and ceremony.[73] Ritual concerns the crossing of lines (e.g., baptism) and ceremony concerns the maintaining of lines (e.g., Sunday worship). The 144,000 have undergone the ritual of redemption, that is, status transformation, just like the first fruit. The opposite are those described by the third angel (Rev. 14:9-11), who have undergone a ritual of negative transformation and are now shamed in perpetual public (in the presence of the holy angels and the lamb), humiliation further indicated by the fact that they have to labor (no rest). The status transformation (both positive and negative) is brought about by God asserting his honor in the face of public shame, that is, blasphemy, false worship, lying, and so on. There may be a hint of ritual in the description of the first angel in the interlude (14:6-7): everyone on the face of the earth apparently will hear the loud voice (φωνῇ μεγάλῃ) of the angel's "eternal good news" as he urges fear and worship of God. The stern message of the third angel in the interlude functions as ceremony to focus the group's attention on the matter of beast worship and its consequences (14:9-13).

(3) Personal identity. Only by embeddedness in the group can one be saved. Salvation belongs to those who are in the group that stands beside the Lamb on Mount Zion. The notion of personal identity is intensified in that only the members of the latter group can learn the "like a new song" (ὡς ᾠδὴν καινὴν) of salvation

---

[73]Malina, *Christian Origins and Cultural Anthropology* (Atlanta: John Knox Press, 1986), pp. 139-143.

that they sing before the throne, the four creatures, and the elders (14:3). Those to whom John writes understand themselves also as "the ones who keep the commandments of God and the faith of Jesus" (14:12).

(4) Body. The physical and social body is not a symbol of life and is in need of transformation. The 144,000 appear in a transformed state on Mount Zion (14:1-3): they have divine names on their foreheads, and they sing something like a new song. There is no mention of the fully transformed state, that is, white robes (3:5; 7:9, 13; 19:14); but a new name is promised, though this will be written on a white stone (2:17). In the interlude, as in the previous two tableaux, the physical body and the social body become further defiled by the marks of the beast upon them.

(5) Sin. Sin is deviance in the social order, which lodges itself in individuals and groups. Mount Zion, a place of salvation and rest for the 144,000, lacks any presence of disorder. The fourth tableau is a conscientious shift away from a description of sin. In fact, in the message of the second angel in the interlude, the symbol of sin in the social body, Babylon the Great, has become dislodged (ἔπεσεν) from its infectious location (14:8).

(6) Cosmology. Events that happen in the world are described anthropomorphically in order to uncover the personal causal factor behind them. The fourth tableau and the interlude both underscore the role of God and the Lamb, not the dragon, in the development of human affairs.

(7) Suffering and Misfortune. The 144,000 are standing on Mount Zion as a direct result of the dragon and the beasts' oppressive regime (persecution ended their lives) and as a direct result of the salvific interference of the Lamb (salvation renewed their lives). The followers of the Lamb felicitously benefit from the ongoing dualistic struggle between God and the dragon.

The Fifth Tableau--The Son of Man on a Cloud (14:14-16). The fourth tableau evinced a shift from the upper hand of evil; the interlude of the three angels punctuated the shift. The fifth tableau is one of two scenes that cursorily depicts the judgment of the earth as a time of harvest; the sixth tableau tells of the harvest of grapes (14:17-20). The "earth" (γῆ), humanity, is the object of judgment. Some commentators interpret the harvesting in the fifth tableau as the ingathering of the righteous (the unrighteous are then harvested in the sixth tableau).[74] The anti-

---

[74]See, e.g., Beasley-Murray, *Revelation*, pp. 228-229, who also listed Swete, Lohmeyer, Behm, Farrer, and Rissi as holding to such an interpretation.

language has predominantly used "earth" for unbelieving humanity, and this is most likely the sense it has in the fifth and the sixth tableaux. The beasts are not even mentioned, but they receive special attention, along with the dragon, in 20:10.

Setting and Content. The fifth tableau consists of the following characters: one like the Son of Man, another angel, and the earth. As John looks ("and I saw") he sees one like the Son of Man sitting on a cloud and holding a sharp sickle (14:14). One in a series of "another" angels (Rev. 10:1; 14:6, 8, 9, 17; 18:1) departs the heavenly temple and gives the command to the one like the Son of Man to harvest the "ripe" earth (14:15).[75] No sooner has the angel spoken than the harvesting is done (14:16).

In terms of White's metahistorical model, the fifth tableau evinces a satiric tragic mode of emplotment. The historical flow of events can only be altered by extrahistorical agents. The tableau is solely concerned with what not humans but divine agents can accomplish on the earth (mode of formal argument). The radical mode of ideological implication is indicated by the image of harvest; the restructuring of society first requires chopping down of the existing structure.

Relexicalization. Jesus is relexicalized as "one like the Son of man" ($\ddot{o}\mu o\iota o\nu$ $\upsilon \dot{\iota} \dot{o}\nu$ $\dot{a}\nu\theta\rho\dot{\omega}\pi o\upsilon$) as in 1:13. In both passages the Son of man image functions more in terms of Christophany than Christology, that is, more as an eschatological figure than as an expression of a particular Christological title.[76] The

---

[75]The reference is to the harvest of judgment in Joel 4:13a (LXX): $\dot{\epsilon}\xi a\pi o\sigma\tau\epsilon\dot{\iota}\lambda a\tau\epsilon$ $\delta\rho\dot{\epsilon}\pi a\nu a$, $\ddot{o}\tau\iota$ $\pi a\rho\dot{\epsilon}\sigma\tau\eta\kappa\epsilon\nu$ $\tau\rho\dot{\upsilon}\gamma\eta\tau o\varsigma$ ("send out the sickles, for the harvest is near"). Note Joel 4:11-12 and the active role of the nations (they are told to gather for battle; in the anti-language of the fifth tableau the previously actively evil earth is not passively awaiting judgment.

[76]van Schaik, "$\H{A}\lambda\lambda o\varsigma$ $\dot{a}\gamma\gamma\epsilon\lambda o\varsigma$," p. 223: "Es handelt sich in 14, 14 [1:3 as well], also bei der als Mensch erscheinenden Figur, um Christus als Richter der Endzeit." Barnabas Lindars, *The Son of Man* (London: SPCK, 1983), p. 159, also noted that Son of man occurred in the Apocalypse of John "without the slightest hint of the titular usage found in the gospels." See also Ulrich Müller, *Messias und Menschensohn in jüdischen Apokalypsen und in der Offenbarung des Johannes* (Gütersloh: Gerd Mohn, 1972), pp. 191-197; Holtz, *Christologie*, pp. 128-134.
The Son of man is a reference to Daniel 7:13-14, in which "with the clouds of heaven there came one like a son of man . . . and to him was given dominion and glory and kingdom, that all peoples, nations, and languages should serve him." John Collins "The Son of Man and the Saints of the Most High in the Book of Daniel," *JBL*, 93 (1974), p. 50, noted that Son of man in the Daniel passage "is identical with, or symbolizes, or represents the 'holy ones of the Most High'" (which are referred to in Dan. 7:18). As a referent to Jesus in the fifth tableau, according to Adela Collins, "The Origin of the Designation of Jesus as 'Son of Man,'" *HTR*, 80 (1987), p. 407, Son of man functioned as an "alternative to other symbols of authority," in the anti-language, namely, the Roman Empire. See also Mogens Müller, *Der Ausdruck*

voice of God is relexicalized as "another angel."[77] When the time of judgment arrives, according to Matthew 24:30, the Son of man sends his angels. In the fifth tableau the situation is reversed; the angel sends the Son of man. One should not, however, that the angel comes out of the temple just prior to speaking and thus represents the hypostatic prophetic word of God, which constitutes relexicalization in the anti-language.[78] The angel relexicalizes God's voice, showing us God in command. Humanity is relexicalized as the "earth," which, corresponding to the shift away from the upper hand of evil, has lost any active connotations (14:3-4, 8, 12, 14, 16) but lies passively awaiting harvest.

Overlexicalization. One finds the following overlexicalizations with regard to the figures of eschatological judgment. The one like the Son of man "is sitting upon the (white) cloud" and "has upon his head a crown of gold and in his hand a sharp sickle" (14:14), which are images of authority and judgment.[79] Authority

---

"Menschensohn" in den Evangelien: Voraussetzungen und Bedeutung (Leiden: E. J. Brill), 1984), pp. 148-150.

No consensus exists on the origin of the title Son of man in the synoptic gospels. For an update of the discussion see Collins's "The Origin of the Designation," pp. 391-407; also see Mahlon H. Smith, "No Place for a Son of Man," *Forum*, 4 (1988), pp. 92-96; Günther Schwarz, *Jesus "Der Menschensohn"* (Stuttgart: Verlag W. Kohlhammer, 1986); John Donahue, "Recent Studies on the Origin of 'Son of Man' in the Gospels," *CBQ*, 48 (1986), 484-498); Müller, *Der Ausdruck*; Lindars, *Son of Man*; Norman Perrin, *A Modern Pilgrimage in New Testament Christology* (Philadelphia: Fortress Press, 1974); Edward Schillebeeckx, *Jesus*, trans. John Bowden (New York: Crossroad, 1979), pp. 459-472.

[77]van Schaik, ""Αλλος ἄγγελος," pp. 224-225.

[78]van Schaik, ""Αλλος ἄγγελος," pp. 224-225; Holtz, *Christologie*, pp. 132-133; Kraft, *Offenbarung*, pp. 197-198; Beasley-Murray, *Revelation*, p. 229.

[79]The cloud (νεφέλη) is associated with judgment (cf. Dan. 7:13; Isa. 19:1; 2 Esdras 13:3; Mark 13:26; 14:62; Matt. 26:64; Luke 22;69; Rev. 1:7) and white is the heavenly or eschatological color: Rev. 1:14 (white hair of the son of man); 2;17; 3:4, 5, 18; 4:4; 6:11; 7:9, 13; 19:14 (white garments); 6:2; 19:11, 14 (white horses); 14:14 (white cloud); 20:11 (white throne). One may also note that the Son of man is seated (καθήμενον) on the cloud, which may denote enthronement (Ford, *Revelation*, p. 238), the divine character of the royal judge (Prigent, *L'Apocalypse*, p. 233), or the eschatological horse (Kraft, *Offenbarung*, p. 197). See Swete, *Revelation*, p. 188; Charles, *Revelation*, vol. 1, p. 18; Holtz, *Christologie*, pp. 129-130; Beasley-Murray, *Revelation*, p. 229; Mounce, *Revelation*, p. 279.

The golden crown (στέφανον χρυσοῦν) may denote royalty (cf. Rev. 4:4) or victory (cf. Rev. 2:10; 3:11; 6:2). The headdress of a ruler was the diadem (διάδημα) (cf. Rev. 19:12), but the notions of royalty and victory probably merge in the fifth tableau. See Charles, *Revelation*, vol. 2, p. 20; Prigent, *L'Apocalypse*, p. 233; and Mounce, *Revelation*, p. 279.

The sharp sickle (δρέπανον ὀξύ) is an instrument for harvesting grain as well as a vine dresser's tool; the latter would be appropriate in light of the following tableau that describes the harvesting of grapes. J. P. M. Swete, *Revelation*, WPC

and judgment are displayed as well in the cursory description of the harvest of humanity (14:16): "and the earth was harvested" (καὶ ἐθερίσθη ἡ γῆ). The "other angel," as the relexicalized hypostatic voice of God, enters the scene from the temple and shouts with a loud voice to the one like the Son of man.

Verbal Play. Verbal play in the anti-language is indicated by alliteration and paronomasia.

(1) Initial alliteration: ἔχων ἐπί (14:14); ἄλλος ἄγγελος (14:15).[80]

(2) Pun (Paronomasia): καὶ εἶδον, καὶ ἰδού (14:14); ἐξῆλθεν ἐκ (14:15); (δρέπανον) . . . θέρισον . . . θερίσαι . . . (ἐξηράνθη) . . . θερισμός (14:15); γῆν . . . γῆ (14:16).

Anti-language and Strong Group/Low Grid. The anti-language of the fifth tableau indicates the following strong group/low grid concerns.

(1) Purity. Lines continue to be drawn sharply between "us" and "them." The Son of man and an angel on one side and the earth on the other.

(2) Rite. The harvest judgment will be the ultimate "time out" to focus on boundary lines. The fifth tableau does not give sufficient evidence to be interpreted as the gathering of the saints, as opposed to the gathering of the wicked in the sixth tableau.[81]

(3) Personal identity. The group that the prophet John represents identifies itself with the Son of man on a cloud. In the two previous tableaux identification with

---

(Philadelphia: The Westminster Press, 1979), p. 229, however, conjectured that the prophet John, following the parable of the seed growing secretly in Mark 4:28-29, is referring to a grain harvest.

Swete, *Revelation*, p. 188, invited comparison of the three images of the Son of man in 1:13-16; 14:14-16; and 19:11-13: "In each case the ornaments and instruments are appropriate to the character sustained. In *c. i.* the royal Priesthood of Christ is the predominant thought; in *c. xix.* He appears as the true *Imperator*; here the writer's aim is to bring together the thought of Christ's victory over sin and death with the hope of His return to raise and judge mankind."

[80]Note that the interlude (14:6-13) mentions three "another" angels and the fifth and sixth tableaux mention three "another" angels (14:15, 17, 18). In the midst of the six "other" angels sits one like the Son of man: "So steht der Christus als Siebenter inmitten der Engel, indem er ihre Zahl voll macht. Damit scheint er einer der ihren zu sein. Die Stellung in der Mitte aber und die besondere Ausstattung hebt ihn weit uber sie hinaus" (Holtz, *Christologie*, pp. 130-131).

[81]Lohmeyer, *Offenbarung*, p. 129; Holtz, *Christologie*, p. 133; Ladd, *Revelation*, p. 200; interpret the fifth tableau as the harvest of the righteous, but see Beasley-Murray, *Revelation*, p. 228; van Schaik, "Ἄλλος ἄγγελος," p. 224; Mounce, *Revelation*, pp. 279-280.

the Lamb held tragic consequences, but the fifth tableau evinces identification with the Son of man as a victorious association.

(4) Body. The key perception of body, physical and social transformation, is symbolized by the cutting down of the earth at harvest.

(5) Sin. The harvesting of the earth takes place in order to dislodge sin, deviance, from God's creation.

(6) Cosmology. World affairs are directly controlled by the divine extrahistorical agent, which is the Son of man, who in turn waits to hear from the hypostatic voice of God (the angel) from the temple.

(7) Suffering and misfortune. The unbelieving world can expect misfortune as a direct result of divine and angelic intervention, just as the saints had earlier experienced persecution as the direct result of the dragon's and the beasts' intervention.

The Sixth Tableau--The Harvest of the Grapes (14:17-20). The sixth tableau, as well as the fifth, is dependent on Joel 3:13. The first harvest is likely the harvest of grain; the second is unmistakably the harvest of grapes. Both harvests are two moments of the one inclusive eschatological judgment. The description of the actual harvest is not left totally to the hearer's imagination as in the fifth tableau. John's vision is of complete judgment, including the cutting of the grapes, the filling of the wine press, and the stomping of the fruit. The latter process, when applied to humans makes for a powerful if not terrible symbol. In the Apocalypse of John the seer, already encompassed by persecution, responds by one of the few means available to him: anti-language, that is, "back talk" against the dominant society.

Setting and Content. The sixth tableau consists of the following characters: two "another" angels and the grape clusters of the earth's grapevine. The fifth tableau ends with the harvesting of the earth. The sixth tableau begins the process again, focusing on "the violent carnage of that judgment."[82] The temple is again closely connected with the onset of judgment (14:17; cf. 14:15): "Another angel came out of the temple himself also having a sharp sickle." A second, "another," angel, who has authority over fire, came out from the altar and gives the command to the first angel (14:18): "Send your sharp sickle and gather the grape clusters of

---

[82]Mounce, *Revelation*, p. 281.

the earth's grapevine. John sees and describes the complete harvest process, noting how the blood deeply overflowed the lower basin of the wine press and consequently flooded the city (14:19-20). [83] The sixth tableau follows the fifth tableau identically in terms of White's metahistorical mode of emplotment, formal argument, and ideological implication.

Relexicalization. The two angels in the sixth tableau bring the total number of angels to six (14:6, 8, 9, 15, 17, 18), with the one like the Son of man making a complete seven.[84] The angels continue to function as the hypostatic voice of God.[85] The first angel comes out of the heavenly temple (14:17) must like the angel in 14:15. The second angel is more nuanced: "And another angel came out of the altar, the one who has authority over the fire" (14:18).[86] The second angel is still a relexicalization for the voice of God, but the connection with the altar introduces the notion that the prayers of the saints play a part in the divine decree of judgment.[87] The third relexicalization is again unbelieving humanity, which is conceived as "the grape clusters of the earth's grapevine" (14:18).

Overlexicalization. One finds the following overlexicalizations with regard to the figures of judgment. The first angel has a sharp sickle (14:17), which, in the hand of the angel, begins a process that is described in full (14:19-20); thus the overlexicalized elements of gathering ($\dot{\epsilon}\tau\rho\dot{\upsilon}\gamma\eta\sigma\epsilon\nu$), filling the wine vat ($\ddot{\epsilon}\beta\alpha\lambda\epsilon\nu$ $\epsilon\dot{\iota}\varsigma$ $\tau\dot{\eta}\nu$ $\lambda\eta\nu\dot{o}\nu$), trampling the grapes ($\dot{\epsilon}\pi\alpha\tau\dot{\eta}\theta\eta$ $\dot{\eta}$ $\lambda\eta\nu\dot{o}\varsigma$), and the resulting

---

[83]The wine press, or wine vat, consisted of two parts: an upper vat (גת; $\lambda\eta\nu\dot{o}\varsigma$) and a lower, deeper vat (יקב; $\dot{\upsilon}\pi o\lambda\dot{\eta}\nu\iota o\nu$), which was connected to the former by a channel. The vats, either square or round, were usually hewn out of rocky ground. See J. F. Ross, "Wine," *IDB*, vol. 4, ed. George Buttrick (Nashville: Abingdon Press, 1962), p. 850. In the sixth tableau (14:20) the $\dot{\upsilon}\pi o\lambda\dot{\eta}\nu\iota o\nu$ becomes the city and its surroundings.

[84]Kraft, *Offenbarung*, p. 198; Ford, *Revelation*, pp. 235-236.

[85]van Schaik, ""$A\lambda\lambda o\varsigma$ $\ddot{\alpha}\gamma\gamma\epsilon\lambda o\varsigma$," p. 225.

[86]The verse seems to be a paraphrase of Joel 3:13. Some commentators have noted the connection between the angel's authority over fire and the developed angelology of the intertestamental period, in which, according to 1 Enoch 60:11-21, e.g., angels were set over the natural elements; see Charles, *Revelation*, vol. 2, p. 23; Ford, *Revelation*, p. 239. The connection, however, between the altar and fire (see esp. Rev. 8:3-5) would appear to limit the angel's authority to the fire of the altar; see Kraft, *Offenbarung*, p. 198.

[87]See Mounce, *Revelation*, p. 281; Lohmeyer, *Offenbarung*, p. 125. Martyred saints cry out from under the altar (6:9) and the prayers of all saints are offered on the altar (8:3-5).

expressed "juice" (ἐξῆλθεν αἷμα ἐκ τῆς ληνοῦ). The second angel, with an identical role as the angel in the fifth tableau, does not have a sickle but "a loud voice" (14:18).

Verbal Play. Verbal play in the sixth tableau takes the following form: initial alliteration and paronomasia, concatenation of genitives, and a word play involving substitution of "blood" for "wine" (14:20).

(1) Initial alliteration: ἄλλος ἄγγελος (14:17, 18); ἔχων ἐξουσίαν ἐπί (14:18).

(2) Paronomasia: ἐξῆλθεν ἐκ (14:17, 18, 20); ἐφώνησεν φωνῇ (14:18).

(3) Concatenation of genitives: (καὶ ἐπατήθη ἡ ληνὸς ἔξωθεν) τῆς πόλεως (καὶ ἐξῆλθεν αἷμα ἐκ) τῆς ληνοῦ ἄχρι τῶν χαλινῶν τῶν ἵππων ἀπὸ σταδίων χιλίων ἑξακοσίων.[88]

(4) Word play--"blood" for "wine": The wine press--as a sign of God's wrath-- is that of God's socially required satisfaction to restore and proclaim his honor.[89] If persons act as though they can worship other gods (which is treating God as though dead), they have to shed their blood to return to God what is God's, that is, life. God's honor requires it. The complete wine making process is described, but since "judgment juice" is being trampled John describes the liquid that is expressed as αἷμα (14:20). The word play extends to the description of the depth of the blood: "And the blood went out of the wine press up to the bridles of the horses as far away as 1,600 stades." A literal interpretation, while detracting in no way from the grossness of the image, misses the probable symbolic intention of denoting the

---

[88]The noun for wine press (ληνός) may be feminine or masculine; feminine is the common construction and the masculine is found only in the LXX in Isa. 63:2. The reading τὴν ληνὸν . . . τὸν μέγαν, though solecistic, is probably original, for otherwise one cannot easily explain its presence in the light of the grammatically correct reading in ℵ R 1006 1854 2053 al. See Metzger, *Textual Commentary*, pp. 752-753; *GGNTLHR*, p. 253; Lohmeyer, *Offenbarung*, p. 126; Charles, *Revelation*, vol. 2, p. 24. Anti-language consists in variations in grammar as part of the verbal play, although this dissertation has not undertaken an investigation into the latter.

The city, outside which the blood flows deeply, is probably Jerusalem, which would correspond to the parallel passage of Joel 3:12-14 ("Let the nations . . . come up to the valley of Jehoshaphat"); see, among others, Mounce, *Revelation*, p. 282.

[89]See Malina's description of the acquisition of honor through the process of challenge and response in *The New Testament World* (Atlanta: John Knox Press, 1981), pp. 30-33. God's honor has been challenged in the earth, and his response, in order to restore his honor, is to harvest the earth and crush the earthlings. Blood here marks the transformation and reduction of the wicked to blood, God thus reclaiming their life force and allowing it to flow outside.

cosmic extent of the blood bath (which is based on the traditional number of punishment, that is, forty).[90]

Anti-language and Strong Group/Low Grid. The anti-language of the sixth tableau is identical to that of the preceding tableau. The motif of harvest judgment, though intensified in the sixth tableau, indicates the concern to dislodge deviance from God's creation, which action is the prerogative of the divine historical agent.

The Seventh Tableau--The Hymn of the Lamb (15:1-4). The fourth tableau began the shift away from the upper hand of evil and focused on the positive images of the Lamb and his 144,000. While the images were positive, one should bear in mind that the anti-language is always aimed against the dominant culture: the 144,000 symbolize those whose lives are diametrically opposed to the regime of the beast. One may view the seventh tableau in the same light. The images in the seventh tableau are images of salvation that simultaneously exalt God and portend the end of the evil dominant culture. With the seventh tableau God, not the dragon, has the upper hand. The question now is not "Who is like the beast?" (13:4) but rather, addressed to God, "Who will not fear and glorify your name?" (15:4).

Setting and Content. The seventh tableau consists of the following characters: "seven angels who have the seven last plagues" (15:1) and "the ones who have victory over the beast and over his image and over the number of his name" (15:2).[91] As the scene unfolds the seven angels are standing in heaven. These angels have been entrusted with the plagues that will finally quell God's anger (15:1). What John describes as a glassy sea mixed with fire (cf. 4:6) separates the first image from the second, which stands upon the Glass Sea singing the song that signals God's victory over the dragon. The vision is a prolepsis of "the faith and patience of the saints." Though prophetic in tone the seventh tableau still evinces the lexicalizations and verbal play of the anti-language.

---

[90]See Charles, *Revelation*, vol. 2, pp. 25-26; Kraft, *Offenbarung*, p. 200; Beasley-Murray, *Revelation*, p. 230; Prigent, *L'Apocalypse*, p. 235; Mounce, *Revelation*, p. 282.

[91]*BDF*, p. 212, explains the peculiar construction "the ones who have victory from the beast" (τοὺς νικῶντας ἐκ τοῦ θηρίου) as probably influenced by τηρεῖν ἐκ (as in Rev. 3:10) and thus equals τηρήσαντες ἑαυτοὺς ἐκ τοῦ θηρίου.

The "Song of Moses" that the conquerors sing (15:3-4) is an explicit "intertextual appropriation"of the politically motivated code of the Exodus tradition.[92] The song not only provides commentary on the preceding events in chapter 13, but, by invoking the Exodus typology, it identifies the Roman Empire as "Pharoah *redivivus.*"[93] The Song of Moses thus functions as a further overlexicalization of social evil in the anti-language of John. The sight of the singing of the song, as well the works of God to which it refers, is described as "great and marvelous" (15:10) undoubtedly because the persecutor will finally be persecuted.[94]

The satiric tragic mode of emplotment is indicated by those who conquered the beast, for they lived helpless in the world as they looked to God for ultimate rescue. The occurrence of divine plagues, according to the mode of formal argument, stresses the control by extrahistorical agent of events within a given location (the earth). The acts of the extrahistorical agent--plague and non-plague-- are extolled in the seventh tableau (15:3). The mode of ideological implication, the radical restructuring of society, is indicated as the time when "all the nations will come and worship before you [God]" (15:4).

Relexicalization. The interlude (14:6-13), the fifth tableau (14:14-16), and the sixth tableau (14:17-20) involved six angels of judgment (their number made complete by the Son of man figure) which were simply called "another angel." The six angels were described as the hypostatic voice of God relexicalized. In the present tableau the angels of judgment are relexicalized as "seven angels who have the seven last plagues" (15:1).[95] The saints are relexicalized as "the ones who have

---

[92]Harris, "Function of the Hymns," p. 172; see also Fiorenza, *Revelation,* pp. 188-189; Jay Casey, "Exodus Typology in the Book of Revelation" (Ph.D. dissertation, The Southern Baptist Theological Seminary, 1981), pp. 189-194; Klaus-Peter Jörns, *Das hymnische Evangelium: Untersuchungen zu Aufbau, Funktion und Herkunft der hymnischen Stücke in der Johannesoffenbarung* (Gütersloh: Gerd Mohn, 1971), pp. 126-132. John intertwines themes from several parts of the Hebrew Bible, even though he is consciously employing the Exodus tradition; see, e.g., the list in Prigent, *L'Apocalypse,* p. 240.

[93]Harris, "Function of the Hymns," pp. 172-173.

[94]Ibid., pp. 170-171.

[95]Many commentators have compared the seven angels with seven plagues to the divine warning in Leviticus 26:21: "'Then if you walk contrary to me, and will not hearken to me, I will bring more plagues upon you, sevenfold as many as your sins.'" The number seven denotes completeness or finality; cf. the seven trumpet judgments (Rev. 8:7-11:18), which speak of destruction by thirds (8:7, 8-9, 10-11, 12;

victory over the beast" (15:2). In the seventh tableau, as in the fourth (14:1-5), the followers of the Lamb are presented as victors, not victims. The anti-language functions to build and reinforce group solidarity by projecting a most positive image of those who, in the dominant culture's eyes, were viewed negatively.

Overlexicalization. The seventh tableau, as White's metahistorical model indicated, emphasizes the extrahistorical agent and his actions. God is the focus of the vision. Holtz views the Apocalypse of John as a highly theocentric work; the unity of God and Christ is a thoroughly functional unity, in which God remains superior to Christ.[96] While the Son of Moses is also the "Song of the Lamb" (15:3), one finds the following overlexicalizations pointing to God.

(1) The last plagues are equated with the wrath of God (ὁ θυμὸς τοῦ θεοῦ) (15:1, 7);

(2) The conquerors play the "harps of God" (κιθάρας τοῦ θεοῦ) (15:2);

(3) Moses was a "servant of God" (δούλου τοῦ θεοῦ) (15:3).

(4) The song itself consists of numerous overlexicalizations of "the Lord God":
God, as the all powerful, performs great and marvelous works (15:3)
God, as the king of the nations, possesses right and true ways (15:3)
God, as the Lord, is to be feared and his name glorified (15:4)
God alone is holy (15:4)
God, once he has manifested his righteous judgments, will see all nations come to worship him (15:4).

The overlexicalizations of the anti-language sufficiently counteract any propaganda of the beast, the Pharoah *redivivus*. The central question of the beast ("Who is like the beast and who is able to make war with him?" [13:4]) has been displaced in the seventh tableau by another: "Who indeed will not fear, Lord, and will glorify your name?" (15:4). The anti-language has created tension between God and dragon and now points to the positive pole of the tension.

9:18); the fifth trumpet judgment lasts five months (9:10). With the passing of the seven bowl (φιάλη) judgments (16:1-21) one would suppose that the world had been depopulated (Holtz, *Christologie*, p. 167); however, more judgments follow (Rev. 17:1-20:15) to make clear in the anti-language the extreme tension that exists between the saints and the dominant culture.

96"Gott in der Apokalypse," in *L'Apocalypse johannique et l'Apocalyptique dans le Nouveau Testament*, ed. J. Lambrecht, BETL 53 (Leuven: Leuven University Press, 1980), pp. 262-263: "Die Apk [behauptet] den Monotheismus und damit die Theozentrik, Herkunft als bindendes Erbe bewahrt, notwendig eignet. Zugleich aber wird damit doch die einzigartige Stellung und Bedeutung Christi festgehalten, die fur die christliche Apk wesentlich ist, und deren Integration in das theozentrischen Erbe das Buch zu einem christlichen gemacht hat" (p. 265).

Verbal Play. The verbal play follows similar lines of the overlexicalizations above, namely, to emphasize the role of the extrahistorical agent, who acts on behalf of the oppressed followers of the Lamb. One finds initial (and mesial) alliteration, paronomasia, concatenation of genitives, a rhetorical question, and, ironically, the divine passive. The rhetorical question (15:4) is noted above. One should note the verbal play on the word "worship" (προσκυνήσουσιν) closely connected to the rhetorical question. God will be worshiped, not the beast (13:4, 15; 14:9, 11).

Alliteration underscores the divine: θυμὸς τοῦ θεοῦ (15:2); κιθάρας τοῦ θεοῦ (15:2); δούλου τοῦ θεοῦ (15:3).

Pun (Paronomasia: recurrence of the same word or word stem): μέγα καὶ θαυμαστόν (15:1)/μεγάλα καὶ θαυμαστά (15:3); ᾄδουσιν τὴν ᾠδήν . . . καὶ τὴν ᾠδήν (15:2).

Concatenation of genitives: τοὺς νικῶντας ἐκ τοῦ θηρίου καὶ ἐκ τῆς εἰκόνος αὐτοῦ καὶ ἐκ τοῦ ἀριθμοῦ τοῦ ὀνόματος αὐτοῦ (15:2).

The divine passive has been noted in previous tableaux where the extrahistorical agent is the implicit agent in the passive voice. In a tableau that focuses on God, one finds, ironically, two occurrences of the divine passive. The wrath of God "was completed" (ἐτελέσθη) by the seven last plagues (15:1), which is the direct work of God. All nations will come to worship God because "your righteous judgments were manifested" (ἐφανερώθησαν) by God himself (15:4).

Anti-language and Strong Group/Low Grid. The anti-language of the seventh tableau indicates the following strong group/low grid concerns.

(1) Purity. The focus on God reproduces the purity concerns of the prophet John and the Christian communities that he represents: justice, righteousness, truth, and worship of God. The latter, in turn, reinforce the boundary lines between "us" and "them."

(2) Rite. Rite in the seventh tableau focuses on boundary lines, the "us" lines, by means of observance of heavenly worship in this great and marvelous vision.

(3) Personal identity. Only by embeddedness in the group can one be saved. The faithful are relexicalized as the ones who have victory from the beast (and his accoutrements). Individualism is foreign to the Christians in the strong group/low grid collectives that John addresses.

(4) Body. The key perception of body--both physical and social--for strong group/low grid is transformation. One can partake of the bliss of salvation only in a transformed state in which the sea becomes like glass. The transformed social

body, symbolized by "all the nations" (15:4), will worship God, but there is no explicit statement as to how this will come about (one can surely exclude universalistic notions here).

(5) Sin. Sin is deviance in the social order, which lodges itself in individuals and groups. The seventh tableau, in view of the above implied physical and social transformations, is a vision of expunged deviance. The only holy One is extolled.

(6) Cosmology. God as extrahistorical agent stand behinds every action: God's plagues bring an end to God's anger, which brings an end to evil.

(7) Suffering and Misfortune. Ultimate deliverance from suffering will come as a result of the end of the dualistic struggle between God and the dragon.

Anti-Language in the Apocalypse of John

Wayne Meeks noted the recurring interpretation of apocalyptic as "essentially an exegetical literature," which has its own "very peculiar angle of vision."[97] The present chapter, building on the kitbashed theory of Malina (primarily Douglas, White, and Halliday) consists of analysis of how the Apocalypse of John, through the very peculiar angle of anti-language, created and maintained the social tension that the prophet John and other Christians experienced in late first-century Asia Minor. John, the seer and hearer, was convinced that "talking back," often in secretive ways (e.g., numeration), was the best way to respond to the dominant culture. In fact, Jesus appeared to him and initiated the process; John was told simply to write down "the things that you saw and that are and that are about to be after these things" (1:20). John perceived Jesus' invitation as a "warrant-for-innovation," for one finds images and allusions from a wide range of sources.[98]

As apocalyptic language, then, the Apocalypse of John, is an anti-exegesis of contemporary society. The anti-language is indicated by relexicalization and overlexicalization of the central concerns of the group and by verbal play of all kinds. The tension that the anti-language creates in the seven tableaux (11:19-15:4) are between God and the dragon, beast and Lamb, good angel and bad angel, earth-

---

[97]"Social Functions of Apocalyptic Language in Pauline Christianity," in *Apocalypticism in the Mediterranean World and the Near East*, ed. David Hellholm (Tübingen: J. C. B. Mohr, 1983), p. 697.

[98]Ibid., p. 700. Meeks here refers to Paul's use of apocalyptic language, but the result is the same for Paul and for John: extreme circumstances call for new ways to convey meaning forcefully.

dweller and saint. At the heart of the tension is the perception and experience of persecution by Christians at the hands of the evil Roman Empire. The "back talk" (relexicalization, overlexicalization, verbal play) of the Apocalypse of John is the kind of language one would expect from those in a strong group/low grid setting, which also evinces a satiric tragic mode of formal argument, emplotment, and ideological implication.

Chapter 5

CONCLUSION

I decline to accept the end of man. It is easy enough to say that man is immortal simply because he will endure; that when the last ding–dong of doom has clanged and faded from the last worthless rock hanging tideless in the last red and dying evening, that even then there will still be one more sound: that of his puny inexhaustible voice, still talking. I refuse to accept this. I believe that man will not merely endure: he will prevail. He is immortal, not because he alone among creatures has an inexhaustible voice, but because he has a soul, a spirit capable of compassion and sacrifice and endurance. . . . The poet's voice need not merely be the record of man, it can be one of the props, the pillars to help him and endure and prevail.

> "Speech of Acceptance Upon the Award
> of the Nobel Prize for Literature"
> William Faulkner

And I saw what looked like a glassy sea mixed with fire and the ones who have victory from the beast and from his image and from the number of his name standing upon the glassy sea having the harps of God. And they sing the song of Moses the servant of God and the song of the Lamb, saying,
> "Great and marvelous are your works,
> Lord God, almighty;
> Just and true are your ways,
> King of the nations;
> Who indeed would not fear you, Lord,
> and will glorify your name?"

> Revelation 15:2–3
> The prophet John

The preceding study has focused on the ability of persons, as "homo loquens," to resist, endure, and ultimately prevail linguistically in the midst of adverse social conditions.[1] The anti-language of the prophet John functions as one

---

[1]William Faulkner, "Speech of Acceptance Upon the Award of the Nobel Prize for Literature," in *Essays Speeches, and Public Letters*, ed. James B. Meriwether (New York: Random House, 1965), p. 120. Dennis Fry, *Homo Loquens: Man As a Talking Animal* (Cambridge: Cambridge University Press, 1977), pp. 1–3, suggested the term *homo loquens* in view of the fact that *homo sapiens*, which Fry somewhat jokingly noted may not be an accurate term, "is above everything else the talking animal." See also the Palestinian Targumic tradition, for example, Tg. Neof. Gen.

of the props to encourage believers to "keep the commandments of God and have the testimony of Jesus" (Rev. 12:17). In the midst of Roman oppression, both real and imagined, John heard the approaching "last ding-dong of doom." At the command of the risen Jesus, he raised his "puny inexhaustible voice" in triumphant opposition, describing both the troubled sea, from which the first beast arose (13:1) and the glassy sea, upon which the conquerors sing (15:2).

Malina's "kitbashed" theoretical model (Douglas/White/Halliday) emphasized social location of thought in order to achieve proper distancing between interpreted and interpreter, who is essentially an "eavesdropper."[2] The prophet John and the communities he represented were viewed as a sect (employing Stanley's categories of sect analysis) that, because of social experience, followed the "cultural scripts" of a group residing in the strong group/low grid quadrant, that is, they proclaimed salvation only for those who belonged to their persecuted group. The device employed to give ample definition to group boundaries, and provide further indication of social placement, is anti-language. The average Christian in the United States today often finds personal distance and discomfort with sect mentality; and to think of viewing early Christian groups as sects usually escapes one's interpretive agenda.

The chief function of anti-language, according to Halliday, was precisely its group defining capacity: to provide an alternative social and conceptual reality.[3] Halliday noted how the *grypserka*, the anti-language of Polish prisoners, divided persons into two classes: 'people' and 'suckers.'[4] In the *grypserka* the distinction between 'people' and 'suckers' is a replication of the distinction, at a higher level, between 'free' and 'unincarcerated.' Similarly, as formulated below, the anti-language of the Apocalypse of John draws a distinction, at one level, between Roman oppressors and the oppressed (seen clearly in Rev. 18:9-20) and, at another

---

2:7, where God creates the Earthling (Adam) as a homo loquens, "a living being who speaks."

[2]Bruce Malina, *Christian Origins and Cultural Anthropology: Practical Models for Biblical Interpretation* (Atlanta: John Knox Press, 1986), p. 12.

[3]M. A. K. Halliday, *Language as Social Semiotic* (Baltimore, Maryland: University Park Press, 1978), pp. 168–169.

[4]Ibid., p. 168.

level, between those who follow the beast and its regime and those who follow the Lamb with endurance.[5]

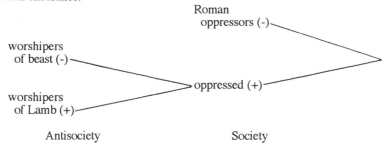

Antisociety   Society

Those who learn and use John's anti-language indicate their embeddedness in the group that worships the Lamb and is destined for salvation. Those outside the group are, as in the *grypserka*, 'suckers,' who are encouraged to remain "outside" (ἔξω) until the time of judgment (Rev. 22:15).

The nature of all language, and of the anti-language in particular, as Kress demonstrated, is to reclassify (metaphor, for example, is reclassification).[6] Kress detected syntactic and semantic reclassification in Donne's poem "A Nocturnall Upon S. Lucies Day." Reclassification, he contended, was "exploited . . . in the direction of negation" (p. 340). In the Apocalypse of John reclassification tended in the direction of reversal, as well as negation: they who receive the mark of the beast will be severely judged; they who refuse the mark of the beast will share in the kingdom of God.

The reclassification of anti-language, indicated by relexicalization, overlexicalization, and all kinds of verbal play, is, like most school yard fights, a provoked process. Roger Fowler reiterated Halliday's contention that the verbal play of anti-language does not exist for its own sake; anti-language arises as

---

[5]Political and economic oppression appear to be the theme of Revelation 18, as Adela Collins, "Revelation 18: Taunt–Song or Dirge?" in *L'Apocalypse johannique et l'Apocalyptique dans le Nouveau Testament*, BETL 53, ed. J. Lambrecht (Leuven: Leuven University Press, 1980), pp. 185–204, has demonstrated. Collins is correct in criticizing those for whom the taunt song/dirge is merely "'stolen poetry, stolen from the old prophets'" (p. 198). Collins, while acknowledging that "originality in the strict sense is not a major characteristic of the Book of Revelation" (p. 198), described John's creative use of images (pp. 198–199), which one finds in the verbal play of anti–language.

[6]Gunther Kress, "Poetry as Anti–Language: A Reconsideration of Donne's 'Nocturnall Upon S. Lucies Day,'" *PTL*, 3 (1978), 331: "Classification [and hence reclassification] is seen as a major link between culture and language, providing the specific input to the syntax of a language."

144

"provoked by, and a creative critique of, the norm [ideology]."[7] There is no agreement as to the nature nor the extent of persecution reflected in the Apocalypse of John; the text does not lead one to believe that oppression was all a product of John's imagination. The persecution was sufficient to provoke the dialogical process of negotiation of anti-language. The language of the visionary prophet becomes the symbolic medium of rejection of the regime of the beast. Anti-language is, in the strict sense, "back talk."

Of the three components to Halliday's sociosemiotic theory--ideational, interpersonal, and textual--the anti-language foregrounds the latter two. Malina noted that the interpersonal component denotes "relation" ("of whom and to whom John speaks") and the textual component denotes "linguistic form" ("how John speaks," "how Jesus and angels speak to John").[8] While the Gospel of John evinces several conversations between Jesus and others to indicate the foregrounding of the interpersonal component, the Apocalypse of John indicates such in at least two of the following ways.

First, one literary component of the Apocalypse is the apostolic letter: John is commanded by Jesus to transcribe and transmit the visions for and to the messengers of the churches (2:1, 8, 12, 18; 3:1, 7, 14); he also received the general command simply to "write" whatever he saw (1:19; also 22:6).[9] The transcription and transmission of the "the book of prophecy" connotes an audience and, thus, the interpersonal (relational) component of language. Second, the seven tableaux are carefully aimed against the norm society and this anti-discourse is an explicit function of the interpersonal component of language.

---

[7]Roger Fowler, *Literature as Social Discourse: The Practice of Linguistic Criticism* (Bloomington: Indiana University Press, 1981), p. 150.

[8]Malina, *The Gospel of John in Sociolinguistic Perspective*, Center for Hermeneutical Studies in Hellenistic and Modern Culture Colloquy 48 (Berkley, California: Center for Hellenistic Studies, 1985), p. 13. Malina wrote, of course, "of whom and to whom Jesus speaks [in the Gospel of John]," etc.

[9]Elisabeth Schüssler Fiorenza, *The Book of Revelation: Justice and Judgment* (Philadelphia: Fortress Press, 1985), pp. 120–125, positing John's kinship to Pauline theology, argued that the prophet most likely appropriated the prophetic–apostolic letter as well in order to provide circulation for his vision. See also Martin Karrer, *Die Johannesoffenbarung als Brief: Studien zu ihrem literarischen und theologischen Ort* (Göttingen: Vandenhoeck & Ruprecht, 1986), for a thorough-going interpretation of Revelation as an essentially epistolary writing that functions as a conversation with the churches of Asia Minor.

In all the verbal contest of the Apocalypse of John, which resounds like "the voice of a trumpet" (4:1), God is conspicuously silent. In the seven tableaux one noted how the divine (impersonal) passive served to underscore the divine role in all the acts of judgment. The one who sits brilliantly on the throne--as those surrounding the throne direct continuous, thunderous worship to him--remains silent. John nevertheless hears the divine voice three times. Immediately following a Christological passage (1:5-7) the first divine statement is made: "I am the Alpha and the Omega, says the Lord God, the one who is and was and is coming, the almighty" (1:8). John hears "a great voice" the second time "out of the temple from the throne," which consists of the ultimate expression "It is finished!" (16:17). God acts (the Apocalypse of John is consistently theocentric), but "the one who sits on the throne" is, for the most part, silent.

God is for the most part silent, until John hears, quite unexpectedly for the hearer, the voice of "the one who sits on the throne" (21:5). The silence of God as monarch holding court is normal.[10] This is the first time one hears the explicit statement that "the enthroned one" is speaking: "And the one who sits on the throne said, 'Behold, I am making all things new!'" Holtz noted that the latter exclamation points to God as creator, whose responsibility as maker necessarily includes redemption, that is, re-making.

Elements of the first two divine utterances are combined in verse 6: "And he said to me, 'It is finished! I am the Alpha and the Omega, the beginning and the end.'" The last (and the fullest!) divine utterance consists, one should note, of relexicalizations for the faithful and for the unfaithful. It is only fitting that when the one who sits on the throne utters the recreative pronouncement that his speech take the form of anti-language.

Faithful (21:6-7)	*Unfaithful (21:8)*	
Thirsty	Cowardly	Fornicators
Conqueror	Unbelieving	Sorcerers
	Corrupt	Idolaters
	Murderers	Liars

---

[10]Malina, in his *Christian Origins*, pp. 76-87, described the "generalized symbolic media of social interaction, through which are encod[ed] real world values" (p. 76): commitment, power, influence, and inducement. As the one who sits as king on the throne, God wields power and commitment. All others have inducement and influence. Commanding is power in words, and once under way, no need to command any more. On the other hand, speaking (praying, hymning, and so on) is influence and should be initiated by lesser persons. See also Bernard P. Dauenhauer, *Silence: the Phenomenon and Its Ontological Significance* (Bloomington: University of Indiana Press, 1980).

The faithful are promised the water of life without expense and adoption; the unfaithful will suffer in a lake burning with sulphur and fire. There is no evil--internal or external, individual or social--that can ultimately destroy the followers of Christ.

The voice whose sound was like a trumpet set the "puny inexhaustible voice" of the prophet John to languaging in such a way as to effectively register opposition to ungodly powers. When the enthroned one himself speaks, his language, so John hears, consists of relexicalization, overlexicalization, and verbal play. When all judgment has been completed ("when the last ding-dong of doom has clanged and faded"), all creation will hear the great, inexhaustible voice of God and the myriads of the divine creation will join their small voices in thunderous praise to the one who sits on the throne.

APPENDIX A

CULTURAL SCRIPTS OF THE STRONG GROUP/LOW GRID QUADRANT OF MARY DOUGLAS[1]

Purity: strong concern for purity but the inside of the social and physical body is under attack; pollution present but purification rites are ineffective

Rite: a society of fixed rites; rite is focused upon group boundaries, with great concern to expel pollutants (deviants) from the social body; fluid sacred places

Personal Identity: located in group membership, not in the internalization of roles, which are confused; distinction between appearance and internal states; dyadic personality

Body: social and physical bodies are tightly controlled but under attack; invaders break through bodily boundaries; not a symbol of life

Sin: a matter of pollution; evil is lodged within the individual and society; sin is much like a disease deriving from social structure; internal states of being are more important than adherence to formal rules; but the latter are still valued

Cosmology: anthropomorphic; dualistic; warring forces of good and evil; the universe is not just and may be whimsical; personal causality; limited good

Suffering and Misfortune: unjust; not automatic punishment; attributed to malevolent forces; may be alleviated but not eliminated

---

[1]Bruce Malina, *Christian Origins and Cultural Anthropology: Practical Models for Biblical Interpretation* (Atlanta: John Knox Press, 1986), p. 15.

APPENDIX B

HAYDEN WHITE'S METAHISTORY MODEL SUPERIMPOSED UPON MARY DOUGLAS'S STRONG GROUP/LOW GRID QUADRANT[1]

Mode of Emplotment = *Satiric Tragedy*: the hero's (dyadic personality or group) interactions pitted against psychological, physical, and/or social constraints result in negative outcomes demonstrating that one cannot overcome one's situation of embeddedness in its manifold dimensions; one can learn how to accept the situation or one can seek and perhaps find a solution lying beyond normal human limits.

Mode of Formal Argument = *Mechanistic*: the meaning of events is to be sought in the latent, implicit, sub– or suprasurface (hence extrahistorical) agencies that control the acts of agents. These agencies are to be found in the scene or location—the physical and/or social environment that is governed by agencies, following predictable "laws" that in fact constrain agents and their acts; discovering and articulating those "laws" and uncovering those agencies are of primary concern.

Mode of Ideological Implication = *Radical*: restructure society in its entirety (revolution)

The best of times is imminent, right around the corner

---

[1]Bruce Malina, *The Gospel of John in Sociolinguistic Perspective* (Center for Hermeneutical Studies in Hellenistic and Modern Culture Colloquy 48 [Berkley, California: Center for Hermeneutical Studies, 1985]), p. 4.

APPENDIX C

A NOCTURNALL UPON S. LUCIES DAY BEING THE SHORTEST DAY[1]

Tis the yeares midnight, and it is the dayes,
Lucies, who scarce seaven houres herself unmaskes,
The Sunne is spent, and now his flasks
Send forth light squibs, no constant rayes;
The worlds whole sap is sunke: 5
The generall abalme th'hydroptique earth hath drunk,
Whither, as to the beds–feet, life is shrunke,
Dead and enterr'd; yet all these seeme to laugh,
Compar'd with mee, who am their Epitaph.

Study me then, you who shall lovers bee   10
At the next world, that is, at the next Spring:
For I am every dead thing,
In whom love wrought new Alchimie.
For his art did expresse
A quintessence even from nothingnesse,   15
From dull privations, and leane emptinesse:
He ruin'd mee, and I am re–begot
Of absence, darknesse, death; things which are not.

All others, from all things, draw all that's good,
Life, soule, forme, spirit, whence they beeing have;   20
I, by loves limbecke, am the grave
of all, that's nothing. Oft a flood
Have wee two wept, and so
Drownd the whole world, us two; oft did we grow
To be two Chaosses, when we did show   25
Care to ought else; and often absences
Withdrew our soules, and made us carcasses.

But I am by her death, (which word wrongs her)
Of the first nothing, the Elixir grown;
Were I a man, that I were one,   30
I needs must know; I should preferre,
If I were any beast,
Some ends, some means; Yea plants, yea stones detest,

---

[1]Gunther Kress, "Poetry as Anti-Language: A Reconsideration of Donne's 'Nocturnall Upon S. Lucies Day.'" *PTL*, 3 (1978), 343-344.

152

And love; All, all some properties invest;
If I an ordinary nothing were,   35
As a shadow, a light, and body must be here.

But I am None; nor will my Sunne renew.
You lovers, for whose sake, the lesser Sunne
            At this time to the Goat is runne
            To fetch new lust, and give it you,   40
                  Enjoy your summer all;
Since shee enjoyes her long nights festivall,
Let mee prepare towards her, and let mee call
This houre her Vigill, and Eve, since this
Both the yeares, and the dayes deep midnight is.   45

BIBLIOGRAPHY

Books

Allo, E.–B. *Saint Jean: L'Apocalypse*, 4th ed. Paris: J. Gabalda, 1933.

Aune, David. *The Cultic Setting of Realized Eschatology in Early Christianity.* Leiden: E. J. Brill, 1972.

Austin, J. L. *How to Do Things with Words.* 2nd ed. Cambridge, Massachusetts: Cambridge University Press, 1975.

Bachmann, Christian, Jacqueline Lindenfeld, Jacky Simonin, eds. *Langage et Communications Sociales.* Paris: Hatier–Credif, 1981.

Barr, James. *The Semantics of Biblical Language.* London: Oxford University Press, 1961.

Beagley, James Alan. *The 'Sitz im Leben' of the Apocalypse with Particular Reference to the Role of the Church's Enemies.* New York: Walter de Gruyter, 1987.

Beasley–Murray, G. R. *The Book of Revelation.* New Century Bible Commentary. Grand Rapids, Michigan: Wm. B. Eerdmans, 1981.

Beckwith, Isbon. *The Apocalypse of John.* 1919; rpt. Grand Rapids, Michigan: Baker, 1967.

Bell, Roger. *Sociolinguistics: Goals, Approaches, and Problems.* London: Batsford, 1976.

Berger, Peter L. and Thomas Luckmann. *The Social Construction of Reality.* Garden City, New York: Doubleday & Co., 1966.

Bernstein, Basil. *Class, Codes and Control,* vol. 3. Rev. London: Routledge & Kegan Paul, 1977.

Beyer, Klaus. *Semitische Syntax im Neuen Testament, I, 'Satzlehre.'* Göttingen: Vandenhoeck und Ruprecht, 1961.

Blevins, James L. *Revelation.* Knox Preaching Guides. Atlanta, Georgia: John Knox Press, 1984.

_____. *Revelation as Drama.* Nashville: Broadman, 1984.

Bloomfield, Leonard. *Language.* New York: Henry Holt and Co., 1933.

Blount, Ben G. *Language, Culture and Society: A Book of Readings*. Cambridge, Massachusetts: Winthrop Publishers, 1974.

Böcher, Otto. "Das Verhältnis der Apokalypse des Johannes zum Evangelium des Johannes." In *L'Apocalypse johannique et l'apocalyptique dans le Nouveau Testament*. Ed. J. Lambrecht. Bibliotheca Ephemeridum Theologicarum Lovaniensium 53. Leuven: Leuven University Press, 1980.

du Boulay, Juliet. "Lies, Mockery and Family Integrity." In *Mediterranean Family Structures*, ed. J. G. Peristiany. Cambridge: Cambridge University Press, 1976.

Bowman, John W. *The First Christian Drama*. Philadelphia: The Westminster Press, 1955.

————. "Revelation, Book of." *The Interpreter's Dictionary of the Bible*, vol. 4. Ed. G. A. Buttrick. Nashville: Abingdon Press, 1962.

————. "Six Hundred Sixty–Six." *Interpreter's Dictionary of the Bible*, vol. 4. Ed. George Buttrick. Nashville: Abingdon Press, 1962.

Brunt, P. A. *Social Conflicts in the Roman Republic*. New York: W. W. Norton, 1971.

Burgess, Anthony. *A Clockwork Orange*. 1962; rpt. New York: Norton & Co., 1987.

Caird, George B. *A Commentary on the Revelation of St. John the Divine*. New York: Harper and Row, 1966.

————. *The Language and Imagery of the Bible*. Philadelphia: The Westminster Press, 1981.

Cathcart, Dwight. *Doubting Conscience*. Ann Arbor, Michigan: The University of Michigan Press, 1975.

Charles, R. H. *A Critical and Exegetical Commentary on the Revelation of St. John*, vols. 1 and 2. The International Critical Commentary. Edinburgh: T. & T. Clark, 1920.

Charlesworth, J. H., ed. *The Old Testament Pseudepigrapha*, vol. 1. Garden City, New York: Doubleday & Co., 1983.

————, ed. *The Old Testament Pseudepigrapha*, vol. 2. Garden City, New York: Doubleday & Co., 1985.

Chomsky, Noam. *Aspects of the Theory of Syntax*. Cambridge, Massachusetts: The M.I.T. Press, 1965.

————. *Language and Responsibility*. Trans. John Viertel. New York: Pantheon Books, 1979.

_____. *Syntactic Structures*, Janua Linguarum Series Minor 4. The Hague: Mouton, 1957.

Clark, Virginia, et al., eds. *Language: Introductory Readings*. New York: St. Martin's Press, 1985.

Collins, Adela Yarbro. *The Apocalypse*. New Testament Message, vol. 22. Wilmington, Delaware: Michael Glazier, 1979.

_____. *The Combat Myth in the Book of Revelation*. Missoula, Mt.: Scholars Press, 1976.

_____. *Crisis & Catharsis: The Power of the Apocalypse*. Philadelphia: The Westminster Press, 1984.

_____, ed. *Early Christian Apocalypticism: Genre and Social Setting. Semeia*, 36 (1986).

_____. "Persecution and Vengeance in the Book of Revelation." In *Apocalypticism in the Mediterranean World and the Near East*. David Hellholm. Tübingen: Mohr-Siebeck, 1983.

Collins, John J. *Apocalypse: The Morphology of a Genre. Semeia* 14. Missoula, Montana: Scholars Press, 1979.

_____. *The Apocalyptic Imagination: An Introduction to the Jewish Matrix of Christianity*. New York: Crossroad, 1984.

Conzelmann, Hans. "ψεῦδος, κτλ." *Theological Dictionary of the New Testament*, vol. 9. Ed. Gerhard Kittel. Trans. G. W. Bromiley. Grand Rapids, Michigan: Wm. B. Eerdmans, 1964.

Court, John M. *Myth and History in the Book of Revelation*. London: SPCK, 1979.

Culpepper, R. Alan. *Anatomy of the Fourth Gospel*. Philadelphia: Fortress Press, 1983.

Dauenhauer, Bernard P. *Silence: the Phenomenon and Its Ontological Significance*. Bloomington: University of Indiana Press, 1980.

Delling, Gerhard. "παρθένος." *Theological Dictionary of the New Testament*, vol. 5. Ed. Gerhard Kittel. Trans. G. W. Bromiley. Grand Rapids, Michigan: Wm. B. Eerdmans, 1962.

Douglas, Mary. *Cultural Bias*. Royal Anthropological Institute of Great Britain and Ireland, Occasional Paper No. 35. London: Royal Anthropological Institute, 1978.

_____. *Natural Symbols: Explorations in Cosmology*. 2nd ed. New York: Random House, 1973.

156

_____. *Purity and Danger: An Analysis of Concepts of Pollution and Taboo.* London: Routledge and Kegan Paul, 1966.

Duke, Paul D. *Irony in the Fourth Gospel.* Atlanta: John Knox Press, 1985.

Elliott, John H. *A Home for the Homeless.* Philadelphia: Fortress Press, 1975.

Ellul, Jacques. *Apocalypse.* Trans. George W. Schreiner. New York: The Seabury Press, 1977.

Farrer, Austin. *A Rebirth of Images: The Making of St John's Apocalypse.* Westminster: Dacre Press, 1949.

Faulkner, William. "Speech of Acceptance Upon the Award of the Nobel Prize." Delivered in Stockholm, Sweden, 1950. In *Essays, Speeches, and Public Letters.* Ed. James B. Meriwether. New York: Alba House, 1965.

Feuillet, A. *The Apocalypse.* Trans. Thomas E. Crane. Staten Island, New York: Alba House, 1965.

Fiorenza, Elisabeth Schüssler. "Apokalypsis and Propheteia: Revelation in the Context of Early Christian Prophecy." In *L'Apocalypse johannique et l'apocalyptique dans le Nouveau Testament.* Ed. J. Lambrecht. Gembloux: J. Duculot, 1980.

_____. "Book of Revelation." *The Interpreter's Dictionary of the Bible,* suppl. vol. Ed. Keith Crim. Nashville: Abingdon Press, 1962.

_____. *The Book of Revelation–Justice and Judgment.* Philadelphia: Fortress Press, 1985.

_____. "The Phenomenon of Early Christian Apocalyptic." In *Apocalypticism in the Mediterranean World and the Near East.* Ed. David Hellholm. Tübingen: Mohr-Siebeck, 1983.

_____. *Priester für Gott: Studien zum Herrschafts und Priestermotiv in der Apokalypse.* Münster: Verlag Aschendorff, 1972.

Firth, J. Raymond. *Papers in Linguistics 1934–1951.* London: Oxford University Press, 1957.

_____. *The Toungues of Men and Speech.* London: Oxford University Press, 1964.

Fishman, Joshua A. *Sociolinguistics.* Rowley, Massachusetts: Newbury House Publishers, 1970.

_____. *The Sociology of Language.* Rowley, Massachusetts: Newbury House Publishers, 1972.

Ford, J. Massyngberde. *Revelation.* Anchor Bible, vol 38. Garden City, New York: Doubleday & Co., 1975.

Fowler, Roger. *Language as Social Discourse*. Bloomington, Indiana: Indiana University Press, 1981.

_____. *Linguistic Criticism*. Oxford: Oxford University Press, 1986.

_____. *Linguistics and the Novel*. London: Methuen & Co., 1977.

Gager, John G. *Kingdom and Community: The Social World of Early Christianity*. Englewood Cliffs, N. J.: Prentice Hall, 1975.

Giglioli, P. P., ed. *Language and Social Context*. Harmondsworth: Penguin, 1972.

Gilsenan, Michael. "Lying, Honor and Contradiction." In *Transactions and Meaning: Directions in the Anthropology of Exchange and Symbolic Behavior*, ed. Bruce Kapferer. Philadelphia: Institute for the Study of Human Behavior, 1976.

Gumperz, John J. and Dell Hymes, eds. *Directions in Sociolinguistics*. New York: Holt, Rinehart, and Winston, 1972.

Guthrie, Donald. *The Relevance of John's Apocalypse*. Grand Rapids, Michigan: Wm. B. Eerdmans, 1987.

Hahn, Ferdinand. "Zum Aufbau der Johannesoffenbarung." In *Kirche und Bibel. Festgabe für Bischof Eduard Schick*. Paderborn: Ferdinand Schöningh, 1979.

Halliday, M. A. K. *An Introduction to Functional Grammar*. London: Edwin Arnold, 1985.

_____. *Language as Social Semiotic*. Baltimore, Maryland: University Park Press, 1978.

_____, and Robin P. Fawcett, eds. *New Developments in Systemic Linguistics*. London: Frances Pinter, 1987.

Hanson, Paul D. "Apocalypticism." *The Interpreter's Dictionary of the Bible*, suppl. vol. Ed. Keith Crim. Nashville: Abingdon Press, 1962.

_____. *The Dawn of Apocalyptic: The Historical and Sociological Roots of Jewish Apocalyptic Eschatology*. Philadelphia: Fortress Press, 1979.

_____. "Prolegomena to the Study of Jewish Apocalyptic." In *Magnalia Dei: The Mighty Acts of God*. Ed. F. M. Cross, W. E. Lemke, and P. D. Miller, Jr. Garden City, New York: Doubleday & Co., 1976.

_____. *Visionaries and their Apocalypses*. Philadelphia: Fortress Press, 1983.

Harris, Zelig. *Methods in Structural Linguistics*. Chicago: University of Chicago Press, 1951.

Hellholm, David, ed. *Apocalypticism in the Mediterranean World and the Near East.* Tübingen: Mohr–Siebeck, 1983.

Hemer, Colin. *The Letters to the Seven Churches of Asia in their Local Setting.* Journal for the Study of the New Testament Supplement Series 11. Sheffield: JSOT Press, 1986.

Hengel, Martin. "Messianische Hoffnung und politischer 'Radikalismus' in der 'jüdisch–hellenistischen Diaspora.'" In *Apocalypticism in the Mediterranean World and the Near East.* Ed. David Hellholm. Tübingen: Mohr–Siebeck, 1983.

Hock, Ronald F. *The Social Context of Paul's Ministry, Tent–Making and Apostleship.* Philadelphia: Fortress Press, 1980.

Holmberg, Bengt. *Paul and Power: The Structure of Authority in the Primitive Church as Reflected in the Pauline Epistles.* Philadelphia: Fortress Press, 1980.

Holtz, Traugott. *Die Christologie des Johannes.* Texte und Untersuchungen, 85. Berlin: Akademie Verlag, 1962.

_____. "Gott in der Apokalypse." In *L'Apocalypse johannique et l'apocalyptique dans le Nouveau Testament.* Ed. J. Lambrecht. Bibliotheca Ephemeridum Theologicarum Lovaniensium, 53. Leuven: Leuven University Press, 1980.

Horbury, W. and B. McNeil. *Suffering and Martyrdom in the New Testament.* New York: Cambridge University Press, 1981.

Hudson, R. A. *Sociolinguistics.* Cambridge: Cambridge University Press, 1980.

Hymes, Dell, ed. *Language in Culture and Society.* New York: Harper & Row, 1964.

Jeremias, Joachim. *Theology of the New Testament.* Trans. John Bowden. New York: Charles Scribner's Sons, 1971.

Jörns, Klaus–Peter. *Das hymnische Evangelium: Untersuchungen zu Aufbau, Funktion und Herkunft der hymnischen Stücke in der Johannesoffenbarung.* Gütersloh: Gerd Mohn, 1971.

Judge, Edwin A. *Rank and Status in the World of the Caesars and St. Paul.* University of Canterbury Publication 29. Canterbury: University of Canterbury, 1984.

_____. *The Social Pattern of the Christian Groups in the First Century.* London: Tyndale Press, 1960.

Kee, Howard Clark. *Christian Origins in Sociological Perspective.* Philadelphia: The Westminster Press, 1980.

Kelber, Werner H. *The Oral and the Written Gospel*. Philadelphia: Fortress Press, 1983.

Koch, Klaus. *The Rediscovery of Apocalyptic*. Trans. Margaret Kohl. Studies in Biblical Theology, new series 22. Naperville, Illinois: Allenson, 1972.

_____. "Vom profetischen zum apokalyptischen Visionsbericht." In *Apocalypticism in the Mediterranean World and the Near East*. Ed. David Hellholm. Tübingen: Mohr–Siebeck, 1983.

_____ and J. M. Schmidt, eds. *Apokalyptik*. Darmstadt: Wissenschaftliche Buchgesellschaft, 1982.

Kraft, Heinrich. *Die Offenbarung des Johannes*. Handbuch zum Neuen Testament, vol. 16a. Tübingen: J. C. B. Mohr, 1974.

Kremer, Kremer. *Lazarus: Die Geschichte einer Auferstehung*. Stuttgart: Verlag Katholisches Bibelwerk, 1985.

Kress, Gunther R., ed. *Halliday: System and Function in Language--Selected Papers*. London: Oxford University Press, 1976.

Labov, William. *The Social Stratification of English in New York City*. Washington, D.C.: Center for Applied Linguistics, 1966.

_____. *Sociolinguistic Patterns*. Philadelphia: University of Pennsylvania Press, 1972.

Ladd, George Eldon. *A Commentary on the Revelation of John*. Wm. B. Eerdmans, 1972.

Lambrecht, J., ed. *L'Apocalypse johannique et l'apocalyptique dans le Nouveau Testament*. Leuven: Leuven University Press, 1980.

Langendoen, D. Terrence. *The London School of Linguistics: A Study of the Linguistic Theories of B. Malinowski and J. R. Firth*. Research Monograph 46. Cambridge, Massachusetts: The M.I.T. Press, 1968.

Lepschy, G. C. *A Survey of Structural Linguistics*. 1970; rpt. London: André Deutsche, 1982.

Lévi–Strauss, Claude. *Structural Anthropology*. New York: Basic Books, 1963.

Lieberson, Stanley, ed. *Explorations in Sociolinguistics*. Bloomington, Indiana: Indiana University Press, 1973.

Lindars, Barnabas. *The Son of Man*. London: SPCK, 1983.

Lindijer, C. "Die Jungfrauen in der Offenbarung des Johannes XIV 4." In *Studies in John*. Ed. A. Geyser, et al. Leiden: Brill, 1970.

Lohmeyer, Ernst. *Die Offenbarung des Johannes*. Handbuch zum Neuen Testament, vol. 16. Tübingen: J. C. B. Mohr, 1926.

Louw, J. P. *Semantics of New Testament Greek*. The Society of Biblical Literature Semeia Studies. Philadelphia: Fortress Press, 1982.

Mâle, Emile. *Religious Art in France: The Late Middle Ages*. Trans. Marthiel Mathew. Princeton: Princeton University Press, 1986.

Malherbe, Abraham J. *Social Aspects of Early Christianity*. 2nd rev. ed. Philadelphia: Fortress Press, 1983.

Malina, Bruce J. *Christian Origins and Cultural Anthropology: Practical Models for Biblical Interpretation*. Atlanta: John Knox Press, 1986.

_____. *The Gospel of John in Sociolinguistic Perspective*. Center for Hermeneutical Studies in Hellenistic and Modern Culture Colloquy 48. Berkley, California: Center for Hermeneutical Studies, 1985.

_____. *The New Testament World: Insights from Cultural Anthropology*. Atlanta: John Knox Press, 1981.

_____ and Jerome H. Neyrey. *Calling Jesus Names: The Social Value of Labels in Matthew*. Sonoma, California: Polebridge Press, 1988.

Martyn, J. L. *History and Theology in the Fourth Gospel*. New York: Harper & Row, 1968.

Meeks, Wayne A. *The First Urban Christians: The Social World of the Apostle Paul*. New Haven: Yale University, 1983.

_____. "The Social Functions of Apocalyptic Language in Pauline Christianity." In *Apocalypticism in the Mediterranean World and the Near East*. Ed. David Hellholm. Tübingen: Mohr–Siebeck, 1983.

Metzger, Bruce M. *A Textual Commentary on the Greek New Testament*. New York: United Bible Societies, 1975.

Minear, Paul S. *New Testament Apocalyptic*. Nashville: Abingdon, 1981.

Mitchell, T. F. *Principles of Firthian Linguistics*. London: Longman, 1975.

Mounce, Robert. *The Book of Revelation*. New International Commentary on the New Testament. Grand Rapids, Michigan: Wm. B. Eerdmans, 1977.

Müller, Mogens. *Der Ausdruck "Menschensohn" in den Evangelien: Voraussetzungen und Bedeutung*. Leiden: E. J. Brill, 1984.

Müller, Ulrich. *Messias und Menschensohn in jüdischen Apokalypsen und in der Offenbarung des Johannes*. Gütersloh: Gerd Mohn, 1972.

Mueller, Claus. *The Politics of Communication*. New York: Oxford University Press, 1973.

Mussies, G. "The Greek of the Book of Revelation." In *L'Apocalyptique johannique et l'apocalyptique dans le Nouveau Testament.* Bibliotheca Ephemeridum Theologicarum Lovaniensium, 53. Leuven: Leuven University Press, 1980.

_____. *The Morphology of Koine Greek as used in the Apocalypse of St. John.* Supplement to *Novum Testamentum 27.* Leiden: E. J. Brill, 1971.

Nickel, Gerhard, ed. *Applied Linguistics: Sociolinguistics.* Stuttgart: Hochschul-Verlag, 1978.

Nickelsburg, George W. E. "Social Aspects of Palestinian Jewish Apocalypticism." In *Apocalypticism in the Mediterranean World and the Near East.* Ed. David Hellholm. Tübingen: Mohr–Siebeck, 1983.

Ong, Walter J. *Orality and Literacy: The Technologizing of the Word.* New Accents. Ed. Terence Hawkes. London: Methuen, 1982.

Osiek, Carolyn. *What are They Saying About the Social Setting of the New Testament?* New York: Paulist Press, 1984.

Palmer, F. R., ed. *Selected Papers of J. R. Firth 1952–1959.* Bloomington: Indiana University Press, 1968.

Patrides, C. A., ed. *The Complete Works of John Donne.* London: J. M. Dent & Sons, 1985.

Perrin, Norman. *A Modern Pilgrimage in New Testament Christology.* Philadelphia: Fortress Press, 1974.

Prigent, Pierre. *L'Apocalypse de Saint Jean.* Commentaire du Nouveau Testament, vol. 14. Paris: Delachaux & Niestlé, 1981.

Ramsay, William. *The Letters to the Seven Churches.* 1904; rpt. Grand Rapids, Michigan: Baker Book House, 1985.

Rist, Martin. "Apocalypticism." *The Interpreter's Dictionary of the Bible*, vol. 1. Ed. G. A. Buttrick. Nashville: Abingdon Press, 1962.

Ross, J. F. "Wine." *Interpreter's Dictionary of the Bible.* Ed.George Buttrick. Nashville: Abingdon Press, 1962.

Rowland, Christopher. *The Open Heaven.* New York: Crossroad, 1982.

Rowley, H. H. *The Relevance of Apocalyptic.* 1944; rpt. Greenwood, South Carolina: Attic Press, 1980.

Rühle, Oskar. "*ἀριθμέω, ἀριθμός.*" *Theological Dictionary of the New Testament*, vol. 1. Ed. Gerhard Kittel. Trans. G. W. Bromiley. Grand Rapids, Michigan: Wm. B. Eerdmans, 1964.

St. Clair, Robert, ed. *Applied Sociolinguistics.* Lawrence, Kansas: The Coronado Press, 1979.

Sabatier, André. "La Place des techniques de communication dans l'Apocalypse de Jean." In *Religion, société et politique: Mélanges en hommage a Jacques Ellul*. Ed. Georges Dmitri Lavroff. Paris: Presses Universitaires de France, 1983.

Saussure, Ferdinand de. *Course in General Linguistics*. Trans. W. Baskin. 1916; rpt. London: Fontana, 1974.

Schaik, A. P. van. *"Ἄλλος ἄγγελος in Apk 14."* In *L'Apocalypse johannique et l'Apocalyptique dans le Nouveau Testament*. Bibliotheca Ephemeridium Theologicarum Lovaniensium 53. Ed. J. Lambrecht. Leuven: Leuven University Press, 1980.

Schieben–Lange, Brigitte. *Soziolinguistik: Eine Einführung*. 2nd ed. Stuttgart: Verlag W. Kohlhammer, 1978.

Schillebeeckx, Edward. *Christ: The Experience of Jesus as Lord*. Trans. John Bowden. New York: Crossroad, 1980.

————. *Jesus*. Trans. John Bowden. New York: Crossroad, 1979.

Schlier, Heinrich. "Vom Antichrist Zum 13. Kapitel der Offenbarung Johannis." In *Die Zeit der Kirche*. Freiburg: Verlag Herder, 1958.

————. "Zum Verständnis der Geschichte nach der Offenbarung Johannis." In *Die Zeit der Kirche*. Freiburg: Verlag Herder, 1956.

Schmidt, Daryl D. *Hellenistic Greek Grammar and Noam Chomsky: Nominalizing Transformations*. Society of Biblical Literature Dissertation Series 62. Ed. William Baird. Chico, California: Scholars Press, 1981.

Schmithals, W. *The Apocalyptic Movement*. Nashville: Abingdon, 1975.

Schneemelcher, Wilhelm, ed. *New Testament Apocrypha*, vol. 2. Trans. R. McL. Wilson. Philadelphia: The Westminster Press, 1965.

Schuetz, John H. *Studien zur Soziologie des Urchristentums*. Wissenschaftliche Untersuchungen des Neuen Testament 19. Philadelphia: Fortress Press, 1983.

Schwarz, Günther. *Jesus "Der Menschensohn."* Stuttgart: Verlag W. Kohlhammer, 1986.

Seland, Torrey. "Jesus as a Faction Leader: On the Exit of the Category Sect." In P. W. Bockman and R. E. Kristiansen, eds. *Contect: festschrift til Peder Borgen*. Trondheim: Tapir, 1987.

Smith, D. M. *Johannine Christianity: Essays on its Settings, Sources, and Theology*. Columbia: University of South Carolina, 1984.

Summers, Ray. *Worthy is the Lamb*. Nashville: Broadman Press, 1951.

Sweet, J. P. M. *Revelation*. Westminster Pelican Commentaries. Philadelphia: The Westminster Press, 1979.

Swete, Henry Barclay. *Commentary on Revelation*. 1911; rpt. Grand Rapids, Michigan: Kregel, 1977.

Tefft, Stanton K, ed. *Secrecy: A Cross–Cultural Perspective*. New York: Human Sciences Press, 1980.

Theissen, Gerd. *The Social Setting of Pauline Christianity*. Ed. and trans. John Bowden. Philadelphia: Fortress Press, 1982.

_____. *Sociology of Early Palestinian Christianity*. Trans. John Bowden. Philadelphia: Fortress Press, 1978.

Thompson, Steven. *The Apocalypse and Semitic Syntax*. Cambridge: Cambridge University Press, 1985.

Trudgill, Peter. *Sociolinguistics*. Harmondsworth: Penguin, 1975.

Turner, Victor. *The Ritual Process*. Symbol, Myth, and Ritual Series. Ithaca, New York: Cornell University Press, 1969.

Vanni, U. *La Struttura lettereria dell' Apocalisse*. Rome: Herder, 1971.

Vermes, G. *The Dead Sea Scrolls in English*. Harmondsworth: Penguin, 1974.

Verner, David C. *The Household of God: The Social World of the Pastoral Epistles*. Society of Biblical Literature Dissertation Series 71. Chico, California: Scholars Press, 1983.

Via, Dan O. *Kerygma and Comedy in the New Testament*. Philadelphia: Fortress Press, 1975.

Vielhauer, Philipp. *Geschichte der urchristlichen Literatur: Einleitung in das Neue Testament, die Apokryphen und die Apostolischen Väter*. Berlin: Walter de Gruyter, 1975.

Voeltz, J. W. "The Language of the New Testament." In *Aufstieg und Niedergang der römischen Welt*, vol. 2, 25.2. Ed. Wolfgang Haase. Berlin: Walter de Gruyter, 1984.

Wengst, Klaus. *Bedrängte Gemeinde und verherrlichter Christus: Der historische Ort des Johannesevangelium als Schlüssel zu seiner Interpretation*. 2nd. ed. Neukirchen-Vluyn: Neukirchener Verlag, 1983.

_____. *Pax Romana and the Peace of Jesus Christ*. Philadelphia: Fortress Press, 1987.

White, Hayden. *Metahistory: The Historical Imagination in Nineteenth Century Europe*. Baltimore, Maryland: Johns Hopkins University Press, 1973.

164

Wilcox, M. "Semitisms in the New Testament." In *Aufstieg und Niedergang der römischen Welt*, vol. 2, 25.2. Ed. Wolfgang Haase. Berlin: Walter de Gruyter, 1984.

Wilson, B. *Magic and the Millennium*. New York: Harper & Row, 1973.

_____. *Religion in Sociological Perspective*. Oxford: Oxford University Press, 1982.

Wuthnow, Robert, James Davison Hujter, Albert Bergesen, Edith Kurzweil, eds. *Cultural Analysis: The Work of Peter L. Burger, Mary Douglas, Michel Foucault, and Jurgen Habermas*. Boston: Routledge & Kegan Paul, 1984.

Zahn, Theodor. *Die Offenbarung des Johannes*, 2 vols. Leipzig: Deichert, 1924.

Periodicals

Ashton, John. "The Identity of the *IOΥΔAIOI* in the Fourth Gospel." *Novum Testamentum*, 27 (1985), 40–75.

Aune, David E. "The Apocalypse of John and the Problem of Genre." *Semeia*, 36 (1986), 65–96.

_____. "The Social Matrix of the Apocalypse of John." *Biblical Research*, 26 (1981), 16–32.

Barr, David L. "The Apocalypse as a Symbolic Transformation of the World." *Interpretation*, 38 (1984), 39–50.

_____. "The Apocalypse of John and Graeco–Roman Revelatory Magic." *New Testament Studies*, 33 (1987), 481–501.

_____. "The Apocalypse of John as Oral Enactment." *Interpretation*, 40 (1986), 243–256.

_____. "Elephants and Holograms: From Metaphor to Methodology in the Study of John's Apocalypse." *Society of Biblical Literature Seminar Papers*. Ed. Kent Richards. Atlanta: Scholars Press, 1986.

Bergmeier, Roland. "Altes und Neues zur 'Sonnenfrau am Himmel (Apk 12)' Religionsgeschichtliche und quellenkritische Beobachtungen zu Apk 12 1–17." *Zeitschrift für das neutestamentliche Wissenschaft*, 73 (1982), 97–109.

Bernstein, Basil. "Codes, modalities, and the process of cultural reproduction: A model." *Language in Society*, 10 (1981), 327–363.

Blevins, James L. "The Genre of Revelation." *Review and Expositor*, 77 (1980), 393-408.

Boring, M. Eugene. "The Theology of Revelation 'The Lord our God the Almighty Reigns.'" *Interpretation*, 40 (1986), 257–269.

Bovon, F. "Possession ou enchantement. Les institutions romaines selon l'Apocalypse de Jean." *Cristianesimo nella Storia*, 7 (1986), 221–238.

Cerfaux, L. "La Vision de la Femme et du Dragon." *Ephemerides theologicae lovanienses*, 61 (1955), 7–33.

Collins, Adela Yarbro. "Early Christian Apocalypticism: Genre and Social Setting." *Semeia*, 36 (1986), 1–11.

_____. "The Origin of the Designation of Jesus as 'Son of Man.'" *Harvard Theological Review*, 80 (1987), 391–407.

_____. "The Political Perspective of the Revelation to John." *Journal of Biblical Literature*, 96 (1977), 241–256.

_____. "Reading the Book of Revelation in the Twentieth Century." *Interpretation*, 40 (1986), 229–242.

_____. "The Revelation of John: An Apocalyptic Response to a Social Crisis." *Currents in Theology and Mission*, 8 (1981), 4–12.

_____. "Women's History and the Book of Revelation." *SBL Seminar Papers*. Ed. Kent Richards. Atlanta: Atlanta Scholars Press, 1987.

Collins, John J. "The Son of Man and the Saints of the Most High in the Book of Daniel." *Journal of Biblical Literature*, 93 (1974), 50–66.

Cook, Michael. "The Gospel of John and the Jews." *Review and Expositor*, 84 (1987), 259–271.

Culpepper, R. Alan. "The Gospel of John and the Jews." *Review and Expositor*, 84 (1987), 273–288.

Donahue, John. "Recent Studies on the Origin of 'Son of Man' in the Gospels." *Catholic Biblical Quarterly*, 48 (1986), 484–498.

Elliott, John H. "The Fear of the Leer: The Evil Eye from the Bible to Li'l Abner." *Forum*, 4 (1988), 42–71.

_____. "Social–Scientific Criticism of the New Testament: More on Methods and Models." *Semeia*, 35 (1986),1–33.

Erickson, Richard J. "Linguistics and Biblical Language: A Wide Open Field." *Journal of the Evangelical Theological Society*, 26 (1983), 257–263.

Feuillet, A. "Les 144.000 Israélites marqués d'un sceau." *Novum Testamentum*, 9 (1967), 191–224.

Firth, Raymond. "Spiritual Aroma: Religion and Politics." *American Anthropologist*, 83 (1981), 582–602.

Ford, J. Massyngberde. "The Meaning of 'Virgin.'" *New Testament Studies*, 12 (1966), 293–299.

166

Gager, John G. "Shall We Marry Our Enemies? Sociology and the New Testament." *Interpretation*, 36 (1982), 256–265.

Gammie, John G. "Recent Books and Emerging Issues in the study of Apocalyptic." *Quarterly Review*, 5 (1985), 96–108.

Halliday, M. A. K. "Anti–languages." *American Anthropologist*, 78 (1976), 570–584.

Hellholm, David. "The Problem of Apocalyptic Genre and the Apocalypse of John." *SBL Seminar Papers*. Ed. Kent Richards. Chico, California: Scholars Press, 1982.

_____. "The Problem of Apocalyptic Genre and the Apocalypse of John." *Semeia*, 36 (1986), 13–64.

Hanson, Paul D. "Jewish Apocalyptic against its Near Eastern Environment." *Revue Biblique*, 78 (1971), 31–58.

Hurtado, Larry. "Revelation 4–5 in the Light of Jewish Apocalyptic Analogies." *Journal for the Study of the New Testament*, 25 (1985), 105–124.

Isenberg, Sheldon R. and Dennis E. Owen. "Bodies, Natural and Contrived: The Work of Mary Douglas." *Religious Studies Review*, 3 (1977), 1–17.

Jeske, Richard L. "Spirit and Community in the Johannine Apocalypse." *New Testament Studies*, 31 (1985), 452–466.

Kress, Gunther. "Poetry as Anti–language: A Reconsideration of Donne's 'Nocturnall Upon S. Lucies Day.'" *P[oetry and] T[theory of] L[iterature]: A Journal for Descriptive Poetics and Theory*, 3 (1978), 327–344.

Kysar, Robert. "The Gospel of John in Current Research." *Religious Studies Review*, 9 (1983), 314–323.

Malina, Bruce J. Book review of Michael N. Ebertz's *Das Charisma des Gekreuzigten: Zur Soziologie der Jesusbewegung*. WUNT 45. Tübingen: Mohr–Siebeck, 1987. In *Catholic Biblical Quarterly*, 51 (1989), 741–743.

_____. "Dealing with Biblical (Mediterranean) Characters: A Guide for U.S. Consumers." *Biblical Theology Bulletin*, 19 (1989), 127–141.

_____. "Normative Dissonance and Christian Origins." In John H. Elliott, ed., "Social–scientific Criticism of the New Testament and Its Social World, *Semeia*, 35 (1986), 35–59.

_____. "Patron and Client: The Analogy Behind Synoptic Theology." *Forum*, 4 (1988), 1–32.

_____. "Religion in the World of Paul." *Biblical Theology Bulletin*, 16 (1986), 92–101.

_____. "Wealth and Poverty in the New Testament and its World." *Interpretation*, 41 (1987), 354–367.

Morgen, Michèle. "Apocalypse 12, un targum de l'Ancien Testament." *Foi et Vie*, 20 (1982), 663–74.

Porter, Stanley E. "The Language of Apocalypse in Recent Discussion." *New Testament Studies*, 35 (1989), 582–603.

Prigent, P. "Pour une théologie de l'image: les visions de l'Apocalypse." *Revue D'Histoire et de Philosophie Religieuses*, 59 (1979), 373–378.

Reddish, Mitchell. "Martyr Christology in the Apocalypse." *Journal for the Study of the New Testament*, 33 (1988), 85–95.

Rissi, Mathias. "The Kerygma of the Revelation to John." *Interpretation*, 22 (1968), 3–17.

Rohrbach, Richard L. "Methodological Considerations in the Debate over the Social Class Status of Early Christians." *Journal of the Academy of Religion*, 52 (1984), 519-546.

_____. "'Social Location of Thought' as a Heuristic Construct in New Testament Study." *Journal for the Study of the New Testament*, 30 (1987), 103–119.

Rowland, Christopher. "Reading the New Testament Sociologically: An Introduction." *Theology*, 88 (1985), 358–364.

Scherrer, Steven J. "Signs and Wonders in the Imperial Cult: A New Look at a Roman Religious Institution in the Light of Rev 13:13–15." *Journal of Biblical Literature*, 103 (1984), 599–610.

Smith, Mahlon H. "No Place for a Son of Man." *Forum*, 4 (1988), 92–107.

Spickard, James V. "A Guide to Mary Douglas's Three Versions of Grid/Group Theory." *Sociological Analysis*, 50 (1989), 151–170.

Strand, Kenneth. "Chiastic Structure and Some Motifs in the Book of Revelation." *Andrews University Seminary Studies*, 16 (1978), 401–408.

_____. "Some Modalities of Symbolic Usage in Revelation 18." *Andrews University Seminary Studies*, 24 (1986), 37–46.

Thompson, Leonard J. "The Mythic Unity of the Apocalypse." *SBL Seminar Papers*. Ed. Kent Richards. Atlanta: Scholars Press, 1985 pp. 13–28.

Ulrichsen, Jarl. "Die sieben Häupter und die zehn Hörner zur Datierung die Offenbarung des Johannes." *Studia Theologica*, 39 (1985), 1–20.

Urban, Greg. Review of *Language as Social Semiotic: The Social Interpretation of Language and Meaning*, by M. A. K. Halliday. *American Anthropologist*, 83 (1981), 659–661.

Vogels, Walter. "Inspiration in a Linguistic Mode." *Biblical Theology Bulletin*, 25 (1985), 87–93.

von Wahlde, Urban C. "The Johannine 'Jews': A Critical Survey." *New Testament Studies*, 28 (1982), 33–60.

White, Hayden. "The Value of Narrativity in the Representation of Reality," *Critical Inquiry*, 7 (1980), 5–27.

White, Leland J. "Grid and Group in Matthew's Community: The Righteousness/Honor Code in the Sermon on the Mount." *Semeia*, 35 (1986), 61–90.

Unpublished Dissertations

Cook, Donald Eugene. "The Christology of the Apocalypse." Ph.D. dissertation, Duke University, 1962.

Creech, Richard Robert. "Christology and Conflict: A Comparative Study of Two Central Themes in the Johannine Literature and the Apocalypse." Ph.D. dissertation, Baylor University, 1984.

Harris, Michael Anthony. "The Literary Function of the Hymns in the Apocalypse of John." Ph.D. dissertation, The Southern Baptist Theological Seminary, 1988.

Hatfield, Daniel Earl. "The Function of the Seven Beatitudes in Revelation." Ph.D. dissertation, The Southern Baptist Theological Seminary, 1987.

Kempson, Wayne Richard. "Theology in the Revelation of John." Ph.D. dissertation, The Southern Baptist Theological Seminary, 1982.

May, David. "The Role of House and Household Language in the Markan Social World." Ph.D. dissertation, The Southern Baptist Theological Seminary, 1987.

Pippin, Tina. "Political Reality and the Liberating Vision: The Context of the Book of Revelation." Ph.D. dissertation, The Southern Baptist Theological Seminary, 1987.

Reddish, Mitchell Glenn. "The Theme of Martyrdom in the Book of Revelation." Ph.D. dissertation, The Southern Baptist Theological Seminary, 1982.

Stanley, John "The Use of the Symbol of Four World Empires to Inspire Resistance to or Acceptance of Hellenism in Daniel 2, Daniel 7, 4 Ezra 11–12, Revelation 13, and *Antiquities of the Jews*: Insights from the Sociology of Knowledge and Sect Analysis." Ph.D. dissertation, Iliff School of Theology, 1986.

Warren, William Leon, Jr. "Apostasy in the Book of Revelation." Ph.D. dissertation, The Southern Baptist Theological Seminary, 1983.

Unpublished Materials

Schmidt, Daryl D. "Semitism vs. Septuagintalism in the Apocalypse." Paper presented at the annual SBL meeting, December, 1987.

INDEX